Improving Learning, Skills and Inclusion

This is the first book to examine the turbulent but important learning and skills sector both from above, by interviewing the officials responsible for it, and from below, by talking to hundreds of learners and front-line staff.

Even though this sector caters for over 6 million learners, it is not well understood by practitioners or policy-makers. For over three years, the authors explored the interactions between these two groups by examining how policy is created and enacted in further, adult and work-based learning.

The data are presented as a series of stories: the learners' experiences, the plans of the policy-makers to bring about radical change, and the struggles of tutors and managers, juggling both change and continuity. The authors also explain how the sector as a whole operates, as policy is mediated and translated by numerous actors at different levels.

The main finding is that the sector is undergoing a fundamental shift from area-based planning to a more marketised 'demand-led' system intended to give employers and learners more say over provision. Their evidence suggests that this high-risk strategy may destabilise education providers and exclude disadvantaged learners.

The book also outlines the elements of an alternative system, underpinned by three principles: prioritising the relationship between tutor and learner; placing equity for once above economic efficiency; and ensuring a more moderate pace of change. This book is an invaluable resource for tutors, managers and institutional leaders in FE colleges, adult and community learning centres and work-based learning sites.

Improving Learning TLRP

Series Editor: Andrew Pollard, Director of the ESRC Teaching and Learning Programme.

Improving Learning, Skills and Inclusion

The impact of policy on post-compulsory education

Frank Coffield, Sheila Edward,
Ian Finlay, Ann Hodgson,
Ken Spours and Richard Steer

Routledge
Taylor & Francis Group

LONDON AND NEW YORK

First published 2008
by Routledge
2 Park Square, Milton Park, Abingdon, Oxon, OX14 4RN

Simultaneously published in the USA and Canada
by Routledge
270 Madison Ave, New York, NY 10016

Routledge is an imprint of the Taylor & Francis Group, an informa business

© 2008 Frank Coffield, Sheila Edward, Ian Finlay, Ann Hodgson,
Ken Spours and Richard Steer

Typeset in Charter ITC and Stone Sans
by Keystroke, 28 High Street Tettenhall, Wolverhampton
Printed and bound in Great Britain by
TJ International Ltd, Padstow, Cornwall

British Library Cataloguing in Publication Data
A catalogue record for this book is available from the British Library

Library of Congress Cataloging in Publication Data
Improving learning, skills and inclusion : the impact of policy on
post-compulsory education / Frank Coffield ... [et al.].
    p. cm.
    Includes bibliographical references and index.
    ISBN 978-0-415-46180-1 (hardback) — ISBN 978-0-415-46181-8
(paperback) 1. Vocational education—Government policy—Great Britain.
2. Labor supply—Effect of education on—Great Britain. 3. Post-compulsory
education—Great Britain. I. Coffield, Frank.
    LC1047.G7I47 2008
    370.11'30941   2007039021

ISBN10 0–415–46180–4 (hbk)
ISBN10 0–415–46181–2 (pbk)
ISBN10 0–203–92899–7 (ebk)

ISBN13 978–0–415–46180–1 (hbk)
ISBN13 978–0–415–46181–8 (pbk)
ISBN13 978–0–203–92899–8 (ebk)

Contents

Boxes and figures

Boxes

Figures

Authors

Frank Coffield is Professor of Education, Institute of Education, University of London.

Sheila Edward, formerly at the Institute of Education, is now Research Fellow at the Centre for Research in Education, Inclusion and Diversity, University of Edinburgh.

Ian Finlay is Senior Lecturer in Educational and Professional Studies, University of Strathclyde.

Ann Hodgson is Reader in Education and Faculty Director of Research, Consultancy and Knowledge Transfer, Institute of Education, University of London.

Ken Spours is Reader in Education and Head of the Department of Continuing and Professional Education, Institute of Education, University of London.

Richard Steer, formerly at the Institute of Education, is now Policy Researcher at City College, Norwich.

Series editor's preface

The *Improving Learning* series showcases findings from projects within ESRC's Teaching and Learning Research Programme (TLRP) – the UK's largest-ever coordinated educational research initiative.

Books in the *Improving Learning* series are explicitly designed to support 'evidence-informed' decisions in educational practice and policy-making. In particular, they combine rigorous social and educational science with high awareness of the significance of the issues being researched.

Working closely with practitioners, organisations and agencies covering all educational sectors, the Programme has supported many of the UK's best researchers to work on the direct improvement of policy and practice to support learning. Over sixty projects have been supported, covering many issues across the lifecourse. We are proud to present the results of this work through books in the *Improving Learning* series.

Each book provides a concise, accessible and definitive overview of innovative findings from a TLRP investment. If more advanced information is required, the books may be used as gateways to academic journals, monographs, websites, etc. On the other hand, shorter summaries and *Research Briefings* on key findings are also available via the Programme's website: www.tlrp.org.

We hope that you will find the analysis and findings presented in this book are helpful to you in your work on improving outcomes for learners.

Andrew Pollard
Director, TLRP
Institute of Education, University of London

Acknowledgements

The six co-authors of this book wish to thank all the people who have contributed to the research. We are grateful to the Economic and Social Research Council (ESRC) and the Teaching and Learning Research Programme (TLRP) for our funding. The scope of our research has taken us into a wide range of organisations in England and Europe: we cannot list them all, but record our gratitude both to the organisations which allowed us access and to the individuals who trusted our assurances of confidentiality and gave us time for interviews. Special thanks are due to the learners and staff in our twenty-four learning sites, especially those who also contributed to our annual seminars and conferences; and to all those who sent us comments on the consultation papers which we distributed to participants. We valued all contributions, supportive and critical, and especially those of the discussants at our project seminars in 2007, John Field in Newcastle and Alan Tuckett in London; and at the symposia we presented at the British Educational Research Association conferences, Stephen Ball (2005), Mary Hamilton (2006) and Lorna Unwin (2007).

We also wish to thank our advisory group: Kate Anderson, Barry Brooks, Alan Brown, Leisha Fullick, Jacqui Henderson, Phil Hodkinson, Esther Saville, Dan Taubman and Alison Wolf. We acknowledge the contributions of Pauline McCormack, research officer on this project for six months in 2004; and of Maggie Gregson, who was funded by the University of Sunderland to attend meetings as a research associate and comment on our work. Finally, we thank Louise Wilson and Jo Lakey, project administrators in Newcastle and London, respectively, for their immense contribution and support throughout the project.

Frank Coffield, Sheila Edward, Ian Finlay,
Ann Hodgson, Ken Spours and Richard Steer
July 2007

Abbreviations

ACL	Adult and Community Learning
ALI	Adult Learning Inspectorate
ALP	Association of Learning Providers
AoC	Association of Colleges
BERA	British Educational Research Association
BTEC	Business and Technology Education Council
CBI	Confederation of British Industry
CEC	Commission of the European Communities
CEL	Centre for Excellence in Leadership
CETT	Centre for Excellence in Teacher Training
CoVEs	Centres of Vocational Excellence
CPD	Continuing Professional Development
CQF	Credit and Qualifications Framework
DBERR	Department for Business, Enterprise and Regulatory Reform
DCLG	Department of Communities and Local Government
DCSF	Department for Children, Schools and Families
DfEE	Department for Education and Employment
DfES	Department for Education and Skills
DIUS	Department for Innovation, Universities and Skills
DTI	Department of Trade and Industry
DWP	Department of Work and Pensions
E2E	Entry to Employment
EEF	Engineering Employers' Federation
EMA	Education Maintenance Allowance
EQF	European Qualifications Framework
ESOL	English for Speakers of Other Languages
ESRC	Economic and Social Research Council
ETP	Employer Training Pilot
EU	European Union

FE	Further Education
FEFC	Further Education Funding Council
FfA	Framework for Achievement
FLT	Foundation Learning Tier
GCSE	General Certificate of Secondary Education
HE	Higher Education
HEFCE	Higher Education Funding Council for England
HMG	Her Majesty's Government
HMT	Her Majesty's Treasury
IiP UK	Investors in People UK
ILP	Individual Learning Plan
JC+	JobCentre Plus
LA	Local Authority
LDA	London Development Agency
LEA	Local Education Authority
LGA	Local Government Association
LLDD	Learners with Learning Difficulties and/or Disabilities
LLSC	Local Learning and Skills Council
LLUK	Lifelong Learning UK
LP	Learning Partnership
LSC	Learning and Skills Council
LSDA	Learning and Skills Development Agency
LSEB	London Skills and Employment Board
LSN	Learning and Skills Network
LSS	Learning and Skills Sector
NDPB	Non-Departmental Public Body
NEET	Not in Education, Employment or Training
NEP	National Employment Panel
NIACE	National Institute of Adult Continuing Education
NLGN	New Local Government Network
NPM	New Public Management
NRDC	National Research and Development Centre for Adult Literacy and Numeracy
NSA	National Skills Academy
NVQ	National Vocational Qualification
OFSTED	Office for Standards in Education
PCDL	Personal and Community Development Learning
PMSU	Prime Minister's Strategy Unit
PSA	Public Service Agreement
QAA	Quality Assurance Agency
QCA	Qualifications and Curriculum Authority

QCF	Qualifications and Credit Framework
QIA	Quality Improvement Agency for Lifelong Learning
QIS	Quality Improvement Strategy
QTLS	Qualified Teacher Learning and Skills
RDA	Regional Development Agency
RSP	Regional Skills Partnership
SBC	Small Business Council
SfL	Skills for Life
SSA	Sector Skills Agreement
SSC	Sector Skills Council
SSDA	Sector Skills Development Agency
StAR	Strategic Area Review
T2G	Train to Gain
TEC	Training and Enterprise Council
TLA	Teaching, Learning and Assessment
TLC	Transforming Learning Cultures in FE (TLRP project)
TLRP	Teaching and Learning Research Programme
TUC	Trades Union Congress
UfI	University for Industry
ULF	Union Learning Fund
ULR	Union Learning Representative
WBL	Work-Based Learning

Part I

What are the issues?

Chapter 1

The turbulent world of learning and skills

Introduction

The media would have us believe that the topic of learning and skills and of vocational education and training is not 'sexy', so they ignore it. Yet our national performance in these areas will influence how prosperous and how fair the UK will be in the future. The official story runs as follows: we are currently the fifth biggest economy in the world, having already been overtaken by China; and within the space of a few years we are going to be overtaken by India as well. How well placed are we to meet this challenge, particularly if these countries pay low wages for the production of high-quality goods and services? On the debit side, we have a history of under-investment in training and a long tale of under-achievement at school. On the plus side, since 1997, the Labour government has devoted more time, energy and resources to the learning and skills sector (LSS) than has any previous administration. So, can the LSS significantly improve the performance of those learners who have been failed by the education system? Will all the young people and adults who study hard to gain vocational qualifications be rewarded with well-paid jobs with training? Can tutors improve the quality of their teaching to ensure that many more people participate, gain qualifications and obtain decent jobs? What new ideas do we need to create an inclusive, equitable and efficient learning system in this country?

These are some of the main concerns which prompted us in 2004 to begin a study entitled *The impact of policy on learning and inclusion in the new learning and skills sector*, funded by the Economic and Social Research Council (ESRC), as part of the Teaching and Learning Research Programme (TLRP).[1] New concerns appeared during our research: for example, are the government's new plans for the sector a move in the right direction or do they pose too high a risk of destabilising long-standing institutions like further education (FE) colleges and centres of adult and community learning (ACL)?

For three and a half years we have tried to understand this sector by simultaneously examining it both from above, by interviewing the officials responsible for it, and from below, by talking to students and front-line staff. Before introducing our project in Chapter 2, however, we need to explain the emergence of the LSS, its main achievements and challenges, its new economic mission and how it is being constantly restructured by government. We also set out to test how well this new sector treats three groups of disadvantaged learners because we thought that this was a good way of judging its claims of being both efficient and equitable. But first we shall introduce the fascinating, turbulent, insecure but desperately important world of learning and skills; a world which remains invisible to most politicians, academics and commentators because, with very few exceptions, neither they nor their children have ever passed through it.

We have chosen to introduce the main issues and debates in this world by providing a brief history of the Learning and Skills Council (LSC), as the fortunes of that organisation are central to all the stories we wish to tell and they provide prime examples of the constant changes that course through the sector. We will then broaden our focus by discussing the main achievements of the LSS, its complexity and two major reviews of its future. Next, instead of attempting to introduce all the major themes with which this book is concerned, we have decided to plunge the reader into the thick of one major controversy – the move to a 'demand-led' system – as that will serve to bring into the open most of the main tensions, debates and anxieties in the sector. This approach also enables us to introduce the main players in the unfolding drama that is post-compulsory education and training in England.

The chapter ends by describing and critiquing the new model of public service reform which the government introduced in 2006. To help any readers who are new to this world, we will explain every initiative and spell out every abbreviation when it is first used (we have also included a list of all such terms at the beginning of the book). Our aim, moreover, is to be even-handed by, for example, welcoming the government's achievements as well as criticising it constructively for its failings.

A brief history of the Learning and Skills Council (LSC)

In 2001 the Labour government introduced a bold reform, which integrated under a new body called the Learning and Skills Council a disparate range of learning opportunities in FE, community and adult learning and work-based training for young people and adults. The LSC was given the power to plan, fund and regulate all education and training post-16 with the exception of higher education; and its significance can in part be judged by its budget, which in its first year was £5.5 billion and which by 2007–8 had more than doubled to £11.4 billion. These are enormous sums of public money, but enormous too are the responsibilities for over five million full- and part-time learners in 385 FE and sixth-form colleges, in school sixth forms and in ACL (with one million people in the latter); for 1,000 publicly funded training providers; for sixth-form and tertiary colleges; for over 250,000 apprentices and those taking National Vocational Qualifications (NVQs) in employment; and for over 246,000 full- and part-time staff in FE colleges alone (DfES 2006a).

Although the LSC has been in existence for only six years, it is already possible to distinguish three distinct phases in its development:

- the first phase, from 2001 to 2003, when its main functions were planning and funding;
- an intermediate phase, from 2004 to 2006, when a business model and a regional tier of administration were introduced;
- the third phase, from 2006 to 2007, concerned first with the move to a demand-led system for adult learners, and, since June 2007, with the forthcoming transfer in 2010/11 of around 60 per cent of its budget for14–19-year-olds to local authorities.

Before we expand on each of these phases, we first need to explain why the LSC was thought necessary and how it was brought into being. When Labour came to power in May 1997, it inherited a diverse array of activities and organisations responsible for post-compulsory education and training apart from higher education:

- the Further Education Funding Council (FEFC), which funded and inspected FE colleges;
- the seventy-two Training and Enterprise Councils (TECs) in England which organised government-funded training and work-force development alongside other enterprise activities;

- school sixth forms, funded by Local Education Authorities (LEAs); and
- ACL run by LEAs and other voluntary and community organisations.

While New Labour had a strong focus on lifelong learning, it did not have plans for large-scale structural change. It soon began to see a case for structural change, however, because of the weaknesses it perceived in funding and planning (e.g., the TECs had seventy-two different funding and planning systems) and in inspection and quality control (e.g., there were three separate inspectorates operating in the same area: FEFC, the Office for Standards in Education (OFSTED) and the Training Standards Council). A White Paper, *Learning to Succeed: a new framework for post-16 learning*, published in 1999, summarised the arguments for change thus:

> There is too much duplication, confusion and bureaucracy in the current system. Too little money actually reaches learners and employers, too much is tied up in bureaucracy. There is an absence of effective co-ordination or strategic planning. The system has insufficient focus on skill and employer needs at national, regional and local levels.
>
> (DfEE 1999: 21)

Some of our interviewees widened this attack upon the previous system. One official, for example, admonished the TECs for 'creaming off' funds from government training programmes to resource their own initiatives; another thought the general quality of the training TECs organised was poor and that some had abused their independence. For Leisha Fullick, a founding member of the LSC, the FEFC's 'obsession with audit trails created a new, but equally burdensome, bureaucratic quagmire to some of those it had cleared away. Its rush for growth through franchising led some colleges into disaster from which a few never recovered, and many others still feel the consequences' (Fullick 2004: 15). The LSC's inheritance was, therefore, challenging: it was bequeathed 'the admittedly chaotic arrangements of three different funding and administrative systems for school sixth forms, FE Colleges and training agencies' (Ainley 2000: 586).

Phase 1, 2001–3: planning and funding

It has already been forgotten how complicated the transition to the new arrangements was in 2001. For example, the seventy-two TECs, all independent companies employing staff on different terms and conditions, had to be wound up. Moreover, the TECs employed around 10,000 staff, but only 5,000 were transferred to the LSC, and this constituted the first major cut in staffing. The LSC also experienced the cultural challenge of merging very different types of organisation: the FEFC was widely regarded as highly centralised and bureaucratic, while the TECs were considered to be more entrepreneurial and autonomous. As one of the policy officials we interviewed observed, the TECs were 'on the other side of the management spectrum in a way. I mean, they'd gone off and done their own thing' (UA10).[2]

The Learning and Skills Act 2000 created the LSC as a single, non-departmental public body with forty-seven local LSCs (LLSC) organised on a sub-regional basis. From its inception, the government had very high expectations of the new organisation and of the whole sector. In a twenty-page remit letter to the LSC in November 2000, David Blunkett, the Secretary of State, charged the new body with drawing up a strategy both to meet the post-16 national learning targets and to enhance equal opportunities. He also added four wider objectives: to encourage young people to stay on in learning; to increase demand for learning by adults; to maximise the contribution of education and training to economic performance; and to raise standards. For the first time, a public body was also given the statutory duty to encourage participation in learning. These high political expectations of the LSC have continued. Each of the annual remit and grant letters has added to the LSC's initial objectives and has provided more detailed targets and new areas of work (see Finlay *et al.* 2007b for further details).

During this phase, planning was based upon three main processes: reviews of the performance of providers; three-year planning agreements between the forty-seven LLSC offices and providers; and strategic area reviews (StAR) of local provision. Provider performance reviews used information from self-assessment reports by providers, inspections, data returns and quality monitoring visits by LLSC staff to judge performance which, in turn, decided rates of funding. From late 2003, LLSCs also required providers to produce three-year development plans with improvement targets, and it was suggested for a short time that these plans would be backed by three-year funding agreements to give providers 'a basis for confident long-term planning' (LSC

2004d: 4) – although this funding stability never in fact materialised. The StAR process involved extensive consultation with local partners to consider radical and innovative options for change as well as to identify weaker provision. The LLSCs soon discovered, however, that they had neither the power nor the political support to reorganise sensitive areas like 16–19 provision, and StAR was quietly dropped in 2005, after two years of concerted effort up and down the country. At the same time, questions had begun to be asked about the capacity and experience of LLSC staff to undertake such comprehensive planning tasks.

From the beginning, the LSC also suffered from a conflict of expectations and values between those of its chairman, Bryan Sanderson, who came from the business sector (BP) and favoured a small central team, and those of the senior management team, headed by John Harwood, who came predominantly from the public sector and wanted a more inclusive approach to decision-making. So the potential for conflicts over values, management style and the relationship between the national LSC and its local arms was built into the structure from the outset.

Phase 2, 2004–6: the business model and a regional tier

In October 2003, after only two and a half years of operation, the LSC appointed a new chief executive, Mark Haysom, and several changes followed quickly. Haysom announced in January 2004 the creation of a regional management team with the appointment of ten regional directors to simplify the reporting structure that had previously involved regular meetings of over fifty LLSC and central LSC directors. The regional directors were also given substantial powers: for example, they 'can move funding and targets around between local LSCs and their providers' (LSC 2004d: 6). This action was swiftly followed by changes to the structure of the national LSC, which, from January 2004, was organised around two directorates: 'Learning' and 'Skills'. Three directorates – 'Quality and Standards', 'Strategic Marketing' and 'Operations' – were closed, which led to the second major reduction in staff, particularly at the centre but also in each LLSC. The whole thrust of the reorganisation was to make the LSC 'more streamlined, manageable and responsive' (LSC 2004e: 2).

So, within its first thirty months of existence, and because its performance in the first two years had not lived up to the expectations of politicians who were impatient for change, the LSC's structure and remit were changed to make it a more strategic planning and funding body. The changes resulted from the promotion of a business model (smaller centre, concentration on key functions and an annual business planning cycle of all its activities) by Mark Haysom, who was joined in July 2004 by a new chairman, Chris Banks, again from the private sector. The business model also meant introducing a 'clear line of sight' between national targets handed down by the Treasury, which were then turned into LSC priorities, plans and funding, which then, in turn, were translated into local targets (see Steer *et al.* 2007).

Our interviewees were convinced that, as a result of these changes, the balance of power shifted away from the national office in Coventry and away from the forty-seven LLSCs towards the regions and, in particular, towards a management board which has a majority of regional directors. The new regional arrangements had no statutory basis; the regional boards were 'purely internally created advisory boards' (UC02). Interviewees also stressed the significance of the new Regional Skills Partnerships (RSP), which were to become the main mechanism for getting 'all the bits of the organisational jigsaw more closely aligned to each other' (X03). The RSP 'will become the core accountable body' (UB08) for the central agencies of the LSC, the Regional Development Agency (RDA), JobCentre Plus (JC+), the Sector Skills Council (SSC) and the Small Business Council (SBC). The plan at that stage was for the RSP to achieve greater coherence in targets and policy among these key players, while the sub-regional level and the LLSCs were to remain the main mechanism for ensuring 'delivery'. The first RSP was launched in the North East in November 2004.

During its first years the main functions of the LSC were to plan and to fund post-compulsory education training. Beyond this, however, interviewees talked of role accretion and confusion as the LSC's remit grew. In August 2004, for example, the LSC took over responsibility for prison education from the Home Office. An official in one of our seminars commented: 'the LSC is suffering from priority overload'.

Role confusion, on the other hand, is the result of contradictions within policy, boundary disputes and political constraints. For example, it appeared to be rife between representatives of the Government Office North East, the RDA, the Regional Assembly and the LLSC. As one official remarked: 'I've been in meetings where all four of those [organisations] claim to lead on 14–19 at the present' (UB05).

Phase 3, 2006–7: moving towards a demand-led system and a divided sector: 14–19 skills and adult skills, 19+

Within five years of its founding, the LSC was expected to develop in a third and radically different way. The Leitch Review of Skills recommended a move to a fully demand-led system as 'the only way to ensure that the UK achieves world class skills' (Leitch 2006: 74). The recommendation that the sector must meet the needs of employers and individuals rather than be centrally planned, which has been accepted by government, will fundamentally change the role of the LSC; and, as the Leitch Report itself recognised, 'will require a further significant streamlining' (ibid.: 76), for the third time in six years. Leitch also proposed another radical change in the role of the LSC, which 'should not undertake detailed planning at national, regional or local level' (ibid.). This recommendation came only five years after the LSC was set up as a planning body and only two years after funding in the sector was to be 'plan-led'. One wonders who would consider building a career in an organisation which is so vulnerable to the capricious nature of such constant policy change. The new proposals for a demand-led system will be discussed in more detail later in this chapter.

In June 2007 the LSC was putting the final touches to the re-organisation from 47 local offices to 9 regional offices and 148 local partnerships, and still moving towards a demand-led system, when it was faced with yet another upheaval. The new Labour administration, led by Gordon Brown, introduced a major change to the machinery of government by dividing the Department for Education and Skills (DfES) in two and abolishing the Department of Trade and Industry (DTI). The new Department for Children, Schools and Families (DCSF) will deal with all aspects of policy affecting children and young people up to the age of nineteen. The new Department for Innovation, Universities and Skills (DIUS) has responsibility for research, science, enterprise and (fourth in the list) the skills of the adult workforce. A new Department for Business, Enterprise and Regulatory Reform (DBERR) is charged with promoting productivity, enterprise, competition, trade and better regulation.

These changes challenge the existence of a unified learning and skills sector because of the split of responsibilities, with DCSF taking the lead for the 14–19 phase and DIUS for adults. This was a possible future which we identified in our first published paper from the project in 2005 (Coffield et al. 2005). Notice that the word 'education' disappears from the title of the DCSF and that the word 'college' does not appear in the title of either of the two successors of the DfES.

The impact on the LSC of this departmental reorganisation can be gauged from the fact that by 2010/11 it will have lost around 60 per cent of its budget (£6.5 billion from £11.4 billion), as funding for school sixth forms, sixth-form colleges and the 14–19 phase in FE colleges is transferred to local authorities. The LSC will eventually lose one of its major powers – to plan and fund the 14–19 phase – and will concentrate instead on the adult skills agenda, principally by regulating the market for demand-led skills. The advantages and disadvantages of the new arrangements will be debated for some time, but the central issue is that government has again resorted to top-down structural change without consultation.

In the midst of such turbulence there is at least one continuity worthy of note. The long, varied and constantly expanding list of roles and tasks given to the LSS by government continues to grow despite the repeated reductions in staffing within the LSC. In Box 1.1, we list the main tasks (but by no means all of the tasks) which the LSS is expected to carry out between 2007 and 2020. Such multiple goals speak volumes for the ambitions that politicians have for the sector, but they prompt the question: is it being asked to do too much? Some of the tasks also call for deep cultural change of a kind we have not managed in fifty years: for example, the government's determination to get individuals and employers to pay much more towards the cost of learning and training.

Box 1.1   Key tasks proposed for learning and skills sector

Year	Task	
2007	1	1.5 million adults and young people to achieve basic skills
	2	Completion rate of 75% for apprentices (53% in 2005)
	3	New Framework for Excellence, a performance management system, to be introduced
	4	Quality Improvement Strategy to be fully operational
	5	Initial trials of Learner Accounts
	6	Fee contribution by learners to rise to 37.5% from 27.5%

continued

Year	Task	
2008	7	5 new specialised Diploma lines to be available for 14–19-year-olds
	8	All poor provision to be eliminated by LSC
	9	8 more National Skills Academies to open
	10	New Framework for Excellence to be used by all providers
	11	DfES to reduce staff specialising in LSS by 325
	12	60% of 16-year-olds to achieve 5 good GCSEs (56.4% in 2005)
	13	50,000 new post-16 places
2009	14	Common funding approach for colleges, sixth forms and training providers
	15	Qualifications and Credit Framework to be operational
	16	5 more Diploma lines to be available
2010	17	All 14 Diplomas for 14–19-year-olds to be widely available
	18	2.25 million adults and young people to improve basic skills
	19	Reduce by 40% proportion of adults without Level 2
	20	All FE teachers qualified or working towards a qualification
	21	Success rates for FE Colleges to be 80% (76% in 2007)
	22	50% of 18–30-year-olds in HE
	23	Foundation Learning Tier to have a full set of progression pathways
	24	200 Academies to be open
	25	Reduce by 2% proportion of young people not in education, employment or training
	26	Fee contribution by learners to rise to 50%
	27	A fully demand-led system to be in place
	28	22,000 Union Learning Representatives
	29	Foundation degree places to rise to 100,000
2012	30	A self-regulating system to be in place, raising standards and tackling underperformance
2013	31	All 14 Diploma lines available nationwide for 14–19-year-olds
	32	85% of 19-year-olds to achieve a Level 2 qualification

Year	Task	
2013	33	Leaving age in England to be raised to 17
2015	34	90% of 17-year-olds participating in education or training
	35	Majority of adult FE budget to be demand-led
	36	Leaving age in England to be raised to 18
2020	37	95% of adults with basic skills (85% literacy and 79% numeracy in 2005): i.e., treble projected rates of improvement
	38	90+% of adults with Level 2 (69% in 2005)
	39	500,000 apprentices (256,000 in 2005)
	40	40+% of adults with Level 4 (29% in 2005)

The main achievements of the sector

This is a good time to take stock of what has been achieved so far by the LSC and by the wider sector. Since its inception, the LSC has met all the major targets set for it by the government, which is more than any other public service can boast, not just within education. For example, nearly 1.7 million people have been helped to improve their basic literacy, numeracy and language skills (LSC 2007c); a network of over 400 Centres of Vocational Excellence (CoVEs) has been put in place; more than 15,000 Union Learning Representatives (ULRs) have been appointed to engage their colleagues in learning; the number of young people starting apprenticeships has risen from 75,000 in 1997 to a record number of 250,000 in 2006; FE success rates have climbed steadily to 77 per cent in 2005–6 (DfES 2006a); and a major investment of over £10 billion has been made in the physical infrastructure, the fruits of which can be seen in the state-of-the-art new buildings on FE campuses up and down the country. See Box 1.2 for a summary of the sector's main achievements.

These are impressive achievements in anyone's book, and yet some glaring deficiencies remain, chief of which is what the policy-makers themselves call 'the scandal of our high drop out rate at 16' (DfES 2004: 71). According to the LSC, 'Currently, around a quarter of young people are not in any form of education or training and 11 per cent (220,000) are' Not in Education, Employment or Training – the so-called NEET group (2006a: 5).

Box 1.2 Main achievements of the sector

Target	Progress
Increase number of 19-year-olds with Level 2 to 69.8% by autumn 2006	69.8% in autumn 2005 (66.8% in 2004)
One million employed adults with Level 2 by 2006	841,000 in autumn 2005
Improve basic skills of 1.5 million adults by 2007 (Skills for Life)	1.619 million in 2007 (337,000 in 2001–2)
Student success rates in FE to reach 78% by 2007–8	77% in 2005–6 (57% in 2001–2)
Reduce proportion of colleges deemed inadequate by inspection	4% in 2005–6 (11% in 2001–2)
Increase number of colleges deemed outstanding by inspection	151 in 2005–6 (25 in 2001–2)
75,500 apprenticeship completions by 2007–8	97,457 in 2005–6 (37,400 in 2001–2)
Introduce Employer Training Pilots	By March 2006, 30,000 employers and 250,000 involved

Sources: ALI (2006a), DfES (2007a), LSC (2006a, 2007a, 2007b, 2007c)

Complexity of the sector

Enough has been said already to indicate that this is an immensely complicated and varied sector, usually defined by its difference from both the school sector (it deals mainly with adults and has links with business) and higher education (it serves local communities and offers a second chance to those who have failed at school) – see Gleeson *et al.* (2005) for further details. Some officials and the FE White Paper (DfES 2006b) have begun to use the phrase 'the FE system' to refer to the wider sector, which includes government agencies such as the Qualifications and Curriculum Authority (QCA), the Quality Improvement Agency for Lifelong Learning (QIA) and independent learning providers as well as FE colleges.

We prefer, however, to use the term 'the learning and skills sector' because it incorporates adult and community learning (ACL) and work-based learning (WBL), alongside FE, which admittedly takes up the lion's share of the LSC's budget. It is only, however, when one tries to pull all the main constituent parts of the sector into one diagram that its complexity becomes apparent. Figure 1.1 mainly represents the institutional architecture of the post-compulsory sector, and includes the rationalisation undertaken by the government in 2006. Only the minimum number of agencies, players and initiatives, needed to understand the sector and this book, has been included but that still called for the use of thirty-seven abbreviations. We can come to one conclusion immediately: this landscape urgently needs to be simplified, and yet there are costs to every restructuring which we explore in the final chapter.

Figure 1.1 looks more like the chart of the internal wiring of an advanced computer than the outline of a 'streamlined', coherent sector; it is also the outcome of years of constant interference and tinkering by successive ministers and civil servants, which has resulted in too many intermediate organisations, particularly at the regional level. What Figure 1.1 cannot reveal, however, is the social impact of these successive changes. For example, the government has been attempting for years to get employers involved in skill formation; and yet those civic-minded employers who gave freely of their time, enthusiasm and expertise by serving on the councils of the forty-seven LLSCs now feel disgruntled about these councils being disbanded. Changing one part of the sector has therefore had perverse consequences for another part by turning supporters into frustrated critics whose goodwill has been squandered. When the sector is so densely interconnected, structural change destroys networks and partnerships which have taken years to build.

Figure 1.1 does, however, have the twin merits of including the six million learners who tend to be omitted from such charts and of encouraging all of us to think how the sector could become a more cohesive and equitable system, despite the seriously unequal power relationships between the main players. Such a diagram may therefore be helpful to newcomers by providing an overview of the sector, as long as they realise that being part of the sector does not guarantee that they understand it.

Figure 1.1 The post-compulsory sector in England, 2006–7

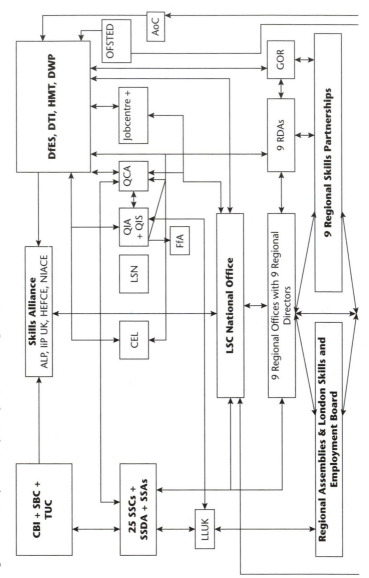

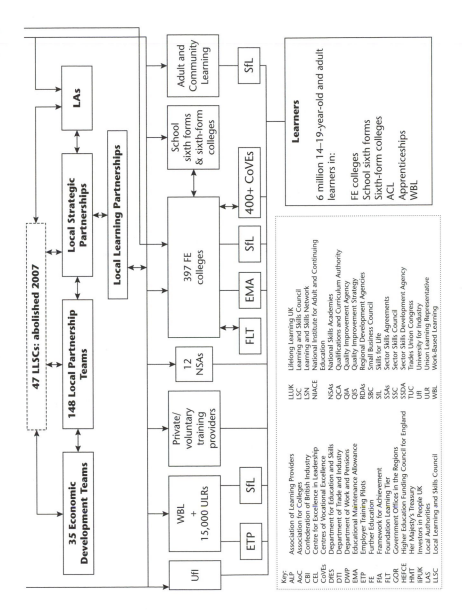

A new mission for the sector

The government also commissioned two far-ranging reviews, the recommendations of which are still reverberating through the sector.[3] First, Sir Andrew Foster (2005) reviewed the future role of FE colleges; and, at the same time, Lord Leitch (2006) was commissioned by the then Chancellor, Gordon Brown, to assess our future skill needs. Nearly all the recommendations of the Foster Report were incorporated into the White Paper on FE and the subsequent FE and Training Bill, which at the time of writing is making its way through the House of Commons.

As we shall see, Foster has set in train some far-reaching changes, but Leitch's proposals, which appear to have been accepted wholesale by the government with minimal public debate, call for a radical break with the past and a move to an entirely new 'demand-led' system. Foster required significant changes to be made, but Leitch opted for a high-risk strategy which could bring about the closure of institutions. Together, their impact on the sector could be seismic. We will defend the use of that adjective, which some may at first find excessive.

Foster characterised FE as the 'disadvantaged middle child' between schools and higher education, which, above all, 'lacks a clearly recognised and shared core purpose' (2005: 5–6). He proposed that 'the unique core focus of FE should be in skill building for the economy' (*ibid*.: 22): that is, the sector is to be 'reconfigured' around skills and employability. For many commentators, however, the new mission of employability is too narrowly utilitarian; in the language of C. Wright Mills, employability turns the public issue of the dearth of good jobs into the private trouble of constant retraining (see Coffield 2007).

Foster made more than eighty recommendations, and only the most significant can be mentioned briefly here. The DfES is no longer 'to micro-manage LSC or FE Colleges . . . Equally, LSC must not micro-manage FE Colleges and other providers' (Foster 2005: 62). In response to the age profile of the workforce (almost a third over fifty) and its casualisation (over 17 per cent do not have permanent full- or part-time contracts), Foster also recommended the introduction of a new workforce strategy to improve leadership, management and continuing professional development (CPD) for all staff.

In addition, the government took the opportunity in the Further Education and Training Bill (2006) to restructure the LSC by establishing nine regional councils and abolishing the forty-seven LLSCs, introduced only five years earlier. Its powers of intervention in FE institutions were also considerably strengthened by the Bill, which allows it to remove all or any member of the governing body (including the principal), to appoint new members and to give that body directions. The Bill also allows FE colleges to apply for powers to award their own foundation degrees.

The move to a demand-led system

The sector was still trying to absorb the significance of all these changes when Lord Leitch published his final report in December 2006. His starting point was the UK's historic deficit in skills: 'The UK's skills base remains mediocre by international standards' (Leitch 2006: 10). Even worse, if all the current challenging targets were to be met, the UK would still remain average by the standards of the Organisation for Economic Co-operation and Development: 'The UK is on track to achieve [in 2020] the same proportion of high skill workers that the US and Canada have today' (*ibid.*: 46).

The analysis carried out by Leitch has been generally accepted, apart from the claim, advanced three times without any evidence, that 'where skills were once **a** key driver of prosperity and fairness, they are now **the** key driver' (*ibid.*: 9; original emphases). His prescriptions have, however, proved to be far more contentious, although welcomed by Bill Rammell, the then Minister for Further and Higher Education (Rammell 2007). Leitch's central recommendation is a move towards a more 'demand-led' system, by which is meant responding to demand from employers and individuals rather than trying, as at present, to plan supply: 'This means all adult skills funding should be routed through Train to Gain and Learner Accounts by 2010' (Leitch 2006: 138).

Briefly, Train to Gain (T2G) is a government-funded scheme that provides both free training for employees to reach a first Level 2 qualification and wage compensation to employers to meet the cost of the time off for training; and, Skills Accounts, the new name for Learner Accounts, will allow individuals to access information, advice and guidance provided by the new universal adult careers service as well as an account card that shows them their entitlement to train (DIUS 2007). Both of these schemes, however, are untried in their current form: the first is in its infancy and the other is still in gestation. Julian Gravatt, the Director of Funding and Development at the Association of Colleges, has noted that both are under the control of government and so it has the power to implement these changes, which will amount to 'nothing short of a revolution in the way that adult learning is funded' (Gravatt 2007: 20).

In short, a market is to be created in the funding of adult skills and the LSC has been given the role of 'market-maker' with powers to intervene with public funding where the market is failing. To give one example of a long-standing failure, one-third of firms in the UK do no training of any kind (Leitch 2006: 12). Moreover, the term 'demand-led' is being interpreted by government to mean that only those learners who take qualifications approved by the SSCs will be publicly funded. (There is a network of twenty-five SSCs which identify the training needs and priorities of employers in all sectors of the economy. They are meant to represent the independent voice of employers, but in effect they were initiated by the DfES and are still largely government- rather than employer-funded.) So employers and individuals will be able to demand only those courses which the government has decided to fund, in a semi-regulated and constrained market, rather than in a genuinely open market. For example, there is currently huge demand from immigrants and asylum-seekers for courses in English for speakers of other languages (ESOL), but there is not the political will to fund these.

For markets to work efficiently and fairly, customers need at least to be knowledgeable about changes in the labour market, the quality of training courses and the economic returns attached to different qualifications so that they can make informed choices. Such conditions do not, however, exist. Indeed, the quality of information, advice and guidance is notoriously patchy in England, particularly for adults, which led Leitch to recommend the establishment of the new universal adult careers service that is now to be taken up by the government (DIUS 2007).

The fundamental flaw in the government's plan, however, is that in essence adult education is *not* a market and it will suffer from being treated as such. It is a process whereby tutors engage students in the knowledge, attitudes and competences associated with their specialism. The relationship between tutor and student is the heart of the matter and all the paraphernalia of the regulated market in the LSS (the concentration on products rather than processes, on customers rather than learners, on funding formulae and administration rather than pedagogy) is a dangerous distraction. If the main objective is to improve the learning of students, tutors and managers, then we have to pay most attention to the central processes of learning: the quality of the relationship between tutors and students; the tutors' subject knowledge and vocational experience; their understanding of pedagogy; and their concern for students. The advantages and disadvantages of the move to a demand-led system are summarised in Box 1.3.

Box 1.3 Moving to a demand-led system

- **The plan** The system will give employers and individuals the power to choose the training they want by responding to their demands rather than trying to plan supply.

- **Funding** Providers will receive funding only as they attract customers, and funding will follow the choices made by employers/individuals. All public funding for adult vocational skills (around £3 billion) will be routed through Train to Gain (T2G) and Skills Accounts.

- **Timetable** Leitch recommends an acceleration of change to a demand-led system by 2010, so the proportion of funds open to competition between providers will increase very rapidly from 2007 to 2008.

- **New roles** The LSC will become 'the market-maker', stimulating competition and providing funding to enable new providers to build their capacity and so enter the market. The LSC predicts it will have to create three different markets: for 14–19 provision, for adults and for employers. The SSCs will provide the LSC with a list of approved qualifications to be funded through the public purse.

- **Official claims for the new system** It will drive up quality, make providers more responsive to employers and learners, and deliver more innovation. Employer engagement and investment in training will increase, as will productivity.

- **Prizes and risks** The plan aims to change the sector once and for all; it is also the highest risk ever attempted by a government in this field. Even the LSC is putting in place 'transitional protection to ensure that the changes do not destabilise institutions' (LSC and DfES 2007: 31). T2G is a new programme, based on Employer Training Pilots (ETPs), which were criticised for too much dead weight: that is, paying for training that employers would have paid for anyway. The initial trials of Skills Accounts have only just begun. So transforming all adult provision by means of these two schemes by 2010 seems very optimistic

continued

> and this has now been recognised by the government (DIUS 2007).
>
> • **Criticisms** The plan will create continuous uncertainty over funding which will undermine short-term and long-term planning. The market will force all providers, public and independent, to 'cream-skim' – compete for those courses which are least costly to mount and attract the most students. Provision for disadvantaged communities and individuals may be badly affected, as may vocational courses which are expensive to run. The market will do little if anything to help the unemployed. The 'product' needs to be valued by the customers but they have not been fully consulted, neither 14–19-year-olds over the diplomas, nor adults over T2G.

Another serious concern about Leitch's proposals is that qualifications are used throughout as a proxy for skills. One of our interviewees made this point graphically:

> Hardly anybody in China is qualified to Level 2. The fact that they manufacture 50 per cent of the world's computers and textiles, and 60 per cent of digital cameras and mobile phones in the world has got nothing to do with qualification levels – it's cheap labour. Qualifying everybody up to Level 2 isn't going to shift mobile-phone manufacture from China to the UK.
>
> (ZA28)

There are therefore real dangers in relying solely on qualifications/skills to secure our economic prosperity, because they are a necessary but insufficient condition for economic success. We also need investment in physical capital, research and development, good industrial relations, an integrated transport system, etc. Moreover, even all five of the Treasury's 'levers' of productivity – competition, innovation, enterprise, investment and skills – may not be sufficient because these levers 'are unconnected with what happens inside the firm . . . productivity is not primarily about inputs but the messy, complex human process of turning them into usable outputs . . . the supply of skills may have increased, but employers' ability to use them hasn't' (Caulkin 2007: 21). Later, we shall be making a similar argument about the slow, painstaking work of reform in classrooms.

The self-chosen mantra of the Leitch Report is 'economically valuable skills' and a distinction is already being drawn between people thought to be 'economically valuable' and those in whom the state thinks it is not worth investing. This is an example of the tendency to increased social inequality and polarisation which Manuel Castells predicted under globalisation: 'a considerable number of humans, probably in a growing proportion, are irrelevant, both as producers and consumers, from the perspective of the system's logic' (Castells 1998: 344). For FE colleges and ACL centres, it is becoming increasingly difficult to protect, as they have done in the past 'because they perceived themselves to have some public duty in respect of those people' (ZA30), valuable learners with learning difficulties or disabilities.

College principals are trying to predict how the new demand-led market will work, with independent training providers competing with them for the same business, and with the LSC actively encouraging new competitors to enter those parts of the market where none exist at present. Colleges claim that the independent providers will concentrate on those courses with high volumes of students which are cheap to deliver – what is known in the trade as 'cream skimming'. To avoid losing large sections of their current income, 'Colleges will be driven to behave in exactly the same way' (ZA30). Three perverse consequences are likely and all are foreseeable. First, courses for the disadvantaged or learning disabled will tend to be dropped, with serious implications for social inclusion. Second, rural areas may lose out because resources will be concentrated in larger, more remote providers. Third, and less obviously, vocational provision which is expensive to deliver, such as engineering or construction, may also become threatened, because the market will tempt all providers, public and independent alike, to offer mainly low-cost courses where the greatest financial returns can be made. But it is exactly the expensive, knowledge-based courses that are the ones needed to boost the UK's productivity.

Policy analysts have become familiar with 'the law of unintended consequences . . . for every policy initiative there will be unpredicted and unpredictable results' (Fink 2003, quoted by Wallace and Hoyle 2005: 3). The actions of this government have also brought into being the law of perverse but foreseeable consequences – policy produces some unwelcome results which could have been avoided, if only professionals had been consulted earlier.

The response of the FE colleges to the Foster and Leitch proposals was, to judge from the comments of the institutional leaders we have interviewed, initially one of shock and mild hysteria which over time has mellowed into a pragmatic determination to protect their institutions. One foresaw 'significant destabilisation of the FE sector, potentially colleges failing financially' (ZA30); another did not think the new demand-led system would work and was likely to break down within five years; a third thought the new measures were more threatening than any previous initiative. The official response of the University and College Union, the largest union representing the LSS workforce, considered that 'the creation of a market driven learning and skills system has the potentiality to destroy over a hundred years of continuous public service by FE Colleges . . . and in doing so perhaps wreak immense damage on the very infrastructures of adult learning and skills development' (UCU 2007: 2).

There is, however, something new in the comments we have collected from our final round of interviews with the key players in the sector. It comes as no surprise to anyone that deeply committed professionals and union leaders are critical of a radical government initiative. But the latest proposals from Leitch have elicited a new type of response from institutional leaders who believe politicians and policy-makers are now living in a parallel universe, having lost touch with the hard realities of running large, complex institutions, which wish to invest long term to protect the needs of marginalised communities and disadvantaged learners as part of their public service ethos. Policy formation in this sector has come to a pretty pass when the first reaction of a senior professional to a major speech on the reforms by a government minister is to enquire: 'What planet is he on?' (ZA28).

The new model of public services reform

In the world of learning and skills, another major feature of the landscape is the government's determination to improve the efficiency, quality and equity of the service. In 2006 the Prime Minister's Strategy Unit (PMSU) published a new model of reform for all the public services, including health, the criminal justice system and housing as well as education. As can be see from Figure 1.2, the model consists of four elements, each of which is intended to exert pressure for change:

- top-down performance management: e.g., targets, standards and inspection;
- market incentives: e.g., competition and contestability (encouraging competitors to enter a market where none exists);

- users shaping the sector from below: e.g., so-called 'choice and voice';
- increasing the capacity of organisations and the capability of the workforce.

The PMSU claims that the model represents the lessons learned since New Labour came to power in 1997 – the limitations of top-down performance management and of competition have apparently been recognised. The new approach combines pressure from above (government), from below (citizens) and horizontally (competition and building capacity), with the intention of creating a self-improving system based on continuous improvement and innovation. 'Continuous improvement', however, as David Sherlock, who was Chief Inspector of Adult Learning, argues, 'demands continuity' (Sherlock 2007: 1).

It is immediately obvious that the experiences, concerns and innovative ideas of the professionals who run the sector are conspicuously absent from the model. This is not an oversight but deliberate policy, as can be seen from the identical treatment of staff in the National Health Service. The co-chair of the Consultants' Association commented recently: 'this government has deliberately disempowered the profession . . . There has been no meaningful involvement of the profession

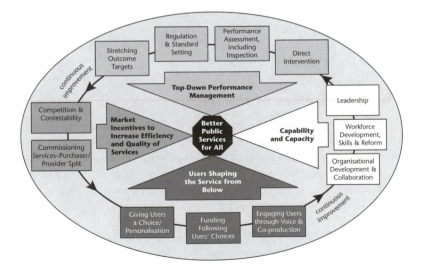

Figure 1.2 Government model of public service reform

Source: PMSU (2006: 8)

in the frenetic and incoherent reforms' (Davis 2007: 33). The same can be said for professionals within the LSS, which means that the story told in this book has a much wider relevance beyond learning and skills: it is a study of the strengths and weaknesses of policy as a means of 'transforming' a major public service and it contains salutary lessons for all the other services.

The government has apparently had a change of heart towards professionals since the publication of the PMSU discussion document, because in the policy review paper entitled, *Building on Progress: public services*, published in March 2007, it promises to 'harness the commitment, dedication and skills of public service workers' (PMSU 2007: 55). It proposes four mechanisms to involve staff in planning: reducing the number of top-down controls, encouraging leading Whitehall figures to 'shadow' front-line staff, developing new policy, and setting targets in partnership with policy-makers.

Towards the end of its ten years in office, this administration, which has imposed a continuously toughening regime of command and control from the centre, now recants and advises its successor to behave in a very different fashion, while simultaneously introducing (without consultation) new measures, like demand-led, which threaten to destabilise public institutions. Will union learning representatives be consulted about T2G and the setting of local targets? Will ministers finally refrain from dreaming up initiative after initiative and from constant interference? It could happen and only time will tell. But, after three and a half years of studying this sector, we shall not be holding our breath.

The organisation of the book

In Chapter 2 we introduce our project by describing its main aim, its objectives and methods of collecting and analysing the data. We also explain our theoretical stance, begin to explore the separate worlds of policy and practice and show how we sought to understand the interactions between these two worlds by examining the role of five policy levers in the management of change. The chapter ends with a set of crucial questions which we have asked ourselves throughout this study, and which we attempt to answer in the final chapter.

We have decided to present the data we collected as a series of narratives or stories, partly because narrative is a useful structure for organising it and partly because, as Jerome Bruner pointed out, 'stories worth telling . . . are typically born in trouble' (Bruner 1996: 142). And the stories we have to tell, when taken together, speak of a turbulent world which is entering a new and uncertain phase.

In Chapter 3 we begin with the stories the learners have to tell – their positive experiences of learning in the LSS, but also the problems of progressing to higher-level courses. We also return to the learners in Chapter 6 by discussing whether governmental and institutional strategies aimed at including ever-more learners are effective and what is needed to make them more so. In Chapter 4 we offer the perspectives of the policy-makers, their key texts, achievements and plans for the future. In Chapter 5 we tell the stories of the tutors and managers who have to juggle both change and continuity. Chapter 7 is rather different in that we try to explain how the sector as a whole operates: the different ways in which policy instruments are translated and mistranslated by different actors at different levels within the sector. In the final chapter we pull together all these stories into a brief summary of what we have learned; then we look forward and outline the features of an alternative system which is more equitable, effective and democratic, elements of which are already present in the LSS and in other areas of the public services.

There is a rationale for this framework which relates directly to one of our main purposes: namely, attempting to understand the interactions between the different levels within the sector. So we have deliberately chosen to move from a 'bottom-up' perspective (the chapter on the views of learners) to a 'top-down' approach (the chapter on the concerns of policy-makers) to a 'view from the middle' (the chapter on the tensions felt by managers and tutors) and so on throughout the book. By this means we hope to convey something of the complexity, scale and richness of the LSS, as well of the inherent difficulties in pulling it together into one cohesive system.

This chapter has sought to introduce some of the main themes and debates which currently run through the LSS and which will be picked up and dealt with in more detail in subsequent chapters. We have tried to indicate the pivotal importance of the sector, the radical character of the reforms proposed for it and the high risks to the institutions and courses on which millions of people depend. The next few years will prove to be decisive for this sector as its resilience is put to the test as never before by government policy. We fully expect to see closures, mergers and new federations of FE colleges, school sixth forms and perhaps even independent providers. This is a space to watch.

Notes

1   The researchers wish to acknowledge the funding of this project by the ESRC – reference number RES-139-25-0105.
2   For an explanation of the codes we use to protect the confidentiality of interviewees quoted, see the Appendix.
3   The Tomlinson Report on the reform of the curriculum and qualifications for 14–19-year-olds is not dealt with here as its main conclusions were not accepted by the government, but it is discussed in Chapter 4. See Working Group on 14–19 Reform (2004).

Chapter 2

Studying the learning and skills sector

Introduction

We began work in January 2004 and finished forty-three months later in July 2007, and in the process we became one of the few constants in the learning and skills sector, where staff, agencies and initiatives come and go. Our overall aim was to explore the impact of national policy on learning and inclusion in this sector. Our three main objectives were:

- to study the roles and relationships between the key partners within the LSS, by studying the impact of five policy levers: targets, funding, planning, inspection and initiatives such as Skills for Life (SfL);
- to test how inclusive the new sector is;
- to develop and test a model of an effective and inclusive local learning system.

It was clearly impossible to study everything in such a massive system, so we decided to focus on three disadvantaged groups of learners: unemployed adults taking basic skills courses in adult and community learning centres; low-skilled adult employees in work-based learning; and younger learners on Level 1 and Level 2 vocational courses in FE colleges.

We wanted to capture the perspectives of these learners and the tutors who worked with them, but also those of the officials responsible for making and enacting policy at all levels in the sector – national, regional and local – as well as the international perspective of our European partners, as an alternative source of ideas and approaches. In addition, we have analysed the main policy documents in the sector, amassing a database of over 300 papers.

Box 2.1　The levels of the sector we studied

1　**International Level** e.g., European Commission
2　**National Level – Central Government** e.g., Cabinet Office
3　**National Level – Departments** e.g., DfES
4　**National Level – 'Arm's-Length' Agencies** e.g., national LSC, QIA, QCA, ALI, OFSTED, SSC; **Independent Organisations** e.g., awarding bodies, Unions, CBI
5　**Regional Level** e.g., regional LSCs, RDAs
6　**Local Level** e.g., LSC partnership teams, local authorities

	FE	ACL	WBL
7	**Institutional Level** College Principals	**Centre** Managers	**Firm** Managing Director
8	**Departmental Level** Faculties	**Course Level** Leader Training Manager, ULR	**Training Department**
9	**Course Level** Managers, Leaders	**Classroom Level** Tutors	**Classroom Level** Tutors
10	**Classroom Level** Teachers	**Learners**	**Learners**
11	**Learners**		

Key:

ACL	Adult and Community Learning
ALI	Adult Learning Inspectorate
CBI	Confederation of British Industry
DfES	Department for Education and Skills
FE	Further Education
LSC	Learning and Skills Council
OFSTED	Office for Stanards in Education
QCA	Qualifications and Curriculum Authority
QIA	Quality Improvement Agency
RDA	Regional Development Agency
SSC	Sector Skills Council
ULR	Union Learning Representative
WBL	Work-Based Learning

Box 2.1 shows both how many levels there are within the sector and the range of participants who contributed to our research. We deliberately chose to include so many different levels because at each level policy is changed as it percolates down to practice. Our attempts to understand the intervening levels between policy-making in Whitehall and practice in the classroom helped us to formulate our ideas on what principles and features might underpin a more equitable, effective and inclusive learning and skills system; we explain these in the final chapter.

Data collection and analysis

We began collecting data when the LSC was entering its second phase at the beginning of 2004 and continued to do so for more than three years. The data fell into two broad categories:

- That collected from policy-makers and officials forming and enacting policy. This 'view from above' is about the aims and objectives of policy, and the mechanisms by which these are to be achieved.
- That collected in learning sites, from managers, teachers and learners. This 'view from below' is about what is happening in practice and the perceptions of impact both of policy and of other factors on learning and inclusion for learners in 2004–6.

'Above' and 'below' are, of course, relative terms. Although the first group were, from the perspective of the learning site staff, promoting the 'view from above', we note that within the first group were many officials who saw themselves as 'in the middle', mediating policy messages 'from above', as they worked with practitioners in the sector, and with other organisations at the same level as their own. Similarly, senior managers in some sites who saw themselves as recipients of policy instructions 'from above' were seen by tutors as agents of policy.

In the course of the project, however, an important third type of data collection emerged, through observation and participation in events which bring together 'the view from above' and 'the view from below'. A very important part of our methodology was a series of annual seminars, one in Newcastle and one in London each year, bringing practitioners, managers and tutors from the learning sites, together with officials and other players in the policy scene, to hear about our findings to date and to have an opportunity to discuss and challenge them in a forum of those who all work in the learning and skills sector, but who have no official opportunity to meet.

The format was fruitful in many ways. In 2006, for example, DfES and LSC officials were so surprised by the gap between their own understandings of policy and the impacts which practitioners were describing that they encouraged us to organise a special one-day seminar, in November 2006, on the Skills for Life target. The many interviews described below are therefore not the only data upon which we have drawn for analysis. Box 2.2 provides an overview of the different ways we collected data. More detail of these processes is provided in the Appendix.

The project began with an analysis of key policy documents and an intensive series of confidential interviews with officials, identifying

---

Box 2.2 Gathering the data

- **From policy**
  - Analysis of over 300 policy documents.
  - 131 interviews with 123 policy actors at many levels, including 52 interviews with LSC staff, national, regional and local; 27 with officials in national ministries and agencies; 5 with staff based in and around the European Commission; 47 with other national, regional or local bodies.

- **From learning sites**
  - 12 sites in London and 12 in the North East.
  - 8 ACL, 8 FE (4 Level 1 courses; 4 Level 2 courses) and 8 WBL sites.
  - Each site visited 4 times (5 for FE), to interview a tutor, a manager and up to 6 learners.
  - 333 interviews with students (individual or group), involving 349 learners.
  - 210 interviews with 109 tutors, managers and ULRs.

- **Bringing policy-makers and practitioners together**
  - Annual seminars in London and the North East (2004–7).
  - Additional seminar on Skills for Life targets (2006).
  - Online survey on key findings (2007).

the policies which they believed were effective and exploring how they believed policy levers were working. Interviews were conducted throughout the project with officials and representatives of the DfES, the LSC, the Inspectorate (OFSTED and Adult Learning Inspectorate (ALI)), the RDAs, the SSCs, employer and union organisations, provider organisations, awarding bodies and other players in the sector. In late 2006/early 2007 we returned to many of the same organisations to update their perspective and discuss our emerging findings. In March 2007 we interviewed some key figures in adult education and lifelong learning in Brussels.

Policy interviews helped us to understand the intentions and processes of policy, but the evidence of impact (or lack of impact) could be found only in the sites where learning takes place. We therefore interviewed learners, tutors and course managers in twenty-four learning sites. The reasons for the choice of learning sites need to be explained further. First, the two regions in which we collected data are very different in their local economy, their labour markets, their skill profiles and their demography. Second, the sites we chose were recommended, either by LSC officials or by college senior managers, as places where we might find 'good practice' (see Coffield and Edward forthcoming). We were often impressed by the quality of teaching and learning in the sites, but we are aware that we cannot generalise from our very small sample to all similar provision. Third, we opted for depth, rather than breadth, making repeated visits to the twenty-four sites to monitor change and learn how policy was received over time, rather than investigating a larger sample of tutors, managers and learners on just one occasion.

This research design has, we reckon, given us a far better understanding of the challenges which tutors, managers and learners face than making single visits to 104 different sites could have done. Nevertheless, 24 learning sites represent only a drop in the ocean in the vast LSS, with 531 post-16 institutions (LSC 2006b: 9) each offering many courses, and more than six million learners in FE, community or work-based learning.

The WBL learning sites were very varied in terms of both employment sectors and learning environment. On each of the visits to these sites, typically we interviewed up to six learners, their tutor and the manager of their course, the ULR and, where appropriate, the line manager. Where possible, we interviewed the same group of learners on all site visits. This wider range of interviewees helped us not only to understand the individuals' expectations and experiences of being an adult basic skills learner and the perspectives of their tutors, but to get a sense of how supportive – or obstructive – their working environments were to their learning, and whether their learning was having any impact on those workplaces (see Evans *et al.* 2006 on expansive and restrictive learning environments).

The learners on the FE sites were studying for Level 1 qualifications in Health and Social Care or Childcare, or for Level 2 qualifications in Business Studies or Painting and Decorating. During the first visit in 2004 a group interview was conducted with each group of learners towards the end of their course; on subsequent visits in 2005 (visits 2 and 3) and 2006 (visits 4 and 5) we talked individually to the same six learners in the first few weeks of their one-year course, and again the following summer when they reported on their personal experiences of the course. This pattern enabled us to observe tremendous growth in confidence in some students, and also, if the learner was no longer on the course, to ask the tutor why he or she had left, and indeed to review the expectations of achievement and progression for the whole group. On our fourth visit, we observed a classroom session for most of the groups, seeing at first hand, for example, the challenges of teaching a class with a majority of learners requiring learning support or physical assistance, the patient efforts required to encourage all class members to participate fully, and the mutual support among learners. On our final visit, we also asked the learners to show us their portfolios of work completed over the year, as a visual aid to demonstrating their progress. This gave us an opportunity to see the feedback on assignments which had helped them to this point.

On visits to the ACL sites, we spoke to tutors, managers and up to six learners, although we sometimes found fewer learners available on the day, especially in centres where drop-in provision was the norm. Patterns of basic skills courses, sometimes in weekly twilight classes, sometimes drop-in sessions, sometimes intensive weeks of preparation for taking a national test, also made it impossible for us to interview learners at the beginning and end of their course in the way we had done in FE colleges, although where possible we followed up learners we had met on previous visits.

Four further features of our approach helped to strengthen our confidence in our findings (these are described in some detail in the Appendix, which contains a fuller account of our methods):

- repeated visits by the same small team of researchers;
- iterative data analysis throughout the project;

- feeding back interim findings to participants, for corroboration or challenge;
- bringing together participants from different parts of the sector, who would not normally have a chance to meet.

Theoretical stance

> Theory is a necessary myth that we construct to understand something we know we understand incompletely.
>
> (Sarason 1990: 123)

Our stance towards theory has been unashamedly eclectic and we have used the work of a wide variety of theoreticians to help us understand or test our data, or to sharpen the questions we used in interviews. For example, when we wished to explore with students their inclusion in the life of their college, we turned to Basil Bernstein's ideas about 'a set of pedagogic rights for evaluating democracy in education', which provided us with principles to examine practice (Bernstein 1996: 5). Bernstein reminded us of the right to be included socially, intellectually, culturally and personally, and of the right to be separate and autonomous; but turning his theory into questions which would be easily understood by our 16- and 17-year-old interviewees proved difficult. For instance, Bernstein's first condition for an effective democracy is that 'people must feel that they have a stake in society' (*ibid.*: 6); we would have run the risk of being misunderstood if we had asked the young people in our sample whether they had a stake in college.

Similarly, when we were trying to understand models of change, the practice of policy-making and the diversity, complexity and dynamics within governance, we turned to the writings of Jan Kooiman (2003) and of John Clarke and Janet Newman (Clarke and Newman 1997; Newman 2000, 2001, 2005), whose names and ideas will crop up repeatedly in this and subsequent chapters. Like them, we viewed the state as Gramsci did: as passing through a series of 'unstable equilibria' (that is, temporary settlements and accommodations to changing external conditions and internal relationships), which are so contested and contradictory that the resulting instabilities repeatedly call for new settlements (see Clarke and Newman 1997: 140); and we shall be calling for a new settlement ourselves in the final chapter. By reference to their work, we were able to place our analysis of policy and practice in the LSS into a wider theoretical, political and social context.

In what follows the theories of many experts (e.g., Ball, Bruner, Lave and Wenger, Rawls, Wenger) and the ideas of many specialists in the sector (e.g., Field, Fletcher, Hamilton, Hodkinson, Keep, Stanton, Unwin) are called upon where we found them helpful in improving our methodology or developing concepts in the building of new theory or in sharpening our understanding or critique of the sector.

The separate worlds of policy and practice

In this project we attempted to understand the complex ways in which some of the official levers of change were used in attempts to affect practice in a variety of organisational settings. In doing so, we studied two very different worlds and how the first world sought to 'transform' the second. On the one hand, we entered the carpeted, controlled and controlling world of policy-makers, who may sit in plush offices but who have been given the daunting task of securing tangible outcomes which will convince ministers that increased investment in the sector has paid off. On the other hand, we witnessed at first hand the vibrant, messy lives of students and hard-pressed tutors and managers, often working in cramped conditions, sometimes in Portakabins, an empty flat or a bus garage (although the facilities in some FE colleges were being steadily upgraded during the period of our research). The task facing this or any government, in trying to improve the achievements of millions of students and the practices of hundreds of thousands of tutors, is therefore immense, and was probably seriously underestimated by the New Labour administrations of 1997 and 2001.

The government's new model of public sector reform, discussed at the end of Chapter 1, represents in part a belated recognition that the public services are too vast and complex ever to be 'transformed' by an apparently simple set of change mechanisms, such as targets, funding and inspection. Hence the new determination to pressurise the sector into enforced self-improvement, where institutions will in future be held accountable for generating the continuous changes considered desirable by the centre.

The stories we wish to tell in this book are complicated. On the one hand, we need to avoid suggesting that all policy-makers are the same (see Chapter 4), or that policy simply determines practice; but on the other, we need to convey that government legislation and policy levers set the parameters for action, while at the same time leaving open spaces for professionals to exercise agency and entrepreneurship, which some are able to exploit better than others. Professionals do feel increasingly constrained, but the plethora of policy documents, initiatives and levers, and the lack of coherence between them, produce what Clarke and Newman (1997) call 'policy vacuums', which provide the more enterprising practitioners with the space in which to adapt rather than to apply policy and, at times, to reshape it in ways more in keeping with their professional values and the needs of their students and their organisations.

For the learners, the first world of strategic partnerships, subtle differences of opinion between policy actors, institutional pressures to change working practices, and hectoring ministerial speeches and interventions is all but invisible, and rightly so. For their tutors and managers, however, policy creates the general atmosphere and sets the conditions under which they have to work; for example, rigorous inspection can act as a stimulus to improvement but also as a constraint on innovation or even minor risk-taking. Indeed, as our project progressed, and despite the significant additional investment in the sector, many staff reported that their room for manoeuvre was being steadily eroded, the risks to their job security were increasing and the talk was of organisational survival.

In other words, our plan to chart the impact of policy on practice did not turn out to be a simple matter of recording linear, evolutionary, rational or cumulative progress. Instead the processes whereby national policy is 'mediated' and 'translated' into local practice proved to be complex, multi-layered, uneven, dynamic, ambiguous, conflictual and often contradictory (Chapter 7 will deal with these processes in detail). As John Clark and Janet Newman (1997: 151) argued: 'Managers are not just the technical conduits through which policies are implemented. The process of institutional elaboration means that the outcomes of reforms are unpredictable.'

These two worlds of policy and practice overlap, and at times collide, when institutional leaders and course managers have to turn national funding regimes, targets and initiatives into viable programmes and procedures, which at the same time must protect the interests of their institutions as well as the interests of their learners. The outcome is a series of competing tensions, pressures and dilemmas which are resolved in different ways in different institutions and in a wide range of professional responses, from enthusiastic compliance to exit from the profession, if values are thought to be compromised (see Chapter 5 for more on this theme). The chief tensions felt by the staff we interviewed were:

- the government's model of reform contains both controlling (e.g., top-down performance management) and enabling (e.g., capacity building through continuing professional development) strategies;
- the regulatory pressures from inspection and the new pressures to develop a method of self-regulation and self-improvement;
- the new insistence to co-operate with other providers who were turned into competitors by an earlier change of policy when colleges became incorporated in 1992;
- the imperative of continuous innovation and the standardisation imposed by the rolling out of 'best practice';
- the government claim that economic and social goals are not in conflict but are interdependent.

Janet Newman (2001: 32) acutely observed that tensions such as these 'are not of mere academic interest but provide the key to understanding the lived experience of public sector staff and the dynamics of institutional change'.

The role of policy levers in the management of change

In its quest to modernise the public services New Labour has employed a variety of strategies which include centralising measures (such as the imposition and monitoring of standards) and decentralising measures (such as investment in professional development). A central aim of our project was to explore the intensification under New Labour of external controls (e.g., targets, inspection) as well as the growing movement to devolve responsibility for change to self-regulating institutions. This led us to track the redistribution of power and resources between different levels within the sector, to examine how institutions adapted to changes in policy and to explore the differing reactions of professionals to the same policy instruments. In so doing we were studying not so much a simple change from government to governance as a move to 'multi-level governance', a concept that draws attention to the vertical interface between transnational bodies such as the EU, the nation-state and so-called '"sub-national" tiers of governance' (Newman 2005: 9).

The literature is replete with references to 'policy drivers' and 'policy levers' and these terms are often used loosely and interchangeably; we wish to distinguish clearly between them (see Steer *et al.* 2007 for a fuller account). By 'policy drivers' we mean the broad aims of government policy as explained, for example, in the White Paper on FE: 'The FE system must be the powerhouse for delivering the skills at all levels that are needed to sustain an advanced, competitive economy and makes us a fairer society' (DfES 2006b: 3). Such overarching aims remain politically uncontroversial because, as Stuart Hall has pointed out, New Labour 'constantly speaks with forked tongue' by combining economic neo-liberalism with a subordinate social democratic programme (Hall 2003: 6). Policy drivers, often expressed through official documents, ministerial exhortation or statements of government priorities in the mass media, provide the broad framework within which policy levers are constructed and evaluated in the struggle to make them more effective.

We use the term 'policy levers' to refer to the instruments that the state has at its disposal to direct, manage and shape change in the public services. Policy levers thus serve as shorthand for the wide array of mechanisms which the government and its agencies employ to implement its policies. The engineering metaphor suggests that these 'tools' are politically neutral: however, 'To the contrary, there is always battle and conflict around their design, choice and application' (Kooiman 2003: 45).

Certainly, in our project we found little evidence of practitioners mechanically responding to policy levers in simple and predictable ways. The full story of how levers were mediated and translated by institutions and professionals will be told in Chapter 7. Here, it is sufficient to note that, out of a wide range of measures that we could have studied, we chose to examine the impact on teaching and learning within the LSS of planning, funding, targets, inspection and initiatives. Our criteria for this selection of levers were significance (we chose those widely thought to be the most influential), variety (a range of initiatives, as well as targets) and manageability (studying as many as five stretched our resources to the limit).

We have sought to understand how these policy levers interact at different levels within the sector, within different phases of policy, with different local ecologies and at various levels within institutions. Moreover, we observed the interactions between policy levers (such as funding and targets), which led to some powerful and unpredicted outcomes; unpredicted, we suspect, even by those who had devised the levers. In studying the use of policy initiatives as policy levers, we encountered some with quite narrow, specific goals (e.g., the Education Maintenance Allowance) and others, such as Skills for Life, which had an impact on almost every aspect of teaching and learning of basic skills – curriculum, assessment, qualifications, funding, teacher qualifications, to name but a few. Box 2.3 gives more detail on the major initiatives which will be mentioned throughout this book.

Box 2.3 The major initiatives we studied in the learning and skills sector

- **Skills for Life (SfL)** Introduced in 2001, Skills for Life is the national strategy in England for improving adult literacy and numeracy skills. With a budget of £1.5 billion in the first three years alone, SfL was introduced following the Moser Report in 1999, which stated that up to seven million adults have problems with literacy and numeracy. SfL is targeted at: unemployed people and benefits claimants; prisoners and those supervised in the community; public sector employees; low-skilled people in employment; and other groups at risk of exclusion. The initiative has seen the introduction of national core curricula in literacy, numeracy and ESOL, and new national tests, the development of teaching materials, professional development and training, and it is associated with the 'Get On' campaign (featuring the 'gremlins' characters). By 2007, SfL had reached its target of 1.5 million adults improving their basic skills and was on target for 2.25 million to have done so by 2010.

- **Employer Training Pilot (ETP) and Train to Gain (T2G)** Employer Training Pilots were introduced in September 2002 to encourage employers to invest in skills and qualifications, particularly for low-skilled employees. The pilots aimed to provide training to a first Level 2 qualification, or in basic skills for employees, and featured combinations of: paid time off work to train; wage compensation for employers; free or subsidised training; and information, advice and guidance for employers and employees. Despite concerns about dead weight (i.e., that the funding was used to pay for training that would have taken place anyway), the initiative has been 'rolled out' nationally to become Train to Gain. T2G operates through 'Skills Brokers' whose role is to offer free advice to businesses, seek to match their training needs with local training providers and ensure that the training is delivered to meet those needs. This initiative is at the forefront of the drive to create a more 'demand-led' system that is more responsive to the needs of employers and learners.

- **Education Maintenance Allowance (EMA)** Introduced in 2004 to encourage young people aged 16–18 to stay on in education or training after the end of their compulsory schooling. There were more than half a million recipients of the EMA in 2006/7, each receiving a direct weekly payment of £10, £20 or £30, depending on household income (the threshold for eligibility for the allowance was £30,810). The EMA is credited with having helped boost participation in learning among 16–18-year-olds, with one evaluation of the pilots estimating that the EMA had increased participation in learning among eligible 16-year-olds by 5.9 percentage points. In July 2007 the government announced that all 16-year-olds who qualify for EMA will be guaranteed a minimum level of maintenance support at university, in an effort to encourage greater participation in higher education.

Sources: Centre for Research in Social Policy and Institute for Fiscal Studies (2005), DfEE (2001), DfES (2007a), DIUS (2007), Hillage and Mitchell (2003), LSC (2006f, 2007b), Train to Gain website: <http://www.traintogain.gov.uk>

Some levers (e.g., targets) became goals in themselves and the eclectic mix of controlling and enabling levers used by government also conveyed confusing messages to practitioners. Janet Newman captured the subtle, complex and contradictory dynamics of policy levers when she commented, 'social policy reforms not only constrain social actors, subjecting them to new forms of governance and new technologies of power, but also open up the possibilities of new forms and sites of social agency' (Newman 2005: 6). This raised for us the question of how much scope managers and tutors felt they still had for professional agency. We discuss their responses in Chapter 5.

Critical questions

To help the reader make sense of this journey into the LSS, we suggest that the following questions be kept in mind as a way of holding on to the most important themes which we have been wrestling with for over three years. As always, there is a danger of being so submerged by the detail that the crucial issues disappear from view. We shall return to these questions in the final chapter, in the belief that 'the art of raising challenging questions is easily as important as the art of giving clear answers . . . and the art of cultivating such questions, of keeping good questions alive, is as important as either of those' (Bruner 1996: 127).

- Are government reforms creating the 'radical and enduring change' envisioned by David Blunkett when he set up the LSC (Blunkett 2000: 1)?
- Are the reforms creating a healthy, innovative and self-confident sector? Is it heading in the right direction?
- Are learners at the heart of the sector?
- Is the LSS well integrated with the schools sector and higher education in order to provide for all types of students clear progression routes in a system of lifelong learning?
- How much radical change can the sector accommodate?
- What changes are needed to create a more equitable, effective and democratic system?

Part II

What does the research show?

Chapter 3

The learners' stories

Introduction

The increased investment in the learning and skills sector since 2001 and the plethora of strategies designed to increase participation, improve standards and raise achievement have undoubtedly brought benefits to learners. In particular, we have seen major initiatives extend learning opportunities for some of the key groups targeted by government: the Education Maintenance Allowance has helped to encourage record numbers of 16–18-year-olds to stay in education and training (LSC 2006a); the Skills for Life initiative and the high-profile campaign prompting people to tackle their literacy and numeracy gremlins have seen 1.5 million learners improve their basic skills since 2001 (DfES 2007a); initiatives such as the Employer Training Pilot, involving around 9,000 employers (DfES 2005a); and the activities of ULRs have introduced new opportunities for learning in the workplace. We saw first hand how such interventions made a real difference to individuals who might not otherwise have participated in learning. In the words of one grateful learner, who was returning to learning at the age of fifty-eight to improve her numeracy skills, 'I think it is amazing how someone my age can have the opportunity to learn and survive ourselves. This is the best thing the government gave us' (LL9).

Despite the real success stories that lie behind headline statistics and comments such as this, the six million learners in the LSS occupy a paradoxical position in relation to policy. The official rhetoric is that 'The experience and success of learners are at the heart of what we do' (LSC 2004c: 5); and the drive towards a demand-led system, which 'purposely sets out to give more control to its customers in order to enhance their individual and business competitiveness' (LSC and DfES 2007: 6), further reinforces the idea that learners should be at the heart of the system. However, there is a danger that the diverse interests and voices of learners become lost in the sheer complexity of the LSS and the constant changes to which it has been subjected.

Strengthening the voice of learners is not just a problem for policy; it is also a major challenge for learning providers (QIA 2007). As pointed out by Kat Fletcher when she was president of the NUS, this requires effort because 'students' views do not just appear out of thin air, they need time, space, encouragement and organisation in order to be able to produce and create those opinions' (House of Commons Select Committee on Education and Skills 2006). Furthermore, research on pupil voice in schools indicates that consultation is most difficult with the least advantaged learners (McIntyre et al. 2005). In spite of the difficulties, there is a need at all levels actively to seek out and listen to the views of learners, for, as we have argued elsewhere, policy assumptions about learners may only be 'half-right' (Hodgson et al. 2007c).

This chapter will tell some of the main stories that emerged from our interviews with learners. We do not claim that the sample of 349 whom we interviewed is representative of learners in the sector as a whole, and this ambitious goal was never our intention. We chose to focus instead on: younger learners on Level 1 and Level 2 courses in general FE colleges; adults (most of whom were unemployed) improving their basic literacy and numeracy skills in community-based learning; and employees in work-based learning where basic skills acquisition forms a part of workforce development. All three groups have in common the fact that they were learning at the lower end of the spectrum of post-compulsory education and training. Most had not done well at school and had left with few or no qualifications. Notable exceptions were some of the learners from overseas who had come to the UK as economic migrants or asylum-seekers, holding qualifications up to degree level from abroad but needing support with English because it was not their first language; they comprised about one in ten of our sample. Whichever category the learners belonged to, their learning needs were significant and they experienced various forms of disadvantage. We were particularly interested in how these learners were faring within the LSS because their experiences shed light on how inclusive the sector is in practice.

There are four parts to this chapter. We begin by introducing the learners, looking at their diverse backgrounds and reasons for learning; we then consider the various disadvantages these learners faced, which had often resulted in disruptions to their learning at school; next, we look at what they said about their current experiences of teaching, learning and assessment; then we look at learner achievement and opportunities for progression. We conclude by suggesting some implications for policy and practice from these stories.

The learners' backgrounds and their reasons for learning

Younger learners on Level 1 and Level 2 courses in FE colleges

The learners in FE were all taking either Childcare or Health and Social Care (at Level 1) or Business Studies or Painting and Decorating (at Level 2). Five out of the eight sites were highly gendered: unsurprisingly, the courses in Childcare and Health and Social Care were female-dominated, whereas the Painting and Decorating students were mostly male; Business Studies had a roughly even gender balance. This selection of courses meant that overall we spoke to more female than male students. Over 80 per cent of the FE learners were aged 16–19, with most of the remainder in their early twenties. The learners in the two North East colleges were predominantly white, while in the two London colleges eight out of ten of those interviewed were from minority ethnic backgrounds. Among the students who had been through the UK school system, the vast majority had achieved a handful of GCSEs (mainly grades D–G) that were variously described as 'not brilliant', 'not very good' or just plain 'bad'.

The motivations of the FE learners varied between courses. Like James and Biesta (2007), we found that students' dispositions towards their courses were linked to the 'vocational culture' of the course. Those on what Stanton (2004) terms 'strongly vocational' courses – features of which are that they are taught by well-qualified and highly motivated staff with up-to-date experience of the vocational area, have facilities that are of industrial standard (e.g., training restaurants), with a programme integrated around the common theme of the particular vocational area – tended to be motivated by a clear intention to go on to work in that area. For example, a Childcare student explained that:

> I love children. I have always wanted to work with kids. I want to be a nursery nurse.
>
> (A1L14)

Those in the more 'weakly vocational' area of Business Studies, meanwhile, had often chosen this course as a fallback option:

> When I came to the college last year I wanted to do Childcare, but I didn't get a place on the course so I thought I would try Business Studies instead.
>
> (D2L3)

For many learners, the appeal of Business Studies lay in their desire to achieve a Level 2 qualification in a broad-based subject that would enable them to progress further with their education:

> This course leads to BTEC National and then you can go on to university.
>
> (D2L1)

An important attraction of FE was the promise of a learning experience that would be different from school, in the expectation of 'a more grown-up environment' (B2L2).

Adults improving their basic skills in community learning settings

The learners in our eight adult and community-learning (ACL) sites were all attending daytime provision, working in the main on literacy from Entry Level 1 to Level 2; some were also doing numeracy. Female learners outnumbered male learners by more than two to one. Of the three groups, these learners spanned the widest range of ages (from sixteen to seventy-seven), with a fairly even distribution of learners between the ages of twenty and sixty. In the North East sites nine out of ten of the ACL learners were white British, while in the London sites there was greater diversity (over half of the learners were from minority ethnic backgrounds). Around 70 per cent of the ACL learners we interviewed were not in paid employment, but this group was diverse, including retired people, full-time mothers, those caring for relatives, volunteers, people who were living with physical or mental health problems and a small number who were actively seeking work. Of those who had jobs, almost all were working part-time.

Around one in three of the ACL learners cited employment-related reasons for wanting to improve their literacy and/or numeracy. This included those who were in work and wanted to perform their existing roles better – such as a care assistant working in a home for the elderly who wanted to avoid making mistakes on medication records – and others who were seeking a change of career. For example, the following learner was taking a numeracy course because he wanted to leave his job in a shop and join the British Transport Police:

> I'm looking to further my career and Maths is a weak point.
>
> (EL13)

For many of those not in work, improving their basic skills was seen as a way to enhance their chances of finding a good job, in some cases following an earlier job loss through redundancy, accident or health problems. However, there was widespread recognition that further qualifications might be needed before these employment goals could be realised:

> I want to do my GCSEs and I want to do a degree as well, because I want to become a nursery reception teacher. So I've got quite a bit of work to do yet!
>
> (IL8)

In line with other research on adult learning (Crowther and Tett 1997; Percy 1997; Brooks et al. 2001; Eldred 2002; NIACE 2005), we found that the ACL learners had a wide range of other reasons or 'organising circumstances' for participating in learning. Personal development motives were prominent among these, with learners seeking to 'do something for me':

> I came here six years ago, but my mum was in a wheelchair and the kids were smaller and things got in the way, and then I ended up not doing anything for myself, as usual. So this time I am. I got divorced in January, and I want to do something for me.
>
> (GL8)

It was not unusual for the decision to return to learning to have been spurred by a major life event, such as divorce, bereavement or illness. Other frequently cited reasons for learning were: wanting to be able to help children with homework; the desire to function better in daily life (e.g., being able to fill in medical forms, understand transport timetables and manage personal finances); and social reasons that were sometimes linked to feelings of isolation and depression.

I was lonely, and I come to class and I can meet people and read and write and enjoy myself.

(LL4)

Finally, for learners whose first language was not English, improving their communication in a variety of contexts was paramount.

Employees in work-based learning with a basic skills component

The learners participating in work-based learning were the most diverse of the three groups. Their characteristics, the programmes they were on and their reasons for learning were all deeply bound up with the particular workplace in which they were employed. These very different workplaces included: a council depot for street care and housing maintenance; a medium-sized food manufacturing company; a bus garage; a school where teaching assistants were engaged in learning; nurseries, GPs' surgeries and offices (younger learners on apprenticeships in Customer Service and Administration); and work in the community (domiciliary care workers). As in the other two groups, a major difference between the sites in London and the North East was that in the former we encountered more learners from minority ethnic backgrounds, many of whom had ESOL needs.

The younger learners on apprenticeships were similar in many ways to the FE college students: they wanted learning that was vocationally relevant; they were attracted to a form of learning that was very different from school; and an important priority was to get a qualification equivalent to five good GCSEs.

My GCSEs weren't perfect, so I thought . . . I'm more of a hands-on person . . . [I'm doing this apprenticeship] to gain more qualifications, because it does say equivalent to five GCSEs. It's just generally improving my CV.

(QL8)

Others among the work-based learners, notably the care workers and some of the council employees, were learning because they were required by law to hold the relevant NVQ qualifications in order to be licensed to practise. (See Box 3.1 for the successful working of this approach in social care.) One learner commented:

We will not be allowed to work without the constant update.

(ML4)

Another important motivation for participating in WBL was the desire to learn new skills to improve future job prospects. As one of the factory workers put it:

It's just to give me more job prospects in the long run . . . It tends to be all the old-timers that are going through all the courses and stuff . . . They're not really older; they've just been here a while. They're wanting to better themselves and realise there's more to life than working on a production line.

(NL4)

As with the ACL learners, such work-related motivations were often combined with wider reasons for learning, the most common being personal development, wanting to help children with schoolwork and needing to improve English for everyday life.

Box 3.1 Licence to practise in social care

The health and social care sector provides a good example of how employer regulation can act as a major stimulus to learning in the workplace. The Care Standards Act 2000 brought a range of previously unregulated care services under the regulatory authority of the Commission for Social Care Inspection. New National Minimum Standards for registered care services require that all care workers be qualified to at least Level 2 in Health and Social Care. This has acted as a major spur to training.

Two of the WBL sites in our research, Roundview Carers and Top Training, involved care agencies that provide home-care services for minority ethnic communities. The new legislation not only prompted these agencies to put their unqualified staff on to NVQ training but resulted in them putting on ESOL classes for their employees where language needs were a barrier to them achieving the NVQ. As one tutor noted, 'The NVQ tends to be a driver for most things in the sector' (TT2).

A detailed discussion of the impact of the introduction of licence to practise in the care sector can be found in Evans et al. (2006).

Disadvantage and disrupted learning

Experiences of socio-economic disadvantage and disruptions in their learning at school were two recurrent themes underpinning the learners' stories. Social class and initial experiences of education are well established as two of the major determinants of participation in lifelong learning (Rees *et al.* 2000; Aldridge and Tuckett 2006) and major longitudinal surveys (e.g., National Statistics 2005) highlight the strong and enduring association between parental social class and educational attainment. Although we did not set out to investigate the backgrounds of the learners in detail, it was clear from our interviews that they faced many significant disadvantages that had hindered their life chances in general and, specifically, represented potential barriers to their participation in learning. For example, many of the learners faced financial pressures stemming from unemployment or having to get by on low-paid, part-time work. A wide range of other disadvantages were also mentioned, linked to physical wellbeing (including long-term illness, accidents and disability), mental health problems, familial difficulties (such as the effects of divorce or the death of a parent), as well as the particular challenges faced by migrant communities.

Difficult and sometimes traumatic personal circumstances often compounded these disadvantages. One such case was that of a 17-year-old who had been trafficked into the UK to be forced into prostitution. Fortunately, this young woman had been rescued by social services and, when we met her, was embarking upon a course in Health and Social Care. For many others their struggles were more routine, but equally challenging, such as the 44-year-old mother of three who was juggling her Entry Level Literacy class with her family commitments and holding down three different part-time jobs, while coping with a long-standing hearing problem. Box 3.2 gives an example from one of the college sites of the types of challenge that staff faced in dealing with multiple disadvantage.

Box 3.2 Challenges in working with Level 1 students

At Beechtree College the CACHE Childcare Foundation course (which is not a qualification to work with children, but a stepping stone to the Level 2 course) was attended predominantly by female students who had left school with few or no qualifications. Around three-quarters received EMA and half the group also had part-time jobs. Challenges identified by staff in working with this group included:

- **Physical, learning and other difficulties** One of the groups we observed included one wheelchair user, and seven (out of sixteen) students who required classroom support. Problems included anorexia, coping with illness in the family, Crohn's disease, serious loss of hearing, dyspraxia and being a young carer.
- **Attendance, timekeeping and behaviour** The students had difficulties with attendance and punctuality, 'because they just don't recognise these things as being important' (B1M1). The tutor had concerns about the behaviour of four or five students in one group of eighteen.
- **Learning how to learn** 'They don't have the social skills and the ability to sit and listen while somebody is talking, or the respect for them to wait for others to finish' (B1T1).
- **Low levels of key skills** Even though the students were receiving key skills support, their tutor was shocked by their 'appalling levels of grammar and spelling' (B1T1).
- **Retention** In spite of intensive classroom support, dropout rates were high. In the tutor's opinion, 'the dropout is not necessarily anything to do with college work, but things to do with home life . . . sometimes they have an awful lot of baggage' (B1T1).

With the exception of those whose previous education had been in other countries, many of the learners recounted negative experiences of learning at school. For the younger learners in FE and on apprenticeships, their time at school was frequently described in terms of having been treated 'like babies' or 'like little kids'. Some complained of 'teachers nagging at you all the time' (B1L3) and about not having been treated with respect:

> At school, they talked to you as if you did not know anything whatsoever.
>
> (A1L11)

Other aspects that had turned some of these young people off school included: a lack of variety in how they were taught; being picked on in class by teachers; experiences of bullying; receiving insufficient attention within large classes or feeling that teachers were interested only in 'the brainy ones'; and not being given enough help and support.

> At school it's . . . if you can't do it, then tough luck. They don't want to help you.
>
> (QL4)

While school had not met the needs of many of these learners, it is important to point out that there were others who had enjoyed their schooling. Moreover, some of the young people who did not like school admitted that their own attitude and behaviour had been lacking:

> I just never did anything at school . . . just sat in the class, that was it, just sat there and did not join in.
>
> (B1L7)

Many of the learners in FE had already experienced significant disruptions and/or difficulties in their learning up to this point. Only around one in three had progressed directly from school on to their college course. The remainder had taken a variety of routes, including a significant minority who had previously been to a different college (such movement between colleges being more common in London), been on different courses within the same college, spent time on work-based programmes such as Entry to Employment (E2E) or apprentice-ships, or experienced spells when they had simply been out of learning altogether. Often these students had experienced several disruptions in their learning, as illustrated by Rebecca's story in Box 3.3.

Box 3.3 Disrupted learning: Rebecca's story

Rebecca, an 18-year-old Business Studies student we met at Central College, had ambitions to become a solicitor. However, because of illness, she had done less well in her GCSEs than she had hoped and did not achieve five A*–C grades. From school she went to an intermediate Business Studies course in another college, but decided that she was 'not really a college sort of person' because she found full-time studying difficult. So she left college and started an office-based apprenticeship instead, finding that she enjoyed the balance between working and learning that this gave her. However, her apprenticeship was abruptly cut short after the placement was terminated by her employer (who, it turned out, was not fully committed to the scheme). Despite feeling angered and upset by this experience, Rebecca decided to return to college and chose Central because it was the nearest to her home. She was desperate to achieve the Level 2 qualification in Business Studies because, in her words, 'I need to find my life', and she still harboured aspirations of working her way towards becoming a solicitor.

When we met Rebecca again towards the end of her course, we learned that she had been struggling to keep up because of continuing problems with her health. Despite having been in and out of hospital, she was determined to complete the course, saying, 'there's no way I'm wasting the year'. The tutors in the college had been very understanding and supportive during this difficult period for Rebecca, regularly phoning her to check when she would next be coming into the college and letting her know when assignments were due. This was taken by Rebecca as a sign that the college staff cared about her progress, strengthening her resolve to succeed and to go on to do an access course and then a degree.

The accounts that the adult learners gave of their school experiences echoed many of the themes that were present in the younger learners' stories. However, the adults were even more likely to report that their schooling had been cut short or seriously disrupted. An unstable home environment – such as family break-up, the loss of a parent or frequently moving house – was one of the major reasons cited:

The thing was that we moved around a lot, partly because of my dad and my mam. I did not fit in at school, it was not a good start, and when I got to high school I was really behind, and if I went, I couldn't keep up. I wagged it, only because I couldn't keep up – it was not because I did not like it. I couldn't keep up and, if I was there, I would just copy off my friends. I never learned much.

(HL6)

Others had left school early because their family needed them to work, such as one learner who had left school at the age of twelve to work on a fairground. Illness, accidents, bullying at school, having to care for relatives and pregnancy were also mentioned as reasons for having missed substantial chunks of schooling.

As we have already suggested, the experiences of those who had stayed in school were often far from positive. Learners frequently cited difficulties with learning in large classes – the lack of individual attention, and in some cases shyness within this environment, caused them to fall behind. This could lead to marginalisation at school: 'if you didn't keep up, you were just pushed to one side' (FL2). Others recalled how their learning had been undermined by disruptive pupils:

> I left at sixteen, but I don't regret it because the school I was in, it was not very nice really. The children were quite disruptive and I don't think I would have passed really if I had stayed. I was quite sensitive at school.
>
> (HL2)

A small minority of the adults we met had been put into special schools or classes, which were variously referred to as 'backward school', a school 'for waifs and strays', 'remedial' classes and 'subnormal classes'. Some of those in mainstream education had also been subjected to damaging labelling, such as one young man who said:

> I was told at school that I must be thick, lazy, or both.
>
> (SL7)

This individual, who in fact came across as being very intelligent and articulate, struggled with learning – he later discovered – because he had dyslexia and dyspraxia, which had not been identified when he was at school.

In the ACL and WBL sites there were not the same behavioural issues as with Level 1 college students, but in many other respects the tutors faced similar challenges of dealing with learners' personal, social and economic problems. In particular, they faced the same task of helping their learners gradually to reconstruct fragile or even damaged learning identities. The task of overcoming previous negative experiences of learning at school should not be underestimated, for as Lave and Wenger (1991: 115) argue, 'learning and a sense of identity are inseparable: They are aspects of the same phenomenon.' This brings us to what the learners had to say about their current experiences of teaching, learning and assessment.

Current experiences of teaching, learning and assessment

Teaching and learning: the central role of the tutor–learner relationship

In line with national learner satisfaction surveys (LSC 2006c, 2006d, 2006e), the learners we met were, with very few exceptions, extremely positive about their experiences of teaching and learning. In the learners' stories, the relationship they had with their tutors emerged time and again as being of crucial importance. For the learners in adult community and work-based learning a key element of this relationship was the tutors' ability to make them, and the rest of the group, feel comfortable:

> It is so relaxing . . . it is just a nice little group. I think when you think back, when you were at school, there was a big class, and I would shy off and I would not like to answer questions and that. But I feel quite happy and relaxed in here. They don't make you feel stupid.
>
> (FL8)

In the words of another learner from the same ACL site, the teachers 'are more like friends than tutors' (FL9). But the success of these learner–tutor relationships was not simply down to the tutors' undoubted interpersonal skills and empathy for their learners. It was also the result of providing a very different approach to learning from that which most learners had experienced at school.

One important feature of this approach lay in providing plenty of opportunities for one-to-one learning and support. One learner commented that she liked this more 'personal' approach adding,

> I find that if I work in a group I lose concentration. With it being one-to-one, it's more direct.
>
> (EL12)

Learners also valued a highly differentiated approach, in which they could focus on the areas on which they needed to improve and were able to work at their own pace:

> The tutor . . . is very easy-going, but she knows that everyone cannot learn the same thing at the same time. Some people understand some things, some people don't. But she lets you get on, and if you need help, you ask, but she prompts you as well.
>
> (HL3)

These adult learners frequently spoke of a positive group ethos, in which 'everybody gives everybody help – because we're all in the same boat' (GL10). The commitment and flexibility of the tutors were also singled out, particularly in some of the WBL sites where learning had to be fitted around employees' shifts:

> Sometimes they will stay late so that they can accommodate me.
>
> (SL6)

At their best, these tutor–learner relationships could transform a learner's identity, by changing 'the relationships between a learner's personal identity, his or her material and cultural surroundings and dispositions to learning' (Hodkinson and Bloomer 2002: 38). An example of the transformative effects of learning is given in Box 3.4. For Yvonne, as with many others we met, gradual improvements in her basic literacy led to a dramatic increase in her self-confidence.

The younger learners in FE also highlighted the central role played by their tutors and lecturers in providing them with a more positive learning experience. There was a number of dimensions to this, which included being given greater freedom, the existence of a more relaxed atmosphere in which it was possible to 'have a laugh' with teachers, smaller class sizes and receiving more one-to-one attention. Students frequently spoke of the more grown-up relationship they had with college staff than that which they had experienced at school.

Students also appreciated the greater variety of learning experiences which they felt they were getting in college, often alternating between practical activities, group discussion and individual or small group exercises. Those on more 'strongly vocational' courses, such as the following Childcare student, particularly valued activities that they saw as equipping them with vocationally relevant skills:

> The best lessons are Play and Practical. We get to be creative and stuff, and then they will say: 'This is what you need to remember, because if you work in a nursery you might have to do it.'
>
> (B1L10)

Box 3.4 Learning transformations: Yvonne's story

Yvonne was briefly mentioned earlier as the 44-year-old mother of three who juggled family commitments and three part-time jobs with her learning. When we first met Yvonne she had been attending the Island Estate learning centre for about three years. Of her school experience, she said, 'I wasn't very good at school, I know that.' She left school with no qualifications and worked in a variety of jobs, including factory work, cleaning, and as a nanny and child-minder.

Her return to learning was somewhat accidental – a friend had enrolled on a Floristry course, but then could not attend, so Yvonne went in her place. After two years of doing Floristry, she moved on to the Literacy class. Her motivation was simply to do something for herself: 'I'm not aiming to get a job out of this course, I'm just doing this for me. I've come here, I've met people, I've made a lot of friends through coming here.'

The relaxed atmosphere in the group gave Yvonne the confidence, for the first time, to speak in front of others: 'I could never talk openly in discussion in front of people and I can do that now. I never dreamed . . . when I was at school, I never put my hand up for any help, I never put my hand up to speak and answer a question. I can do that now. I know it's only a small group of us, but I can do that quite confidently.' Gradually she began to make progress in her writing and spelling. Whereas previously she would stick to writing simple words that she could spell, Yvonne said, 'Now I'm much more adventurous and I can put a lot more into my words.' As her confidence grew Yvonne decided that she would have a go at the Entry Level 2 Literacy 'exam', which she passed.

We met Yvonne again several months later, by which time her growing confidence and improving literacy were helping her to carry out her part-time supermarket job more confidently and competently. Of deeper significance to Yvonne, however, was the fact that she was now planning a project for herself, which was to write a book telling the life story of an elderly friend of hers. With this goal in mind, Yvonne was happy to continue progressing at her own pace; 'it takes me time to learn, but I get it in the end'.

Most students also regarded the support and encouragement of their teachers, and, in some cases, of additional learning support staff, as playing a vital role in helping them to succeed in their learning. One commented appreciatively:

> You can get help with anything you want. They just help you . . . They use all kinds of methods of learning and you can use what helps you best.
>
> (B2L6)

In contrast to most of the adult learners, the FE students exhibited a greater reliance upon their tutors to challenge them and chase them up when they had not done assignments:

> I'd probably say the lecturers have been the biggest thing to help me, because they've helped me with my work, pushed me on and made me more self-motivated. So that when I've got work, if I've fallen behind or something, I have to get on with it and get it done instead of just sitting there chatting to someone. I have to sit there and get it all done . . . [The lecturers] make sure that [you get assignments] in on time and that you don't miss deadlines.
>
> (C2L2)

In spite of the importance that Level 1 and 2 students attached to being treated like adults, the reality was that their learning was often highly directed and very closely monitored. Like Wahlberg and Gleeson (2003), we found that the students' status as adults was somewhat ambiguous.

Assessment: opportunities and constraints

The qualifications that the learners were working towards, and the ways in which they were assessed, were major factors shaping their learning experiences. These factors presented both potential opportunities and constraints upon learning, depending crucially on how teachers managed their approach to assessment. In the ACL and some of the WBL sites, assessment centred upon the core curricula in literacy and numeracy and the national tests that were introduced through the Skills for Life initiative. Although a number of staff expressed concerns that taking a test might be off-putting for some learners, in the vast majority of cases these fears were unfounded (partly because tutors were careful to ensure that learners were not put under pressure to take a test until they felt ready to do so). If anything, taking the tests, and the subsequent sense of achievement when learners passed, proved highly motivating for learners and staff alike. One tutor recalled the moment when a group of learners from Moorcroft Depot received their results on the mobile learning bus that visited this site:

> If you'd have seen the people's faces on the bus when they got off . . . with a certificate in their hand . . . getting off the bus with their result. I think we had an eighty-something pass rate and everyone passed one thing . . . But just to see the faces. I think you just have to watch that. Some of them have never had a qualification in anything . . . So [the national test] has a place, although it is limited in some ways.
>
> (MT1/1)

One of the major limitations alluded to here, which was frequently mentioned by the basic skills tutors, was that the national tests in literacy do not test writing.

While recognising the value in having the core curricula and a clear specification of levels against which learners' progress could be measured, some tutors and managers expressed concerns that this standardisation might diminish their ability to respond to the learners' needs. One manager succinctly expressed this conundrum when she wryly asked, 'Skills for whose life?' Our evidence from speaking to the learners, however, indicated that most tutors were able to meet both the learners' needs and the requirements of the core curricula. Leaving aside the question of the associated paperwork for tutors, we found learners who were clearly benefiting from the combination of diagnostic assessments, Individual Learning Plans (ILPs) and planning against the core curricula. This process was described to us by one of the learners at Eastway:

> [The tutor] assesses where you are on the diagnostic. She will show you where you came off, which sections, and then she will run through with you on your ILP what she feels you need to cover to be able to get you through your Level 2. She does evaluation which tells her how you perform better – by text, by speaking – she can tell you where you are on that scale, so she will have all that information in your file. And she will go through it with you and

you sign it to say that you are happy with everything, and the way she is teaching you. And you know exactly where you are.

(EL15)

While this termly exercise sounds intensive, we found plenty of examples where tutors were still able to tailor learning to the everyday needs of their students (e.g., in helping them to understand a letter from the bank or to complete job applications or other forms).

For the students and staff in our FE sites there were different issues around assessment. These centred upon the tension between, on the one hand, the need to break coursework down into manageable units for the sorts of students described in Box 3.2, in order that they could succeed, and, on the other hand, the danger that this becomes an intensive exercise in spoon-feeding, or chasing the assessment criteria, resulting in superficial learning that limits students' development as independent learners (Ecclestone 2005; Torrance *et al.* 2005). As one manager put it, when you are dealing with students 'for whom it is an achievement of self-management to be here by nine o'clock', how can they manage 'to plan a piece of work that's going to take six to ten weeks – I mean how can they achieve that properly?' (C2M2). The result was that:

You end up, some would say, nannying them through, and I've got staff who are now splitting up what's supposed to be one assessment into little assessments. That has implications for what the tutors and the lecturers need to do, to help students give them in. But there are horrendous implications for managing and monitoring the collection of it all.

(C2M2)

From the point of view of the students, such assessment practices – which often involved them getting a second chance to improve their assignments (and in some cases third or even fourth chances) – were welcomed as helping them to better their grades:

We get feedback and corrections right up to the end, so we can keep changing and get the best mark possible.

(C2L2)

It was unclear how far these exercises in 'criteria chasing' represented a successful strategy for giving students the early gains needed to go on to further (more independently achieved) success, and how far they represented a mechanical approach to learning that would ultimately prove limiting once students moved on to higher levels.

Achievement and progression

Bearing in mind Veronica McGivney's observation that 'learners' notions of their own progress and progression are often different from those of policy makers, funders and education practitioners' (McGivney 2003: 1), we found a large majority of learners who felt that they had been successful in their learning. Moreover, many of the learners in our sites had achieved qualification outcomes or were well on the way to doing so. For example, success rates on the FE courses we followed were either around, or above, the national average of 77 per cent (LSC 2007c). In many cases the learners we met were experiencing the taste of success in education for the first time in their lives. One learner who had come to learning late, at the age of sixty-four, having covered up her illiteracy throughout her whole adult life, reflected on her achievement of an Entry Level Literacy certificate by saying, 'It's amazing really.' More important than the certificate, however, was the fact that

> I can write notes and things like that now; and do my own business, like if I have to go to the Post Office . . . I'm much more independent now.
>
> (KL5)

Although the overall picture we found was of widespread satisfaction and achievement, learners' future progression in learning was often far from certain. A key factor in the success of many of the WBL sites, for example, was that the learning was offered in or close to the learners' place of work and at times that could fit in with their working hours. However, the drawback to this was that once learners had completed the courses that were on offer it could be very difficult for them to access other learning opportunities. A bus driver at Southern Transport put it starkly:

> Going to college is not an option in a job like this.
>
> (SL7)

There were two other issues that affected the WBL sites in particular. First, learning opportunities could be restricted by what employers were able or willing to support. For example, we met domiciliary care workers at Top Training who wanted to progress from the Level 2 NVQ to Level 3, but we were told by their tutor that they were unlikely to be able to do so because there were not the opportunities for them to carry out the tasks needed for the higher-level qualification within their current job roles:

> [NVQ Level 3 is] more of a supervisory level. And people need to be doing supervisory-level stuff to be able to do it, or be able to at least involve themselves in that. So when people say, 'Oh, I want to do a Level 3,' great, but you have to be doing that job role.
>
> (TT1)

Another potential barrier to further progression within WBL was the heavy reliance of many of these sites upon initiative funding. Elsewhere we have likened this provision to 'flowers in the desert' (Finlay *et al.* 2007a), because short-term funding means that successful provision can wither away as quickly as it appeared.

Funding uncertainties were also prevalent in the ACL sites. Although Skills for Life provision is a government priority and has been protected from recent funding cutbacks in adult learning, there were signs that this wider funding climate, and the prioritisation of attainment at Levels 1 and 2, was having negative repercussions for basic skills provision at the lower levels (see also McGivney 2005). A striking example was the learning centre on the Island Estate, where the loss of funding for a wide range of embedded basic skills classes (literacy and numeracy embedded in general adult education classes such as IT, Floristry and Aromatherapy), and the loss of funding for childcare, had a devastating impact on the 'social capital' (i.e., the social relations of 'belonging', trust and confidence) generated across the centre as a whole: learner numbers plummeted from around two hundred to fifty; rows of computers sat idle; and the once vibrant atmosphere at the centre turned decidedly quiet. One learner said, 'There's not many people around here so much because the courses have been shut down' (IL1); another felt that the loss of the embedded courses would limit the numbers coming in to do literacy and numeracy because they 'haven't got the confidence, because they're adults, to say they've got a problem with their English' (IL6).

For the younger learners in FE, progression appeared, on the face of it, to be less problematic: progression pathways were clearer; the opportunities were more secure (in that they were not subject to the same funding uncertainties affecting adult learning); and there were not the same difficulties of accessing higher-level courses. Colleges were undoubtedly making efforts to support student progression, and one manager proclaimed that

> We, as a college, bend over backwards to support progression . . . You could walk out of the door with a degree in six years' time.
> (B2M4)

Notwithstanding how unrealistic this would sound to many of the Level 1 and 2 students we interviewed, most of whom did not have the stability and confidence to be thinking this far ahead, the emphasis on progression was none the less clear.

However, the actual numbers of students progressing between levels was highly variable and, in some cases, worryingly low. In three sites we found that only around one in three students was successfully progressing on to the next level. A variety of reasons were given for such low progression rates, which included unaddressed ESOL needs, financial constraints and some screening out of students whose attitude and behaviour were not deemed suitable for the higher level (specifically in relation to Childcare). One consistent factor appeared to be that the prime focus of attention, as reflected in the targets that college managers were under pressure to meet, was on retention and achievement ('the big buzz words', according to one tutor). There was not a correspondingly high focus on student progression.

Conclusion: implications for policy and practice

At the beginning of this chapter we suggested that learners are central to the rhetoric of policy but lack a forum to exercise an effective voice within the sector. As the learners' stories outlined here indicate, we have tried as far as possible to let the learners speak for themselves and in the process found a number of paradoxes. First, we found significant and deeply rooted combinations of social, economic and other forms of disadvantage affecting many learners, and yet, despite their evident needs, learners within the LSS receive less funding than other, more advantaged groups of learners. For example, it is estimated that FE colleges receive 8 per cent less funding per student than school sixth forms for educating 16–18-year-olds (DfES 2006b). Second, we found very high learner satisfaction with provision that was generally extremely successful in meeting their needs, and yet the provision for adults was subject to major uncertainties about its future viability. Third, we found a strong desire among learners for further progression in their learning, but in all types of site the focus on learner progression was weak (largely because the emphasis of funding and targets is on retention and achievement).

All of this points to a somewhat mixed picture of how effectively the LSS meets the needs of some of its most disadvantaged groups of learners. Policy constructs of learners as confident and informed consumers within a 'demand-led' system are far removed from the realities of these learners' lives, and this is one reason why we doubt whether the mechanism of learner choice will significantly improve things for these groups. A more equitable and inclusive system, in our view, would not simply be focused on achieving better outcomes for the most marginalised groups of learners but would seek to enhance their voice and participation within the sector. Following Bernstein, we would stress the importance of a democratic approach to inclusion in education, in which all learners could benefit from the

---

Box 3.5 Implications for policy and practice

- Policy needs to refocus on supporting and sustaining the tutor–learner relationship.
- Success at the lower levels depends upon a flexible, patient and informal approach that starts where learners are, is tailored to their needs, and can gradually build their confidence through small-group learning and one-to-one support.
- More needs to be done to support learner progression by, for example, providing step or bridging courses 'for those who find the gap between levels too great' (McGivney 2003: 21).
- Provision for the most disadvantaged groups needs to be properly resourced. This could mean an adult equivalent to the Every Child Matters agenda, requiring different agencies to work much more closely to address multiple needs.
- A truly effective lifelong learning strategy needs to pay greater attention to failings within the school system, to problems of transition and to the impact of poverty and deprivation on educational attainment.

institutionalisation of three interrelated rights: at the individual level, the right to enhancement, which supports individual transformations and creates confidence; at the social level, the right to inclusion, socially, intellectually, culturally and personally; and at the political level, the right to participation, defined by Bernstein as the 'the right to participate in procedures whereby order is constructed, maintained and changed' (Bernstein 1996: 7).

It is clear from the learners' stories that they enter the LSS with complex and multifaceted needs that are not just educational, but social, economic and personal; many have been scarred by their learning experiences in the school system. For these reasons, the recommendations we have to make in light of the learners' stories (outlined in Box 3.5) apply within the LSS but also extend beyond its boundaries.

Chapter 4

The policy-makers' stories

Introduction

If prizes were given for responsiveness to change, then those working in the learning and skills sector would undoubtedly sweep the board. Since 2001 and the establishment of the Learning and Skills Council in England, there has been a constant stream of policy documents, initiatives and structural changes affecting the sector. This has led to a highly complex landscape (see Figure 1.1, p. 16 above) which, although employing thousands of staff and affecting the lives of over six million learners, is not well understood, even by those who work within it. In this chapter we attempt to paint a picture of the LSS in England in 2007, based primarily on an analysis of 131 in-depth interviews with 123 European, national, regional and local officials over the period 2004–7 and key messages from nine major policy documents mentioned by these policy-makers.[1] We will also refer briefly to four more recent policy texts, which have been published since the majority of interviews took place, but figured strongly in our final round of interviews (see Box 4.1). We examine these three years from the perspective of the policy-makers we interviewed who, like the teachers, trainers, lecturers and managers in FE and adult and work-based learning, have had to make sense of (or 'translate') rapid successions of politicians' pronouncements, respond to several major restructuring exercises and take up new roles and responsibilities or even face redundancy during this period. And this was even before the most recent announcements of changes to national ministries in 2007, as described in Chapter 1. We use the policy-makers' stories to identify what they hope to achieve in the LSS, what structural changes have taken place, how the new arrangements operate, what the new terminology used in policy documents signifies, and what debates and issues they see as important to the future of post-16 education and training in this country. We conclude with five policy implications for the sector.

What are the policy-makers trying to achieve?

It is perhaps worth getting two things out into the open before plunging into an analysis of policy-making in the LSS. The first is what we mean by 'policy-makers'; the second is how we can be sure we are describing their views accurately.

Other chapters in this book recognise the fact that policy can be viewed in different ways depending on your position in the LSS. They also demonstrate that policy is made and translated by teachers and managers, as well as by those who are usually referred to as policy-makers – ministers, civil servants, political advisers and officials of national, regional and local government organisations. In this chapter, however, we confine ourselves to the accounts of the latter group. While we do not claim that we are representing the views of all policy-makers, the large number of interviews, the fact that they are taken from different levels of the system, that they have been captured at different points in time, that key officials have been interviewed more than once, that their views have been seen within the context of official policy texts, and that their transcripts have been analysed by six people all make us confident that we have attempted to grind out obvious error and that we have a strong evidence-based story to tell.

Chapters 1 and 2 of this book highlighted both the achievements (see Box 1.2, p. 14 above) and the frenetic pace of change in this sector, with hundreds of policy documents relating directly to the LSS published by the DfES, the Treasury, the LSC and other national, regional and local bodies. In addition, several influential government-commissioned independent inquiries (e.g., Tomlinson on 14–19 education and training; Foster on FE; and Leitch on skills) have reported on issues affecting the sector and added to the policy brew.

How can we make sense of this plethora of policy and its impact on the shape and behaviour of the LSS? How can we tell which texts drive policy and policy-makers and which are merely elaboration or mood music? One way (and this is the approach we take in this chapter) is to focus on those texts that policy-makers themselves cited as important; those they used to explain or legitimate their views or actions (see Box 4.1).

Box 4.1 Thirteen recent policy texts

- *14–19 Education and Skills* (DfES 2005a)
- *Realising the Potential: a review of the future role of further education colleges* (Foster 2005)
- *Skills: getting on in business, getting on in work* (HMG 2005)
- *Learning and Skills: the agenda for change* (LSC 2005b)
- *Further Education: raising skills, improving life chances* (DfES 2006b)
- *Framework for Excellence: a comprehensive performance assessment framework for the further education system* (LSC 2006b)
- *Prosperity for All in the Global Economy: world class skills* (Leitch 2006)
- *The UK Government's Approach to Public Service Reform* (PMSU 2006)
- *Pursuing Excellence: the national improvement strategy for the further education system* (QIA 2007)
- *Delivering World-Class Skills in a Demand-Led System* (LSC and DfES 2007)
- *Building on Progress: public services* (PMSU 2007)
- *Raising Expectations: staying on in education and training post-16* (DfES 2007c)
- *Place-Shaping: a shared ambition for the future of local government* (Lyons 2007a)

The twin 'policy drivers'

Taken together, these thirteen documents broadly cover both the age range of the sector and the scope of learning opportunities provided through public funding. Here we focus on the two underpinning 'policy drivers', a term we use in the project to describe the broad aims of government policy that pervade these documents.

The first concerns the importance of raising skills levels in the UK to ensure the country remains economically prosperous. It is asserted in the foreword of the FE White Paper by then Prime Minister Tony Blair, Secretary of State for Education and Skills Ruth Kelly and Chancellor Gordon Brown: 'Our economic future depends on our productivity as a nation. That requires a labour force with skills to match the best in the world' (DfES 2006b: 1). It is endorsed in Lord Leitch's report, beginning in the foreword where he talks about the importance of unlocking the skills potential of the British people and adds: 'The prize for our country will be enormous – higher productivity, the creation of wealth and social justice' (Leitch 2006: 6). And it is taken up in the initial government response to this report: 'despite significant advances in the skills and qualifications of individuals . . . we have to raise our game if we are to continue to compete – as individuals and businesses – in an increasingly competitive global context' (LSC and DfES 2007: 2).

The final two words of the quotation from Lord Leitch – 'social justice' – lie at the heart of the second and, in the Government's mind, related key policy aim of increased social inclusion and social mobility. The *Skills* White Paper, for example, talks of the need for 'a step change in productivity and social mobility' (HMG 2005: 4). While *Delivering World-Class Skills in a Demand-Led System* makes the relationship between the twin policy drivers plain:

> These are sobering economic statistics, but there are also powerful social reasons for concentrating on reform. Young people and adults should have every opportunity to increase their value in the job market, and to seek self-improvement and to build self-esteem.
>
> (LSC and DfES 2007: 2)

Interestingly, these twin drivers chime very much with European policy-makers' views (CEC 2006c), as one of our interviewees pointed out:

> There is also a political recognition (within the European Commission) that education and training has something to contribute to Europe's competitiveness and employment and social inclusion.
>
> (Y4)

In English policy documents, a direct link is made between skills, employment and social inclusion. There is an assumption that the first leads to the second and on to the third, even though there are many who question this assertion (e.g., Wolf 2002). Indeed, a close reading of these thirteen policy texts suggests that the second aim of social justice is not only dependent upon but subordinate to the first aim of developing skills for economic competitiveness. Moreover, some of our interviewees saw the two in tension with each other.

The focus on these twin drivers and the connection between them has, in fact, remained remarkably constant as the rationale for policy within the LSS in England throughout its whole lifespan, 2001–7. Rather, it is the policy language, structures, initiatives and mechanisms that have been used to realise the policy drivers that have changed, and it is to these that we now turn.

How has the organisation of the LSS changed as a result of recent policy?

When the LSC was established in 2001, it comprised a National Council, located in Coventry, with forty-seven local councils across the rest of England. However, this structure lasted only until January 2004, when the newly appointed chief executive, Mark Haysom, announced the creation of a regional management team. This was just the first step towards restructuring the LSC, which currently comprises nine regional offices responsible for 153 'local partnership teams' normally covering the same areas as local authorities. The original forty-seven local councils were effectively decommissioned, although technically they could not be dissolved until the passage of the FE Act 2007, and regional councils were set up in their place. This structure, which was highlighted in the FE White Paper (DfES 2006b) and came into operation in autumn 2006, was described in the following pictorial terms by one official:

> What we have now is more of an onion, where we've got this very much slimmer national office and a fatter region and also quite fat local areas . . . So the structure was deliberately designed to give more authority and responsibility at regional level and to build up the picture from the local areas.
>
> (UA14)

Roles and relationships – national, regional and local

The new LSC structure with its reduced staffing raised questions about the relationship between each of the levels within the organisation and about how it would operate on a day-to-day basis in supporting providers to meet the government's twin goals of improving the nation's skills for economic competitiveness and ensuring social cohesion. In addition, as we pointed out in earlier publications (Hodgson *et al.*

2005; Coffield *et al.* 2005), the way that the LSC works with the DfES (and now its successors) and with other partner agencies in the LSS also has a strong bearing on what it can achieve and how it is perceived by the providers who translate policy into practice.

One of the major criticisms in the final report of the Foster Review of FE was of 'micro-management' by the DfES with regard to the LSC (Foster 2005: 51) and by the LSC in relation to colleges (*ibid.*: 52), leading to potential confusion between the roles of the two organisations. According to officials we interviewed from the DfES and LSC, these two criticisms are now being addressed. The DfES role was described by one interviewee as being 'to performance manage the national partners who deliver for us' (WO7), while an LSC official asserted, 'I would say we have a robust relationship with the DfES, which means we can be frank, but we also work together' (UA14). Although those outside these two organisations are less convinced:

> I think one of the difficulties is that still DfES and LSC are not quite clear about who is doing what, in my view, in terms of policy and strategy.
>
> (V12)

While having ministers who are 'big fans of FE' (WO8) is seen as both unusual and 'very, very positive' (V12), it also means that ministerial pressure on DfES civil servants can be intense and is very evident in policy-making even at local level:

> It's just been eye-opening for me on a personal level, how hands on, I suppose, and how direct individual ministerial involvement is with the whole learning and skills sector.
>
> (UB13)

But what about the way in which the new LSC structure operates at national, regional and local levels? Where does power lie and who makes the decisions that will impact on local provision? The term 'tight–loose' was often used to describe the relationship between 'what must be tight and nationally prescribed and where it is loose in terms of regional and local flexibility' (UA15). There was particular enthusiasm within the LSC, but also more widely among policy actors, about the potential of the new structure to facilitate work at the local level. To support this local role, and to address earlier criticisms of lack of capacity at the local level, appointments to posts in local partnership teams were made at higher grades. These staff members work directly with individual providers to negotiate their contributions to regional targets.

Where there seems to be less agreement, even within the LSC itself, is to what extent this new structure requires planning at the local level. One interviewee stated: 'one of the things we need to start doing is real planning' (UC15), but another commented: 'it is naïve in the extreme to think that the LSC's job is somehow to come up with perfect plans for provision in local communities and somehow sort of mastermind this' (UA13).

Far more of the non-LSC policy-makers we interviewed in 2006–7 were positive about the new structure of the LSC and the way it had delivered on its key performance targets (see Box 1.2, p. 14 above) than those we interviewed in 2004–5, before the organisational changes had taken place. Nevertheless, there were criticisms about the slow pace of change within the organisation itself, with one official commenting, 'If they were a private organisation, they'd have been dead by now' (X12). Another believed that constant restructuring had detracted from 'vision and standards' (ZA21). There was still concern about the human capacity within the organisation ('we've got these people who are not necessarily experts and some of them, in one or two cases, have absolutely no background' (X12)); its lack of democratic accountability; its bureaucratic way of working ('it is still a huge organisation . . . and a costly overhead on the system' (ZA24)); and whether it would be able to retain any independence from the DfES ('it's a delivery body and ultimately its policy is dictated by the DfES' (ZA20)).

Moreover, the new regional structure with LSC partnership teams in local authority areas was not always perceived as the optimum level of governance for meeting either employer or learner needs. As one interviewee pointed out:

> It's a nonsense in terms of learners. They don't give a monkey's whether they stay in the borough; they just go where they want to go and where their transport links are.
>
> (UC15)

This suggests that at least in large metropolitan areas like London, there may be a role for sub-regional and sub-borough levels of governance (see Fullick *et al.* 2007 for further details).

Yet more quangos – rationalisation but continuing turbulence and complexity

While the restructuring of the LSC undoubtedly meant a huge upheaval for policy-makers and providers in the LSS, by no means has it been the only important organisational change to take place since 2001. Key national agencies have been merged (OFSTED and the Adult Learning Inspectorate (ALI)) and new ones born (the Sector Skills Development Agency (SSDA), Sector Skills Councils (SSCs) and the Quality Improvement Agency for Lifelong Learning (QIA)).

The policy-makers we interviewed differed in their views about the contribution that these new organisations would make to the LSS, although there was a general recognition that, as one person bluntly put it, 'The less national quango-type organisations that we've got, the better, really' (UC17) and that there was a need for clarification about the specific functions of the various agencies.

With regards to the OFSTED/ALI merger, the main concern was the difference in ethos between the two organisations and the dominance of the former in the newly merged structure. The establishment of QIA in 2006 was described by one official as part of central government's desire 'to devolve the delivery of national programmes as far to the front line as we could and to take them out of the Department' (WO7). It was also an attempt to clarify the reciprocal roles of the LSC, OFSTED and QIA in quality assurance and improvement within the sector, although some interviewees were sceptical, with one claiming that QIA was 'actually making the landscape more complex' (V10). Others were more charitable, but suggested that it was possibly too small to achieve its stated objectives and that it appeared anomalous as a national organisation responsible for quality improvement in an era when institutional 'self-regulation' was being promoted.

The SSDA[2] was set up in 2002 to encourage the formation of twenty-five SSCs to cover all employment sectors within the UK. This took five years to put into place. While government money was made available for this task, the SSCs were intended to be independent, employer-led organisations that would support the government's skills strategy, improve National Occupational Standards and provide a forum for employers to articulate the skills needs of their particular sector though Sector Skills Agreements (SSAs). Latterly, they have been given a role in the design of vocational qualifications in their sector (LSC and DfES 2007).

According to our interviewees, SSCs have more union involvement than their predecessors, the National Training Organisations, and, as a result, 'there's a potential in the sector agenda to look at building that social partnership road' (ZA20). The majority of the policy-makers we spoke to, however, and this included employer organisations themselves, were very sceptical about SSCs. As the Engineering Employers' Federation (EEF) commented in its written submission to the Education and Skills Select Committee on Post-16 Skills and Training:

> While these bodies are intended to be led by employers, for employers, some . . . appear to be dominated by public sector representatives from the learning and skills sector, such as the regional LSC, Job Centre Plus, Higher Education, the Government Office and the RDA, among others.
>
> (EEF 2006: 8)

And again, there were concerns from interviewees about bureaucracy and complexity.

Perhaps, then, there are two main responses to the question: how has the organisation of the LSS changed as a result of recent policy? First, there has been a move towards more regional and local levels of governance and there is a continuing rhetoric of institutional autonomy. However, to what extent this actually constitutes genuine devolution of power from the centre or simply clearer 'lines of sight' between national, regional and local delivery is still up for debate. Second, the turbulence of the first three years of the LSS has continued throughout the last two, with continuous organisational change and, despite efforts at rationalisation, the introduction of yet more agencies into an already complex landscape. As one policy-maker commented:

> It's a bit like town planning . . . The plan's very clear in the mind of the planners . . . but in terms of the people actually living on the streets . . . it's kind of, at times, anything but clear.
>
> (V13)

Is this town planning or is it, as Ewart Keep (2006) provocatively describes it, a government playing with 'the biggest train set in the world'?

What are the main messages for change?

Having described the new organisational structure for funding, planning and improving the quality of the LSS, we now examine the language and mechanisms policy-makers use to explain their aims and to animate the system. Chapters 5 and 7 analyse how managers and teachers respond to these policy messages and levers; here, we focus on four interrelated themes that have been ubiquitous in policy documents and regularly referred to in our policy interviews over the last two years (see Box 4.2). Interestingly, these themes are not the same as those we found in the first round of interviews we undertook in 2004: policy language, it appears, has moved on as fast as the structures within which it is conceived.

Box 4.2 Four major policy themes in the learning and skills sector, 2005–7

1 'Prioritisation'.
2 A 'demand-led system', including 'market making' and 'contestability'.
3 The drive for quality and excellence, including 'specialisation', 'personalisation', 'clarity of mission', 'the trust agenda' and 'self-regulation'.
4 'Simplification'.

'Prioritisation'

The LSS, like all other public services, has its own Public Service Agreement (PSA) targets (see Box 4.3). Introduced in 1988 under the Conservatives as part of the Comprehensive Spending Review process led by the Treasury, PSAs have also played an important role under New Labour as part of its centralised performance management system by focusing policy-makers on the areas they need to address. The LSC translates these targets and the messages from DfES policy documents and ministerial statements into an annual statement of priorities for the sector, which indicates to providers what will be government funded and, by implication, what will not be. One policy-maker described the way prioritisation works, seeing it as different from the way the LSC had operated in its early days:

For me, it's a system now, because we have a delivery chain that very clearly starts in government, with government prioritising its funds. It goes to the LSC, that's the first part of the delivery arm . . . When it gets to a college or a private provider, they know what part of the delivery chain they're in, how they're meeting government objectives or their own objectives.

(WO6)

In practice, the position is more complex than this because, as one official explained, prioritisation is of two types: there are priority *learners* (e.g., those with learning difficulties and disabilities) and priority *provision* (e.g., adult basic skills) – and this, he said, was 'not well understood' (UA14).

Box 4.3 Key targets for the learning and skills sector

- **Young people** 90% of 17-year-olds to be in learning in 2015 with more than 85% of them achieving at least a Level 2 by age 19.

- **Adults** Reduction by at least 40% of the number of adults in the workforce who lack an NVQ at Level 2 (or equivalent qualifications) by 2010. Improvement in the basic skills of 2.25 million adults between 2001 and 2010, with a milestone of 1.5 million by 2007.

Source: LSC and DfES (2007)

PSA targets for the sector are seen by some policy-makers as positive because they ensure that there will be money from the Treasury for provision (e.g., adult basic skills) for those who might otherwise not have access to it. Several too saw prioritisation as working very effectively in focusing colleges and work-based training providers more tightly on the type of provision that government wants to fund, so that 'the outcomes are more closely linked to the policy changes' (UA17). To illustrate this point, one policy-maker cited the fact that in his local area in 2002–3 less than 10 per cent of the adult provision the LSC funded was contributing to PSA targets, whereas in 2006 it had risen to 45 per cent (UC15). Moreover, there was a general recognition by both providers and policy-makers we interviewed that, as one put it, where 'there is a tightening of the budgetary climate' (ZA23), prioritisation is a necessary and logical step. On the other hand, there are downsides to prioritisation. It was described by one policy-maker as being 'centrally driven and normative' and having 'all kinds of turbulent effects on providers' (ZA23), and another admitted that there was 'fallout' from moving money away from unaccredited adult learning (see Taubman 2007 and Hodgson *et al.* 2007a for more detail). Moreover, tightening national priorities means reducing the flexibility to meet local needs and conditions.

A 'demand-led' system and the role of 'contestability'

The concept of a demand-led FE system and the role of contestability within this (i.e., giving 'employers more choice over who provides training without being limited to a particular college or training provider' (HMG 2005: 24)), derive both from sector-specific policy documents, such as the FE White Paper and the final report of the Leitch Review of Skills, and from the broader public sector reform agenda laid out in Cabinet Office documents (PMSU 2006, 2007). The first talks about 'a system shaped by the demands of learners and employers' (DfES 2006b: 16), a phrase which is echoed in the Leitch Report's definition of 'demand-led skills' (Leitch 2006: 4). Both are making a sector response to the government's policy intention that 'public services should respond to citizens' (PMSU 2007: 11). Two major changes flow from this: money increasingly follows the 'customer' and there is a move to 'open up the supply side, where appropriate, so that the greatest possible diversity of provision is encouraged' (*ibid.*). Hence, the increasing use of demand-led funding of adult skills provision and the application of 'the principle of "contestability" as an important way of driving up quality' (HMG 2005: 24).

The majority of policy-makers and providers in the LSS would probably agree with the broad thrust of policy, as exemplified in this comment: 'we are quite rightly giving increasing attention to the voice of customers and citizens in shaping the future of public services' (WO7). The way that demand-led funding and contestability will play out in practice for providers, however, is causing considerable anxiety to many in the sector and is polarising positions.

First, there was a difference between the views of colleges and independent learning providers. The former felt that the pace of change was too quick, was already beginning to distort their provision and was not allowing them to meet the needs of their local communities or particular groups of learners. The following quotation is typical of the views of college senior management:

> With contestability comes a different way of funding us, which means that we have got to respond differently, which means that the landscape is not so stable, which means that there are increasing interests being shown by the private sector in what we deem to be our work.
>
> (ZA27)

Independent learning providers, on the other hand, wholeheartedly supported the reforms, but felt that they were not being implemented fast enough, that there was not a level playing field in which to compete and that bureaucracy was getting in the way of a proper market. As one policy-maker rather graphically stated:

> Your policies are great, Prime Minister, but the implementation's balls-achingly slow . . . They still haven't broken through their civil servants and their public quango agencies to deliver a market-place response.
>
> (ZA26)

Meanwhile, the LSC saw its role as 'being more of a market-maker, to enable the sector to organise itself in a market and be responsive' (UC17). An alternative view from within the DfES was that the LSC would only have to 'market-make' when there was a gap and the market was not operating effectively.

There was also a difference of opinion over how much of the LSS budget should be demand-led and contestable; whether this approach should apply to 14–19 provision as well as to adult learning; the extent to which the state should intervene to protect the needs of those who are not well placed to articulate their own demands; and if there should be more emphasis placed on the demands of learners or employers, because these can often be in tension with one another (see Finlay *et al.* 2007a).

Moreover, it was not only providers who wondered whether ministers and civil servants really understood the implications of a fully demand-led system with demand-led funding. One policy-maker expressed his concerns:

There are some real purists here who would like a very pure demand-led system that would, from a bureaucracy point of view, be an absolute nightmare and from a management point of view [be] really difficult for providers to manage . . . Even companies and organisations that are totally demand-led get involved in planning. Otherwise you have chaos.

(UA17)

The 'drive for excellence' – relations between policy-makers and providers

Other chapters in this book discuss the fact that the LSS has traditionally been seen (and has seen itself) as a 'Cinderella sector'. However, this view had changed considerably by the end of our project, because of the huge injection of resources into the sector and increased political attention.

Bill Rammell, the then Minister for Further and Higher Education, for example, in the foreword to *Learning and Skills* (LSC 2005b: i) referred to further education as 'the engine room for skills and social justice in this country'. Indeed, from Sir Andrew Foster's final report onwards, national policy documents have been trying to talk up the sector, as have the policy-makers who translate those texts: 'we are actually very committed to the notion of enhancing the prestige and self-esteem of people working in FE' (WO7). Hence one major reason for what Foster called 'the quality imperative' (Foster 2005: 7). Or, as one of our interviewees put it rather more starkly: 'the push is on at the moment and we are going to get rid of the rubbish by 2008' (WO8). It is interesting how the FE White Paper, in responding to the Foster Report, links together the ideas of excellence, a clear mission and specialisation, and suggests that together they will deliver what the economy requires (DfES 2006b: 22), but without really explaining how.

Improving the quality of post-compulsory education and training is also part of wider national and international agendas. One of our European policy-makers asserted that: 'the drive towards quality has been taken on board by most countries' (Y3) and the two recent public sector reform documents published by the Cabinet Office (PMSU 2006, 2007) refer repeatedly to the importance of 'high quality' and 'continuous improvement'. In the case of the latter document this is linked to increased 'personalisation' of services through 'diversity of provision' and 'contestability and incentives to drive innovation and improvement' (PMSU 2007: 7).

However, there were differences of opinion about who was doing the improvement and how it should be done. Recent policy documents, such as the FE White Paper (DfES 2006b) and the Quality Improvement Strategy (QIA 2007), have laid emphasis on 'self-regulation' and 'autonomy', as did many of the policy-makers we interviewed. But those on the receiving end saw it rather differently:

> Government has largely seen the quality improvement agenda as a top-down model and has imposed its own solutions, rightly or wrongly, on the system, without ever allowing it to become a bottom-up model and embedding a quality improvement philosophy within institutions which then deliver the changes.
>
> (ZA24)

The reliance on external benchmarks and outside evaluators, such as inspectors, has become so much part of the culture within the LSS that one interviewee remarked:

> There's actually quite a sea-change needed in terms of helping people to get back the confidence that they used to have before they started being slapped on the wrist the whole time.
>
> (ZA22)

Nevertheless, 'self-regulation' was broadly recognised by both policy-makers and practitioners as a step in the right direction and part of a broader 'trust' agenda that was very welcome. Moreover, while the idea of actively involving professionals as partners in public service reform policy was, for example, conspicuously absent from the first public sector reform discussion document (PMSU 2006), it made an appearance in the latest document on this subject (PMSU 2007). One of the next steps towards more 'tailored' public service is 'to engage with the public service workforce as partners' (*ibid.*: 30) in reform. However, these plans still have to be turned into changed behaviour.

'Simplification' – more than just a new word for 'bureaucracy busting'?

During our first set of policy interviews in 2004, there was much discussion of 'bureaucracy busting', resulting from the reports of the Bureaucracy Task Force, chaired by Sir George Sweeney (LSC 2004b).

In our final set of interviews the term 'simplification' was commonly used and reverberates through recent policy documents. One of our interviewees stressed its ubiquitousness:

> It is now a simplification agenda . . . a simplification of structures, a simplification of processes, a simplification of the delivery chain right down to the front end.
>
> (WO6)

Simplification does then seem to mean more than just 'bureaucracy busting'. The way that the LSC structure had been slimmed down was seen as an example of 'simplification' in action. Great play was made of 'single documents of guidance', 'two big conversations' per year related to the 'Business Planning Cycle' and 'lighter touch' contract management (UC14). However, Train to Gain, which was intended to embody all of these features, had, according to one interviewee, 'created a lot of bureaucracy; it's slowed down decision-making' (UC17) and compared unfavourably with its predecessor, Employer Training Pilots. Moreover, in terms of simplification of structures, in the words of one of our interviewees:

> What we don't see across the system overall is a systematic approach to simplifying the landscape.
>
> (UA17)

What are the burning issues for policy-makers?

This chapter is about the policy-makers' stories, so in this section we summarise the five main issues that they raised about the LSS. Interestingly, however, these issues are also shared by practitioners in the sector, as other chapters in this book will testify.

The policy process – too much, too fast and no time for reflection

The first and foremost issue for policy-makers, and this was true of people we interviewed from all of the organisations involved in our study, was the way in which policy-making is conducted. While there was support for the government's general policy aims, there were many complaints about the speed of policy:

Nothing is really given enough time to bed in before the next thing comes along.

(UC16)

Constant change and restructuring were seen as counter-productive in terms of professional commitment:

It is so destroying of any momentum. It is so demoralizing. It is so anxiety-creating that actually performance suffers.

(V11)

While one official argued that the transactional costs of change could be seen as 'an investment because of a better return that's coming later' (UA17), he was in a minority. There was criticism too of the lack of a joined-up approach to policy, with too many initiatives. This 'policy busyness' (Hayward *et al.* 2005), which was recognised as a feature of the English system by our European interviewees, has undoubtedly been exacerbated by having six different Secretaries of State for Education and Skills and numerous junior ministers since 2000. Each new minister understandably wants to make her or his own mark on the territory. What policy-makers complain about is the lack of 'policy memory' (Higham and Yeomans 2007) that is brought to bear on new initiatives:

Skills for Life started as though it was year zero.

(ZA21)

They also regretted the lack of recognition that proper implementation takes time. As one interviewee explained:

One of the underlying weaknesses of the last three years – and I fear of any government – is the belief on the part of ministers, of politicians, that when they have announced something it has happened.

(V11)

Another official with considerable experience of education and train-ing systems across Europe suggested that what we need in England is 'creeping, not jumping' (ZA25).

Perhaps the sharpest criticisms were reserved for what we have referred to elsewhere as 'policy tensions' (Hodgson and Spours 2003), a term which is used to describe the way that one government policy may work against another. One of the most cited examples in the LSS was the tension between the drive for institutional collaboration and the equally strong drive for institutional autonomy and competition. As one interviewee summed it up:

> So there seem to be two competing forces here. And one is saying, 'It's a free-market economy and the market will configure itself to deliver the best provision' . . . and then there's another one saying, 'But you must plan it.'
>
> (UC15)

The other major policy tensions identified by policy-makers were those between the government's drive towards a high-skills economy and the demands of social inclusion; satisfying the needs of individuals and the needs of employers; and the difficulties of maintaining a balance between regional and sectoral priorities.

Who pays for learning?

An important issue for policy-makers, and one which is played out in all the recent policy documents (e.g., DfES 2007c; LSC and DfES 2007), is: who pays for lifelong learning or, perhaps more precisely, who pays for which type of learning and how are the costs to be shared between the state, the individual and employers? This is not a new debate, of course (e.g., Williams 1999; Piatt and Robinson 2001), nor is it one that is confined to England (e.g., Green et al. 2000). Among our interviewees there was a recognition that the government had been increasingly generously funding the LSS, but that resources were finite, prioritisation of government funding was necessary and individuals and employers would both have to pay more. This was not seen as an easy policy to implement, however. When learning had been free or very cheap in the past, the introduction of fees was highly controversial. There was also a recognition that, as a result of prioritisation, 'adult learning has got squeezed' (ZA24) and this was having an impact right across the country.

Asking employers to pay more was also seen as problematic, even though policy documents in England are increasingly candid about the need for this to happen. Some interviewees were worried about the Train to Gain initiative and whether precious resources might be wasted on what is known as 'dead weight' (i.e., government funding paying for training that employers would have funded themselves). There is also a lively debate among both policy-makers and practitioners about how the overall education budget is divided between schools, higher education and the LSS, and whether the latter is getting its fair share (e.g., Styles and Fletcher 2006; Stanton and Fletcher 2006). Given the nature of many of the learners within the LSS, this is seen as a serious inequity (see Chapter 6).

The role of employers

A related and equally hotly debated issue for policy-makers was the role of employers in the LSS. Many were sceptical about employers' commitment to training their workforce. There is also a broader debate about whether the notion of an 'employer-led' sector is the right concept at all and whether a social partnership approach, such as that employed in other European countries, would be a more effective way of operating. In the Nordic countries there are collective agreements between the social partners to promote a more shared approach to training, changes in the workplace and government policy decisions.

Several policy-makers also highlighted the need for more employment sectors to introduce 'licence to practise' arrangements, as well as greater financial rewards for employees gaining qualifications. A couple suggested that sector levies might be an effective way of increasing the role of employers in training. These are all strategies that the Leitch Report (2006) touched on, but ultimately shied away from, preferring to continue with the 'voluntarist' approach that has traditionally been the hallmark of the English post-compulsory education and training system. What Leitch proposed instead was the introduction of a new 'Pledge' for employers 'to voluntarily commit to train all eligible employees up to Level 2 in the workplace' (Leitch 2006: 4) and for this to be reviewed in 2010 with statutory arrangements to be brought into play if progress was not considered sufficient.

Qualifications

Almost all of the policy-makers we interviewed, including the European ones, commented on the powerful role of qualifications in lifelong learning, although the latter also stressed the importance of non-formal and informal learning, which does not necessarily need to be certificated (see Colley *et al.* 2003 for a discussion of informality and formality in learning). Current qualifications were seen as too inflexible to meet the needs of adults or employers. As a result, several countries in Europe are actively involved in developing a European Qualifications Framework (EQF). England, somewhat behind Scotland, Wales and Northern Ireland, is in the process of developing the new Qualifications and Credit Framework (QCF), previously referred to as the Framework for Achievement (QCA 2004). Progress was seen as too slow, there were concerns about costs and the way that the four countries of the UK still do not seem to be going in the same direction (e.g., Stevens 2007). Particular anxieties were expressed about the greater role of SSCs in qualifications development and about the design and purposes of the new diplomas (see HoC 2007 and Hodgson and Spours 2007).

Capacity to deliver?

While 'fostering workforce innovation and development' is one of the key tenets of public sector reform (PMSU 2007: 56), a number of policy-makers were concerned about the future capacity of the workforce within the LSS. One spoke of the 'crisis of succession' (V11) in terms of governance and leadership of FE colleges, owing to many principals reaching the age of retirement and difficulties in recruiting new leaders and governors. Others mentioned the number of part-time, agency and temporary staff in the sector, their lack of status and the fact that they felt they had no voice in the policy process (see Chapter 5). From the other end of the telescope, practitioners commented on the continuing lack of capacity in the LSC to undertake the new tasks they were expected to perform in a demand-led system.

Conclusion: the researchers' view of the policy-makers' stories

As researchers who have had the privilege of listening to the policy-makers' stories and reading their texts, what can we conclude?

Perhaps the first thing to note is that policy-makers do not speak with one voice. While there was a common view, on some issues there were considerable differences of opinion. All the policy-makers to whom we spoke were strongly committed to the government's twin policy drivers – economic competitiveness and social inclusion. But they tended to disagree about the policy mechanisms employed to achieve these ends. All were pleased about the higher profile being accorded to the LSS by politicians and noted the significant achievements that had been made since the inception of the LSC in 2001 (see Box 1.2, p. 14 above). As an outsider, one sensed tremendous energy, drive and enthusiasm. But discord began to creep in over the conduct of the policy process itself, the way in which the model of public sector reform was being applied to the LSS, the balance of power between local, regional and national governance, and how major deep-seated issues, such as the reform of the qualifications system and the relationship between the education and training system and the labour market, were being tackled (or not).

While those in central government, through either policy documents or the words of ministers and DfES officials, are constantly pushing for faster reform, the majority of those below this level, including the LSC itself, appeared to feel that the pace of change was too swift and did not allow adequate time for effective implementation or reflection on progress before future action was decided upon. There was exasperation about the sheer number of initiatives and the inherent tensions between some of them. The rhetoric of 'demand-led' provision and funding, 'self-regulation', 'prioritisation', 'excellence' and 'simplification' was ubiquitous. The majority of those interviewed saw some merit in these terms and what they represented. However, there was a significant degree of scepticism and anxiety, or even hostility, towards the possible ramifications of turning this rhetoric into reality. 'Demand-led' funding, for example, was viewed with considerable fear by those representing FE colleges, because of the destabilising effects it is likely to have on them. There is a deeper problem too with the way the concept of 'customer-focused' services has been applied by the government to the LSS, because there is not one 'customer' but two highly heterogeneous groups – learners and employers – whose needs and expectations are complex and often very different.

Box 4.4   The policy-maker's world and the world of practice

If the government goes down the path which they have chosen to do, of putting in a lot of structures to get things done, that is just one way of looking at the world. There is another way of looking at the world which is how you get things done.

(ZA30)

A second major area of disagreement among policy-makers was the extent to which the structural changes to the LSC had made it more locally and regionally responsive or simply more effective at carrying out national government priorities. There is no doubt that the government's avowed intention, as part of reforming the public sector, is to devolve more power to the local level (see PMSU 2007; DCLG 2006) and this is certainly the thrust of the recent review of local government, as this quotation from a speech by Sir Michael Lyons, the chair of the review, testifies:

> In my final report, I call for a new partnership between central and local government. This needs to be based on changes in behaviours from all tiers of government to achieve a stronger relationship – creating a shared ambition for the future. Central government needs to leave more room for local discretion and recognise the value of local choice; while local government needs to strengthen its own confidence and capability, engage more effectively with local people, make best use of existing powers, and stop asking for central direction.
>
> (Lyons 2007b)

The move to more local control is also reflected in the way that 14–19 education will be funded in the future – that is, through local authorities (Cabinet Office 2007). However, how this policy will play out on the ground in the LSS is still unclear and, as both our interviewees and recent research in the area (Grainger *et al.* 2007; Steer and Lakey 2007) point out, the local-authority level is probably not the right layer of governance for all aspects of the post-compulsory education and training system, particularly in large metropolitan areas with small unitary authorities. What appears to be needed is a more careful balance of regional and local govern-ance within a supportive national policy framework alongside a more general drive for greater democratisation (see Chapters 7 and 8 for an elaboration of these ideas).

Finally, there are three other long-standing issues that were raised by policy-makers and, despite all the recent reforms and restructuring within the LSS, still need addressing. First, how can we ensure that resources are made available for adults to pursue learning for life rather than simply for qualifications or employment? This is an important message from our learner data and one that several policy-makers raised. Current policy clearly prioritises learning that leads to 'economically valuable skills' (Leitch 2006: 2) and there is a real concern about the loss of broader adult provision. A second, related issue is how the qualifications system can be reformed to meet the needs of the twenty-first century. The development of the QCF is seen by many as a step in the right direction (see Hodgson *et al.* 2006), but the continuing insistence on a divided 14–19 qualifications system – with GCSEs and A Levels on one side and the new diplomas, other vocational qualifications and apprenticeships on the other – is viewed as fundamentally unhelpful by many policy-makers and the vast majority of practitioners and researchers (Hodgson and Spours 2007).

The third, and possibly the most intractable, issue which affects both the supply and the demand for learning in England is the lack of social partnership arrangements that exist in other European countries to underpin the relationship between employers, learners, trade unions, the education and training system and the government. Without policy mechanisms, such as social partnerships, 'licences to practise' and sector levies, there is a limit to how much the reform of policy structures and initiatives can do to meet the challenging targets set by government itself.

Box 4.5 Implications for policy

1   There has been considerable money and attention focused on the LSS since the inception of the LSC. This is entirely welcome and justifiable in both social and economic terms. It is important that it continues to receive a high level of support and that levels of inequity between this sector and other parts of the education system are eradicated.

2   There is a case for slowing the pace of reform, in particular in relation to demand-led funding, so that consolidation and reflection, based on the considerable energy, knowledge and commitment in the sector, can take place before introducing yet more change into what has been a constantly turbulent sector.

3   Top-down and centralised policy has been a hallmark of governance in the LSS. The time has come for a greater balance between national, regional and local decision-making founded on a strong social partnership framework.

> 4   While the broad thrust of education and training policy is supported within the sector, greater emphasis needs to be placed on the wider benefits of learning and on adult provision that is not simply geared to employability.
> 5   The qualifications system is currently not fit for purpose. Further reform, along the lines of the QCF, is necessary to develop the type of unified and credit-based system required to support an inclusive approach to lifelong learning.

Moreover, as the quotation in Box 4.4 suggests, there is only so much that can be done by policy-makers on their own: it is the practitioners, working within the parameters set by policy, who ultimately decide which learning opportunities they can offer and which learners they can serve. It is to these central players we now turn.

Notes

1   The interviews undertaken for this research cover the period up to the change of Prime Minister from Tony Blair to Gordon Brown in 2007. For this reason the discussion in this text will confine itself to changes that took place prior to the restructuring of the DfES. The final chapter of this book will speculate about the implications of this latest round of change for the LSS and more detail is contained in our fifth research report – Hodgson *et al.* 2007b.

2   At the time of writing, yet another change was announced with the UK Commission for Skills replacing the SSDA and the National Employment Panel in 2008.

Chapter 5

The practitioners' stories

Why are the practitioners' accounts important?

The pivotal position of teaching staff and the middle managers with responsibility for course leadership in the learning and skills sector makes their views particularly important. On the one hand, these practitioners are close to their learners, dealing with them on a daily basis and building up experience of what they find useful, motivating and supportive of their learning. As discussed in Chapter 3, in the eyes of the learners, the tutors are the people who respond to their needs and make the sector work. On the other hand, these tutors and their managers are responsible for carrying through the agenda of the policy-makers, as described in Chapter 4, with targets to meet, on which their future funding and the survival of their organisation may depend, and they must also fulfil the requirements of awarding bodies whose qualifications they offer.

The tutors, therefore, stand close to the learners and their learning. They are overseen by local managers, for example in colleges or in local authority community teams, and many told us they also had direct contact with the awarding bodies. Tutors and middle managers are, however, largely remote from the Learning and Skills Council and those who devise policy in central government. Only a few managers – usually managers of adult and community learning (ACL) services, rather than middle managers in colleges – had any contact with even local LSC officials, and none felt that they had the power to influence or change government policy. Some made it clear that they did not know why or by whom decisions were taken, as these comments from an ACL service whose Entry Level provision was under threat illustrate:

We don't know why decisions have been made. It's just very, very isolated.

(JM1)

We don't know what's happening as tutors – we're nearly always the last to know. And it's not been the programme managers' fault: they don't know either.

(JT2)

Tutors' understandings of government policy were also coloured by the management priorities of their institutions and the culture of the teams to which they belonged. In some settings, pressure to meet targets was absorbed by managers, and had not been passed down to tutor level; but in others, where local management stressed the importance of meeting targets, or favoured frequent 'mock' inspections in preparation for OFSTED visits, staff were under pressure to conform. The impact of local cultures and local management 'translations' of policy will be considered in more detail in Chapter 7. Here, our focus is on the tensions described by teaching staff, tensions which arise from reconciling the demands of policy with the needs of learners.

Given their position, as recipients of directives from above, and producers of outcomes on which they would be judged, could teaching staff be construed as the victims of policy – or 'dupes' or 'devils' (Bathmaker 2001)? Did they see themselves as victims? How was their experience of government policy, and in particular of the use of policy levers, such as targets and initiatives, affecting their perceptions of their professional role and their practice? We shall return to these questions, as we review in turn the diversity of interviewees in our sample; their perspectives on the pressures of policy change; and their views on working with both learners and colleagues. We end by considering the provision for professional learning for staff in the sector, their conditions and status, and what the future may hold for them and the sector.

Diversity in our sample

For this chapter, we draw primarily on 210 interviews, of which 184 were with tutors and middle managers and 26 were with union learning representatives (ULRs) or workplace managers with responsibility for staff development. As our Appendix on methodology explains, our rationale was based on a balanced sample of *courses* for Level 1 and Level 2 learners, rather than on selecting a representative sample of *people* working in the sector. The staff we interviewed were simply those who happened to be teaching or managing the courses we had selected. Our schedule of repeated visits over two years also allowed us to gauge the stability of staffing on those courses. At one end of the scale, in one of the eight FE courses we met the same manager and course tutor on all five visits; by contrast, in another college we found one course had four different managers in the space of two years. Other relevant data sources for this chapter are our annual participant seminars and the final online survey (see Steer and Lakey 2007).

These sources tell us a lot about the state of the sector, but we freely acknowledge the limitations of our data. As discussed elsewhere (Edward *et al.* 2007), we can make only a cautious contribution to current debates about the professionalism of staff in colleges (see Gleeson *et al.* 2005; James and Biesta 2007), because of our clear focus on the impact of policy on teaching and learning. Our line of questioning was not designed specifically to draw out interviewees' personal constructs, values or understandings of their professionalism. Insights gleaned from those who chose to relate their personal experience of policy to their values, motivation and professional careers, described below in the section on working with learners, are valuable. However, since we were not collecting such data systematically, we only glimpse, but cannot generalise about, the meanings of professionalism in our sample. Although we learned occasionally that a tutor we had interviewed had left the organisation, unlike the TLRP team who researched Transforming Learning Cultures in Further Education (see James and Biesta 2007), we did not have resources to contact tutors who disappeared from our sites, to explore their reasons for leaving.

We refer readers with an interest in just one of the three types of learning site to our specialised papers elsewhere, on FE (Spours *et al.* 2007), ACL (Hodgson *et al.* 2007a) and work-based learning (WBL) (Finlay *et al.* 2007a). In this chapter, we draw primarily on data from staff directly involved in teaching and managing learning. There are other important figures, however, in the practitioners' stories, some of whom we were able to interview, and some of whom we simply heard about or observed in action. On the WBL sites, for example, ULRs and training managers provided valuable background information about the learning cultures of their organisations and the synergy between their own roles and those of the basic skills tutors who taught there. In some ACL sites, volunteers worked alongside tutors, providing one-to-one support for learners being taught in groups. In FE sites, the presence, or absence, of classroom assistants made a huge difference to learning. In one Level 1 class of eleven students, we observed five adults in addition to the tutor, supporting learners with a range of physical disabilities and learning or behavioural difficulties. Other support staff, including learning mentors and student counsellors, also figured in learners' accounts.

Even among teaching staff, there was considerable diversity. In colleges we met full-time staff and others on fractional or short-term contracts; staff with thirty years of experience behind them, and others so new to their roles that they were still completing teaching qualifications. Such differences were likely to affect perceptions of policy and change: for example, an experienced ACL manager welcomed the availability of Skills for Life funds, and relished the challenge of trying to make the Employer Training Pilot scheme work in her service, because she was looking back over decades of uncertain funding:

> All the time I have been a manager, my biggest problem has been getting the money to run the organisation. I have always been, with my team, under threat.
>
> (GM1)

Understandably, experienced tutors were also more likely than newly qualified staff to have reservations about elements of the Skills for Life initiative, such as the narrowness of the Level 2 National Test for Literacy (which does not test writing) and the inherent temptation for tutors to 'teach to the test', which conflicted with their previous training and professional practice:

> We were trained that it was learner-led, and what the student wanted, that we would provide that to the best of our ability, rather than having to get so many people through the exam.
>
> (KT2)

Are there clear differences between the views of staff in, say, FE colleges and those we met in workplace or community sites? The differences are not as marked as we expected, for three reasons. First, although staff in the three types of learning site were working in slightly different policy environments, common themes emerged from their responses to questions about the factors which affected teaching and learning. Second, we found differences between staff working in different course teams and organisational cultures within the college sector, differences that were at least as great as those between college and community teams. Third, the constituencies overlap and there is mobility between them. Workplace tutors included some from colleges, others from community teams and others from the private sector. Basic skills tutors could choose to work in a range of settings, and some of our interviewees had worked in several. We also learned that sometimes community teams struggled to recruit, because local colleges could offer more attractive salaries and conditions.

In the rest of this chapter, we consider in turn the shared ground of issues about policy change and pressures; then the intervening cultural factors in the sites; and finally, professional and career development for staff in the sector.

Policy change and pressures

We interviewed staff about the impact on their practice of the policy levers – targets, funding, inspections, planning and initiatives – which have been described in previous chapters. Chapter 7 also considers the range of staff behaviour in response to policy levers. Here, as an example, we focus on the responses from staff about the impact of what is perhaps the most pervasive of the five policy levers to which we sought their reactions – targets. Staff in all three types of learning site identified meeting targets as an important influence on their practice, highlighting how targets were often linked to other levers, such as funding, and initiatives (Skills for Life and the Employer Training Pilot), to form an even more powerful triple lever, which could affect the future survival of their courses. Evidence of achieving targets was also important for inspection and indeed for planning, although for many of our interviewees, planning was seen as a necessary local management process, rather than a requirement of national policy.

Pressure to meet targets was mentioned by staff, in terms which ranged from acceptance and (sometimes reluctant) compliance, to 'ethical gaming', by which we mean creative attempts to use the fruits of meeting targets to support other, less well-funded work.

Although many tutors and managers deplored the effects of target-chasing, practices such as payments to encourage learners to take a national test in basic skills were common. If, for example, a local authority had chosen to meet its Skills for Life targets by offering council

---

Box 5.1 Targets, targets, targets

I suppose a year of consolidation would be nice, but it is not likely to happen. We move on in different areas all of the time . . . If we are told basically, 'This is what we do: this is what we suggest you do and your funding depends on it' – then is that not what we do? . . . We are walking a narrow line of getting the job done.

(B2M3)

With funders increasingly regarding success rates as the only indicator of quality and effectiveness, we have no alternative.

(Survey, 42 – senior manager)

We just make sure that we hit our targets and get the money in . . . get the targets and outputs out of the way, and then we get on with what we are really about.

(FM3)

---

employees financial incentives to take the tests, tutors were obliged to comply. A few tutors, however, took a principled stand against the temptation to put learners in for a Level 1 test, and thereby secure the target, rather than take the slower and riskier route to a Level 2 test:

> When they ask me how many I will get, I will say that I will get as many as I can. But I won't put people through a test that is at a lower level, just so that they get a target, if it is not the right one for the person.
>
> (MT1)

Even those who prided themselves on meeting their targets sometimes expressed reservations about whether they were a true measure of success. Alder College, for example, reported being penalised for poor retention, when they had helped NVQ learners find apprenticeships and transfer to that route: a move which tutors, managers, employers and learners all saw as positive for the learners' career, but which led to missed targets on the NVQ route. A manager commented:

The LSC say, 'Work-based learning is looking good, but FE looks terrible' . . . I actually believe that that is progression and success, but it isn't for the LSC.

(A2M1)

Box 5.2 illustrates further tensions between targets and meeting learners' needs.

Box 5.2 Do targets tell the whole story?

The numbers that have gone through the national tests will be used as a medium for how well we are improving our service, and I think it's a bit of an untruth. It's not a true measure of where our strengths lie. I think it's one of the strengths, but I don't think it's the only one. I think it's a bit heavily weighted on that side.

(EM1)

LSC only talk about targets and outcomes, but I want to talk about learners and people's needs . . . Instead of talking about the immediate training needs of firms, we need to talk about the continued existence of an educated society.

(Seminar, 2007 – ACL manager)

A second theme common to all three strands of our fieldwork was the pressure to cope with paperwork and administration, maintaining a balance between bureaucratic demands and meeting the needs of learners. Time which tutors would rather have spent preparing lessons, materials and feedback for learners had to be spent filling in forms to provide evidence to allow the course to continue. Sometimes the same information was required by several parties, such as college management, LSC or awarding bodies. Although in the period of our research some attempts were made to rationalise this, with encouragement from the LSC, complaints about time spent on paperwork continued. A college tutor expressed her frustration:

I really don't feel that I've enough time to produce everything for the courses that I'd like to produce . . . The main thing would be to allow me to have more time to mark and prepare the work –

that is where it's so difficult at the moment. You are really chasing your tail all year . . . The amount of pressure that everybody is under is crazy.

(B2T3)

Paperwork associated with Skills for Life was particularly onerous for teams which offered drop-in provision, in the community or workplace: although flexibility was welcomed by the learners, staff had to pay the price in paperwork to log in each learner's attendance and achievement records, to ensure funding could be claimed. This burden may fall particularly heavily on tutors on fractional contracts, as a respondent to our survey in 2007 suggested:

The current amount of paperwork per session and per month is ridiculous for a part-time tutor.

(Survey, 38 – tutor)

A third common theme in our data was the danger that a policy emphasis on target groups leads to neglect of other needy groups. As discussed elsewhere (Hodgson et al. 2007a), the decline of non-accredited learning for adults in the community has limited opportunities for attracting new learners and offering progression routes for basic skills learners; and many interviewees expressed concerns about the loss of funded ESOL courses and of courses below Level 1 which do not count towards targets. Box 5.3 illustrates some of these concerns.

In colleges too, concerns were raised about provision for learners with learning difficulties and those whose progression from one level to the next was likely to be slow. Our interviews with tutors and managers took place before the publication of the Leitch Report (2006), and the increased emphasis on 'demand-led' systems, but a principal interviewed since then saw dangers ahead:

I think what you would have seen in the past . . . is that colleges would have protected vulnerable learners and expensive provision, because they perceived themselves to have some public duty in respect of those things. But that was before colleges were going to compete on quality and price with the private sector. You are now in a completely different ball-game.

(ZA30)

> ## Box 5.3 Protecting provision for basic skills learners below Level 1
>
> I think the frustrating thing is that a lot of our learners are not even nearly at Level 1, and so therefore in the eyes of these targets that we've been set, they don't count. We could be working with them for years before they actually reach Level 1 and that's a frustration because they are the people who obviously really need help.
>
> (IM1)
>
> And I think it is a danger, because then you are seen as successful, because you have got three hundred people through the tests [at Level 1 or 2], but in actual fact what might be more of an achievement is getting five people from Entry [Level] 1 to Entry 2.
>
> (GT1)
>
> We have traditionally taken young people with learning difficulties and other disabilities. In view of the serious conse-quences of not achieving success rates, we are now having to review this, particularly for people who are hard to place with an employer.
>
> (Survey, 70 – independent training provider)

Working with learners and colleagues

Working with learners

Although staff welcomed the increased resources for their area of work, many were unhappy with some aspects of the impact of policy on their roles. They did not, however, transmit their anxieties to their learners. In both their interviews and our observations we found evidence of motivated staff enjoying teaching and conveying their enthusiasm to learners. When we asked tutors what influenced their teaching and learning, learners and their needs were seen as the most important factors. Staff might be weary of paperwork, anxious about inspection or targets, under pressure to boost student achievement and retention, but, once they were in the classroom and with their learners, most were still enjoying teaching. A college principal recognised the fundamental motivation of the staff, even at management level, commenting:

> Most of us came into education because we feel we want to make a difference, and we do have moral obligations.
>
> (ZA31)

Some tutors in the sector confirmed their personal reasons for choosing to stay there, despite pressures of paperwork:

> I've a passion for education and I feel for these students.
>
> (B2T1)

> Oh, I love working with them . . . I'm used to trying to make learning enjoyable . . . and they were just fun.
>
> (MT1)

The burgeoning literature on professionalism in FE (e.g., Avis 2003; Gleeson *et al.* 2005; James and Biesta 2007) alerts us to the dangers of describing heroic tutors occupying the moral high ground, protecting their learners and battling against the 'audit explosion' (Power 1994) – but we would not be doing justice to the practitioners' stories if we failed to mention the satisfaction and sheer enjoyment many also continue to find in their teaching.

From where does this satisfaction originate? No-one said they relished the paperwork; only a few enjoyed (usually retrospectively) the experience of being inspected; but many stressed their commitment to learners and the satisfaction of seeing success and achievement from people who had struggled in their previous experiences of education and were accustomed to failure. For example, basic skills tutors took pleasure in showing us displays of award ceremony photographs, with learners receiving their first-ever certificates, and described the surprise and satisfaction of overhearing workers at a council depot discussing maths problems in their work breaks, rather than the latest football match. In colleges, too, commitment to learners and their needs perhaps partly explains why tutors stayed in this sector, instead of seeking more lucrative employment in schools or elsewhere. They also derived satisfaction from the fact that so many learners were enjoying their current courses and contrasting that positive experience with their poor treatment at school.

What about the traditional attractions and satisfactions of professionalism? If we trawl back over the last forty years in the literature on professional practice, from Etzioni (1969) through, for example, Johnson (1972), Eraut (1994), Hoyle and John (1995) to Wallace and Hoyle (2005), we see how professional autonomy and scope for the exercise of professional judgement remain important aspirations for professionals. The meanings of those terms have, however, changed over the years. Just as doctors and other health service professionals, for example, have seen their autonomy restricted, so have teachers. The gesture of closing the classroom door no longer shuts out the world and its targets, inspections, peer observations and other elements of heightened accountability.

While we could not explore fully what professionalism meant to our interviewees, we did ask, in 2005, about changes they were planning to make to their teaching. We wanted to know whether they were still able to make changes based on personal professional judgements or on the priorities of their local course team, rather than on the requirements of national or institutional policy. The responses showed reassuring variety, with evidence that some tutors were creating space among the teaching, paperwork and assessment for reflective practice and seeking new ways of engaging and keeping their learners' interest. Two examples illustrate this point. A work-based tutor, teaching one-to-one in a drop-in centre, planned sessions to bring together those scattered learners, so that they could learn together and enjoy peer support. A course manager was developing an incentive scheme collaboratively with her Level 1 Childcare learners and tutors, hoping that this process would reinforce learners' interest and trust in the scheme, and also develop their skills in collaborative working, which would be vital in the nurseries where they would eventually work.

Our data resonate with the findings of Stronach et al. (2002), who distinguish between the 'economies of performance' and 'ecologies of practice'. Like the nurses and schoolteachers they describe, staff in our research talked about their 'economies of performance' – dealing with paperwork, meeting targets and the demands of managers, inspectors and other bodies. But their stories also included reference to their 'ecologies of practice' – in this case their learner-centred values and their own beliefs about learners' needs and how to make a difference to them and help them succeed. Our research suggests that it may be the strength of this commitment to learners which helps some staff keep in perspective and cope with the bureaucratic demands which might otherwise overwhelm them.

This solution did not, however, work for everyone. Like the TLRP team who researched Transforming Learning Cultures, we also found staff whose strong commitment to learners, combined with meeting the demands of accountability, led them to work impossibly long hours, engaging in 'underground working' (James and Diment 2003), and 'routinely engaging in working well beyond their job descriptions' (Hodkinson *et al.* 2005b: 2). While some of those who told us they were working extremely long hours were still in place when we completed the fieldwork, we learned that one such tutor had become ill, and another left abruptly to take a less stressful post outside the sector. Worryingly, we learned at a project conference in 2007 that financial uncertainties in the post-Leitch era had led to shortening of staff contracts to three or six months at a time, reducing goodwill and morale, even in teams that were previously exceptionally committed and enthusiastic. We shall return to the theme of individual choice and agency at the end of this chapter.

As discussed in Chapter 3, learners in this sector, particularly younger learners at Level 1 and 2, are often very challenging, although potentially rewarding, to teach. Tutors working with 16–19-year-olds in FE described learners coping with social and emotional problems, difficult family backgrounds, health problems, involvement with drugs and crime and the demands of part-time working, while trying to meet the same commitments as other students. Particularly at Level 1, lack of academic confidence was sometimes combined with disruptive or challenging behaviour. Some tutors had strategies for building a culture of mutual respect in their classroom, as a strong foundation to enable learners to grow in confidence. Interviewing learners at the end of their course, we saw and heard evidence of their increased confidence, and some told us about the activities they had enjoyed – including those which staff had told us were designed deliberately to strengthen the group learning culture.

Working with adult learners in the community or workplace was not as different from working with adolescents in FE colleges as we might have expected. Confidence and a strong relationship with the tutor again were seen as central to learner success; and helping embarrassed adults feel strong enough to take national tests required skill and sensitivity. But whereas a young person in college might stay and be disruptive, an unconfident adult learner would be more likely to give up and withdraw.

Working with colleagues

Working in a team was the other major source of motivation for teaching staff. Their stories are full of references to the support of colleagues, either in dealing with students or in coping with administrative demands. But teamworking was not universal. In some settings we found relatively isolated tutors, who came in, did their teaching and went home, taking no notice of wider team or college issues:

> I just come in. I've got a job to do and I do it. And there are things on the periphery that I don't get involved with. Simple as that!
>
> (C1T1)

Elsewhere, however, teamworking was more highly valued. The manager of a Level 1 college course, who described her team as 'a tight ship', high-lighted the importance for the learners of strong team communication, co-ordinated by the 'personal tutor':

> They are very aware that this is a team approach to teaching them, that it is not just one tutor coming in who does not disseminate information to others. So we have very clearly defined that the impact of one session and how that session may have gone is discussed and the tutors know they have a port of call . . . the personal tutor.
>
> (A1M1)

Having discussed variations in teamworking more fully elsewhere (Coffield *et al.* 2007), in this context we simply note the diversity of its uses and outcomes. In the example above, teamwork ensured that learners knew that staff members shared information and therefore that they could not play one tutor off against another. In an ACL setting, where staff were still coming to terms with the introduction of Skills for Life, with its associated paperwork, Individual Learning Plans and target-driven pressure to persuade learners to take the national tests, tutors valued highly the peer support of colleagues, and felt their similar professional experience and training helped them cope with changes:

> We support each other with the pressure that we get or the stress that we feel, because it goes against the way we were trained.
>
> (KT2)

In other ACL settings staff were more positive about the changes, but still collaborated to share problems and solutions, both in dealing with the paperwork, which had changed, and in supporting the learners, who had not. Hamilton (2007: 253) notes that ACL, with its traditions of informality and responsiveness to the needs of the local community, is 'the sector where professional values are most out of kilter with the new managerialism and the market/business ethos now being promoted through government policy'. Perhaps surprisingly, it was rare to find 'managerialist' tensions between tutors and managers working in our ACL sites: although all staff there might be frustrated by changes to funding and paperwork, most tutors were not blaming their managers, but voicing the same concerns as those managers about policy-makers and officials above them in the system. If there was a perceived barrier between 'them' and 'us', it did not separate managers from tutors in most of these teams, but rather it fell between those who designed and administered the policy and those practitioners who were trying to make the system work for their learners. Shared values, team ethos and belief in the need to keep the service going for the sake of the learners seemed to help tutors and managers to support one another in coping with the changes.

In FE settings, too, we encountered resentment of policy levers, especially targets; and in one of the eight we found target-related tensions between teaching staff and a manager who had been brought in to solve the problem of low retention and achievement rates and had introduced a tight monitoring system. Tutors were instructed to direct their teaching towards the assignments, to 'chase' all the criteria which students needed to complete assignments and to monitor intensively their attendance and performance. Staff who were unhappy with this mechanistic approach and restricted role were encouraged to leave, with the manager commenting:

> I don't care about the staff, to be honest. If they want to leave, I'll get more.
>
> (C2M1)

That did prove necessary. This example was, however, the exception, rather than the rule. Shared professional backgrounds were particularly valued in 'strong' vocational areas, such as Construction and Childcare, where tutors and managers had previous practitioner experience in the fields that their learners were hoping to enter. Here, tutors were role-modelling to some extent, as well as teaching, and on at least one Nursery Nursing course, the teaching team was also consciously projecting a model of the teamworking skills that learners would require on their placements and in their subsequent careers. Yet even in subjects such as Business Studies or Health and Social Care, taught by staff teams with less homogeneous backgrounds, it was clear that the quality of communication in the team and the team culture were having an impact, not only on the learners' experience, but on tutors' learning and development – to which we now turn.

Learning and inclusion for staff?

Staff development is a very complex and sensitive issue. On the one hand, it can be used as a policy lever: for example, in setting out requirements for FE tutors to acquire a teaching qualification, or for Skills for Life tutors to take the new Level 4 qualifications in literacy and numeracy. On the other hand, for established professionals, development is a very personal matter. Externally imposed programmes of professional development may not meet individual needs, and may also disrupt existing local plans for staff development in teams. In this section we review our findings on the tensions in staff development between activity required to keep pace with policy change and the personal professional development that enables tutors to become more effective teachers and develop their careers.

The sector has clearly seen much top-down, policy-led activity in staff development during our research, although the ultimate impact on students' learning is harder to ascertain. In line with the agenda set out in *Success for All* (DfES 2002), many more staff in colleges now have teaching qualifications, both for FE teaching and for basic skills. The introduction of Skills for Life was accompanied by programmes of staff development, both national and local. The Post-16 Standards Unit has produced and distributed packs of teaching materials to colleges. As we have discussed elsewhere (Coffield and Edward forthcoming), we found this process had provided an excellent opportunity for those involved in the design of these materials, but evidence of the impact of the packs on teaching and learning was less clear, with some staff reporting that materials were not suitable for their learners:

> I think [Standards Unit materials] are too . . . maybe set up for the 14–16-year-olds. There is a card game and I tried that on the apprentices, and for a few minutes they were interested, but they would rather see it on [the electronic whiteboard].
>
> (A2T1)

Neither the subject coverage of the teaching materials available at the time of our fieldwork nor the size of our sample allows us to assess whether these materials will succeed in spreading 'good practice'. Tutors we interviewed were more optimistic about the related project of training subject coaches to work with individuals and groups on developing their own subject teaching skills in context.

As Box 5.4 shows, further measures for workforce development were outlined in the FE White Paper (DfES 2006b) and will affect the future of the sector, although our interviews with practitioners were completed before these changes were introduced.

Box 5.4 Government measures for workforce development

Reform of initial training:

- Qualified Teacher Learning and Skills (QTLS) status;
- establishment of Centres for Excellence in Teacher Training (CETTs);
- access to high-quality initial training for Skills for Life teachers;
- a professional recognition scheme to help experienced staff upgrade through a portfolio process;
- a new management qualification for principals and aspiring principals.

New regulatory continuing professional development (CPD) requirement, applying to FE colleges, for:

- all full-time teaching practitioners to fulfil thirty hours' CPD a year;
- colleges and providers to draw up development plans for CPD, including preparation for the introduction of specialised diplomas and Train to Gain;
- teaching staff to maintain a CPD portfolio, including evidence of industrial/subject updating and development of skills in subject teaching, and to be professionally registered to maintain licence to practise.

Source: DfES (2006b)

The professionalisation agenda has not been universally well received. In ACL, for example, for some long-serving and well-qualified tutors who had taken pride in developing their professional practice for decades, and possessed an array of general teaching and specialist qualifications, the requirement to take additional qualifications late in their careers was viewed as rather insulting. Delays in the establishment of routes to qualification, and in particular of opportunities to gain accreditation of prior learning, caused distress and anger. Once courses were available and tutors began to take them, fresh problems were reported, in the disruption of existing local programmes of staff development tailored to local and individual needs. Tutors' energies had to be diverted into acquiring the Level 4 qualifications, and managers and experienced tutors were also heavily engaged in mentoring new entrants to the profession who were preparing to take those qualifications. In such turbulent times normal practice of regular sessions of staff development for sharing expertise within a staff team was difficult to maintain.

Elsewhere, the pace of policy change was seen to damage opportunities for tutors to learn and improve their practice. A basic skills tutor with both college and community experience commented:

> I think everyone needs to challenge their own practice, but I don't think there is a climate in some places that allows you to do that. It is because people are running too fast. It is: 'Oh God, we are going to stick with this, because we have not got time to think of another way of doing this.' We have got too many new things to do: there is not time to go back and see if what we have done already is OK.
>
> (MT1)

The climate of relentless change, in funding, initiatives, inspection and other procedures, has clearly not been conducive to reflection and considered improvement in practice, at team level or at personal, practitioner level.

Now that Skills for Life and the Level 4 qualifications are well established, the worst of the turbulence in staff development in ACL may be over, but problems remain around the issue of professional status. If tutors are to be seen as professional, should they not have a 'voice', and be consulted by policy-makers? Hamilton and Hillier (2006: 158) point to the particular difficulties for tutors in the community: 'A lack of formal representative networks and associations and (until recently) training has meant that practitioners have only been able to make token contributions to new developments.' Of the practitioners we interviewed, there were very few, mostly senior managers in colleges, who said they had a 'voice' that might be heard by policy-makers, perhaps through involvement in a professional association or Sector Skills Council (SSC). For the rest, the gap between those who design and issue policy and those who try to make the sector work for the learners seemed very wide. As noted in Chapter 2, our seminars provided a rare and welcomed opportunity for people from different levels in the sector to come together. More ways need to be found of reducing this distance between policy and practice.

A second question arising from the professionalisation agenda was raised by several interviewees: should professionals not have professional careers? The manager of a local authority basic skills service argued for better career development structures, on a par with those offered in schools:

> I think the whole Skills for Life agenda has been dedicated to driving up quality, and . . . having had knowledge of some of the other providers, particular training agents, I think there was a need to drive up the quality there, because there was a great inconsistency. But I think what needs to go with it is a career development kind of structure for people who are in this.
>
> (GM1)

Other community staff pointed to difficulties in recruiting and retaining good staff, especially when neighbouring colleges were in a position to offer 'golden hellos' to tutors doing the same work, and could also offer better conditions of service. In the colleges, staff cited comparisons with schoolteachers who were earning more, with greater job security, and we heard of examples of people who had given up posts in FE to return to the school sector. Right at the bottom of the pile, in colleges, community teams and work-based learning, were the staff on short-term and/or part-time contracts, whose ongoing employment depended on the success of recruitment or the next bid for work, and whose opportunities and incentives to engage in staff development were very limited.

Looking to the future

Reviewing themes from the practitioners' stories, we see how the position of the tutors makes them important, but vulnerable, players in the sector. If we start by considering their vulnerability, it is clear that national policy impacts on all aspects of their practice, since funding and, ultimately, the survival of their organisations depend on meeting targets, which they cannot neglect. Moreover, since they are accountable for distinct aspects of their practice to college and local authority managers, inspectors and awarding bodies, all of whom make their own paperwork demands, their autonomy is strictly constrained, to a degree which would surprise colleagues in higher education.

Yet their importance is undeniable. First, they are succeeding where others have failed, in school, to help young people and adults achieve their first qualifications and gain confidence in themselves as learners. From the policy-makers' perspective, these practitioners are the means to the end of meeting targets, and, as shown in Box 1.2 (p. 14 above), the statistics of achievement of the FE colleges and of the Skills for Life programme over the last four years are impressive. The energy and ingenuity of LSS staff in attracting and retaining new learners, and supporting them to success, should be applauded. So too should their flexibility in adapting to new initiatives, new structures, such as the SSCs and the QIA, new inspection regimes and ever-changing funding rules. Much has been expected of staff in the sector, and much has been delivered, against a backdrop of national policy which constantly sets new challenges, and allows little time for one change to be evaluated before the next is introduced. Practitioners who would have appreciated recognition of their achievements and a little time to consolidate, evaluate and improve are instead braced for further changes in the wake of that bold statement in the White Paper on FE: 'We will eliminate failure' (DfES 2006b: 56). While the focus of policy attention on the LSS and the money poured into it have been welcomed by practitioners, there is no doubt that the pace of policy change has confused, frustrated and demoralised them, and has also distracted them from their core task of working with learners.

More will be said in Chapter 7 about the mediating role of practitioners and of other players in the sector. The practitioners' contribution which we have witnessed includes trying to maintain stability and continuity for learners throughout policy changes, and protecting vulnerable learners, especially in basic skills classes below Level 1, who have little hope of contributing to the national targets and may struggle to progress, but nevertheless depend upon the support of basic skills teams to maintain their skills and quality of life. We have seen professionals fighting successfully to maintain such provision, subsidising it from more lucrative work at Levels 1 and 2; and we have also seen them failing to protect some classes which were highly valued in their community. The quotations in the opening section of this chapter express the powerlessness and frustration of practitioners who were neither consulted nor offered an explanation when a decision was taken by a distant official above them in the system.

Gleeson *et al.* (2005: 446), following Grace (1995), raised questions about the scope for professional agency and the ways in which FE teachers 'resolve tension between agency and structure in the changing conditions of their work'. We found some scope for professional agency, primarily in the decisions tutors can make about how they teach, and about how much time they devote to the needs of their learners. Particularly with young learners in FE, some tutors were devoting far more time than they were contracted to spend, helping learners both with academic work and with problems in their lives; and even in colleges where learning mentors and other support staff were available, learners told us they preferred to talk to their tutor. The strength of the tutor–learner relationship in FE is the cornerstone of success for many learners who have failed at school, but it can also put tutors under considerable pressure.

The practitioners' stories have also given us insight into the importance of workplace cultures, both at institutional and at team level, in supporting professional practice and development. While 'loners' may survive in isolation, most tutors stressed the value of collegial support; and even for those teaching basic skills in the workplace, a potentially isolating setting, we found that a strong, synergistic relationship between ULR and tutor was valued by both and could ensure sustainability, since the ULR knew the workforce and could ensure a steady stream of learners. The institutional impact could be positive or negative, either encouraging teamwork around course management, staff development, pedagogy and inspection, or discouraging it by overloading staff with paperwork or mock inspections, or by lowering morale through heavy accountability regimes which created a 'blame culture'.

CPD is both a right and a responsibility of any professional. As Avis (2003) suggests, however, in common with other public service professionals, practitioners in the LSS may not be sufficiently trusted to be allowed to take charge of their own development. We noted how staff development has been used as a policy lever, and certainly the professional learning of staff in the LSS has been dominated in recent years by nationally set agendas, such as Skills for Life. Our findings suggest that too much professional development time has been spent on simply keeping pace with policy-led changes, such as new procedures for inspection, squeezing out such activities as working on new materials, approaches and techniques with colleagues, which might help tutors become more successful teachers.

With the advent of the requirement for all full-time FE college teachers and trainers to attain QTLS status, to undertake at least thirty hours of CPD per academic year from September 2007 and to main-tain a portfolio of evidence (see Box 5.4), staff development in the sector is at a crossroads. There is already a national agenda on staff development, signalled by the distribution of Standards Unit teaching materials, the training of subject coaches, and the funding of eleven new CETTs (DfES 2007b). Many, including Grubb (1999: 363), would argue strongly for institutional approaches to staff develop-ment, creating a culture where good teaching is valued, and 'there is less room for mediocre teachers to secrete themselves away'. But our questioning about changes that staff were planning, or would like to make, to their own teaching indicated the importance of also addressing the individual needs and aspirations of teachers facing different challenges at different career stages. Moreover, some of these needs could be met by having time allocated to work together with colleagues in the teaching team, developing teacher learning communities (Thompson and Wiliam 2007) or by talking the problem through with a subject coach. We can only hope that the new staff development structures will be flexible enough to allow an appropriate blend of all these approaches, and that some degree of agency and a modicum of 'personalised learning' will be permitted for LSS practitioners as well as for learners.

Our final batch of themes all suggest that the LSS is still in some ways the 'neglected middle child' (Foster 2005), despite the amount of money and attention that has been lavished on the sector. The lack of 'voice', of a means of communicating with distant policy-makers and of sharing in the policy process, caused anger and frustration, yet when we brought practitioners and policy-makers together in project seminars, they had a great deal to say to one another, with great civility, and everyone gained from the experience. Such events diminish the sense of distance which practitioners feel and could be used to help policy-makers understand the impacts of their decisions.

Although there was surprisingly little talk of union support in our interviews, discontent about pay and conditions, about lack of parity with schoolteachers – which the government aimed to reduce from 13 per cent to 8 per cent by 2007 (DfES 2006b) – and lack of career structures for ACL staff were frequently mentioned. A recent survey by the National Research and Development Centre for Adult Literacy and Numeracy (NRDC) (Swain 2007) discovered that 35 per cent of part-time teachers wanted full-time positions. Particularly in London, many tutors cannot afford to take community posts, and part-time posts are viable only for those who have other incomes to support them. All these concerns emerged before the new policy emphasis on 'demand-led' funding, which some key players in the sector predict will destabilise the finances and possibly the staffing of smaller centres, and even some colleges.

Box 5.5 summarises some implications which we draw from the practitioners' stories.

Box 5.5 Some implications of the practitioners' stories

- The sector needs fewer, more intelligent targets.
- The pace of policy change needs to be slowed.
- Greater equity is needed in pay, conditions and career structures for professionally qualified practitioners.
- The introduction of licence to practise will need to be handled carefully to ensure that CPD does not become a bureaucratic exercise rather than a useful learning experience.
- Better feedback systems from practitioners to policy-makers should be developed.

Finally, we return to the question posed in the introduction to this chapter: are practitioners victims of policy? Yes, many complain; yes, many have suffered; yes, some have left the sector as a result. But from the evidence of those we interviewed, the sector has held together until now because of the strength of the learner–tutor relationship and because the commitment of staff to what they do in the classroom still outweighs their frustration with the constant changes in policy and procedures. What we cannot know is whether the changes ensuing from the Leitch Report will tip the balance.

Chapter 6

How inclusive is the sector?

> Seen in historical perspective, the attempt to combine the equality
> of civil and political rights, which is of the essence of democracy,
> with the inequality of economic and social opportunities, which is
> of the essence of capitalism, is still in its first youth.
>
> (Tawney 1938, cited in Marquand 2004: 1)

The British Labour Party has made several attempts to resolve or at
least accommodate the tension between economic efficiency and
social equity since 1938. Economic success and social inclusion are the
twin pillars of New Labour's strategy for post-compulsory education in
England. This chapter will argue that the New Labour government
has abandoned equality of outcome (which was a key Labour Party
commitment into the 1980s) in favour of equality of opportunity.
However, targets based on outcomes (e.g., free basic skills development for those who need it; free education up to Level 2 for adults or
Level 3 for under-25-year-olds who have not previously achieved
it) have had positive effects on the inclusion of some disadvantaged
groups. We found improvements of both participation and achievement
of people who had poor prior experiences of education and training.

This chapter will discuss these findings from our research into the
learning and skills sector, but will also highlight the inequitable outcomes of both recent and longer-standing policy decisions. For example,
the continuing funding differentials between provision of education
in schools and other settings, including FE colleges, and between
provision at Levels 1 and 2 and Level 3 and higher education mean that
the most disadvantaged continue to be provided with a cheaper service.
Box 6.1 illustrates these inequities. The effects of policy decisions
on equity and inclusion form the core of the chapter, which starts with
an exploration of the meaning of inclusion.

Box 6.1 Inequities in the learning and skills sector

- The lower the socio-economic status of the family, the more likely the student to be in a general FE college.
- Very little Level 1 or 2 provision in schools or sixth-form colleges.
- Funding gap of 8% between schools and colleges.
- Guided learning hours are greatest for A Level/Level 3 students and least for Level 1.
- 20% gap between funding for Level 1 students in FE and Level 3 students in sixth-form colleges.
- Colleges in areas of greatest deprivation offer less teaching at all levels.

Sources: Coffield (2007), Robson and Bailey (2007), Fletcher and Owen (2005), Stanton and Fletcher (2006)

Inclusion and related concepts

One of the traditional roles of the LSS has been to provide a second chance; an opportunity for those who did not succeed in the compulsory schooling sector to gain an education. The sector could thus be seen as providing an opportunity of inclusion for those who have previously been excluded. Recent government policy for the sector is premised on ideals such as social inclusion and social justice. Tony Blair, when Prime Minister in 2006, wrote the following: 'Tackling social exclusion is at the heart of this government's mission. It is our fundamental belief that everyone should have the opportunity to achieve their potential in life' (Cabinet Office 2006: Prime Minister's Preface). Inclusion and justice are not simple concepts but are parts of a wider family of ideas that includes fairness, equity and equality, viewed by some philosophers as linked terms. Rawls (2001), wrote of 'justice as fairness' and was referring to distributive justice: that is, the basis on which benefits and burdens in society are distributed among the population. He clearly saw equality as the underpinning value in any consideration of fairness. In proposing his position of justice as fairness, he outlined two principles of justice. The first asserts that each person has an equal claim to basic rights and liberties; and the second, recognising that both social and economic inequalities exist, suggests that, for fairness, these inequalities need to satisfy two conditions. First, when they are 'attached to positions or offices, these [should be] open to all under conditions of fair equality and opportunity; and second, they are to be to the greatest benefit of the least advantaged members of society' (Rawls 2005: 5–6). Fairness is a central concept in the definition of equality offered by the Equalities Review set up in 2005 by the British government:

> An equal society protects and promotes equal, real freedom and substantive opportunity to live in the ways people value and would choose, so that everyone can flourish . . . An equal society recognises people's different needs, situations and goals and removes the barriers that limit what people can do and can be.
>
> (Equalities Review 2007: 19)

This final point is particularly relevant to a discussion of education policy, since many inequalities that exist in, for example, university admissions processes or funding arrangements for post-compulsory education appear to favour the most advantaged rather than the least advantaged members of society. Furthermore, when the government or universities attempt to address these inequalities, they are accused of being unfair to the children of the privileged.

Not all systems of distributing benefits have equality at their roots. Rescher (2002) provides a survey of distributive systems such as paternalism and markets and rejects these, concluding that distributive equity is central to a concept of fairness in distributive justice. Paternalism favours those in favour with the *Pater*; and markets favour those who already have sufficient resources to exchange for the benefits in question. Thus paternalism and markets are inherently inequitable, yet it appears that the policies adopted by the current government involve a mix of both. On the one hand, paternalism is evident in centrally directed policies that favour certain groups of disadvantaged learners (some of those with basic skills needs) while neglecting others (some ESOL learners); and, on the other hand, the market figures largely in the plan to move to a 'demand-led' system of resource allocation.

If, however, we accept equality as 'the sovereign virtue' (Dworkin 2000), we are still left with the question of how to operationalise it in educational practice. What does treating people equally mean? Is it sufficient for people to have equal opportunity to access educational benefits or should the government and providers take steps to ensure a more general equality of conditions or outcomes and to remove barriers that hold people back?

As part of its project to modernise public services in England, New Labour has been influenced by both neo-liberalism and by its social democratic roots, with (at the time of writing, July 2007) the former arguably exerting the greater influence. This ideological commitment to neo-liberalism has resulted in New Labour deliberately abandoning the traditional Labour Party aim to progress towards greater equality by redistributing resources in favour of the disadvantaged and adopting an attempt to improve the lot of the disadvantaged by improving the economy as a whole.

Policies on inclusion

In September 2006 the government published *Reaching Out*, its action plan on social exclusion (Cabinet Office 2006). Box 6.2 illustrates the frequency with which some terms were used in this document. In the previous section we explored the meanings and relationships of terms such as 'justice', 'equality', 'equity', 'fairness' and 'inclusion'. We highlighted the centrality of notions of equality when seeking justice, fairness and inclusion; however, we can see from Box 6.2 that the terms 'equality' and 'inequality' do not feature prominently in New Labour discourse. 'Fairness' appears only once. 'Distribution' and 'redistribution' do not appear at all, probably dismissed as the baggage of Old Labour and as terms likely to scare the voters of 'Middle England'. 'Opportunities' and 'outcomes' appear with far greater frequency. Now, of course, this is a crude measure, but in this section we will be exploring in greater depth and with a more thorough contextual focus how New Labour is attempting to combat social exclusion through education and training.

> We need to build a relationship of trust not just within a firm but within a society. By trust, I mean the recognition of a mutual purpose for which we work together and in which we all benefit. It is a Stakeholder Economy in which opportunity is available to all, advancement is through merit and from which no group or class is set apart or excluded. This is the economic justification of social cohesion, for a fair and strong society, a traditional commitment of left of centre politics but one with relevance today as it is applied anew to the modern world.
>
> (Blair 1996)

Box 6.2 Word frequency in *Reaching Out*

Word(s)	Frequency
Inclusion/Exclusion	167
Outcome(s)	121
Opportunities	56
Justice	20
Equality/Inequality	11
Fairness	1
Distribution/Redistribution/Equity	0

In this frequently cited speech that Tony Blair made in Singapore, a year before taking office as Prime Minister, he set out what has become a keystone of New Labour policy on inclusion. The first point to note is that he refers to the creation not of a stakeholder *society* but a stakeholder *economy*. Social inclusion, in New Labour terms, is achieved principally through economic inclusion. One becomes a full member of society through becoming economically active. This point has been reiterated time after time in policy statements and practices since 1997. In the first Green Paper on lifelong learning by the Labour government, published in 1998, David Blunkett, then Secretary of State for Education, started his foreword by emphasizing the function of education in the creation of human capital before conceding that education did also bring wider benefits in that it will 'help us fulfil our potential and open doors to a love of music, art and literature' (DfEE 1998).

This emphasis on economic inclusion is carried through to the latest documents at the time of writing. The Leitch Report (2006) makes great play of the need for greatly improved levels of skills if the UK is to remain competitive. This underwrites the point that economic growth is clearly much more important to New Labour than economic redistribution. The government evidently sees exclusion being tackled primarily through there being more resources all round rather than through a significant redistribution of available resources. This movement away from equality of outcome through redistributive policies has been recognised by several analysts of New Labour policy. Hill (1999: 26), for example, writes: 'The concern with social inclusion and social exclusion in "New Labour" policy and rhetoric disguises, rhetorically replaces, the existence of social class and its attendant inequalities. "New Labour" is determinedly not egalitarian.' Commenting on New Labour policies, Hodgson and Spours (1999) and Prideaux (2005) write of the adoption of measures to improve both the overall economy and individuals' capacities to take advantage of labour market opportunities. These policies took precedence over measures to improve equality through progressive taxation and social benefit payments which were previous commitments of Labour in power and in opposition.

The 2006 Spring European Council identified efficiency and equity as 'twin challenges', noting that they were sometimes seen as mutually exclusive and that greater emphasis was often placed on improving efficiency in education and training. The subsequent communication, *Efficiency and Equity in European Education and Training Systems*, states that it is 'too often the case that existing education and training systems reproduce or even compound existing inequalities' (CEC 2006a: 2). The same paper highlights the costs of inequalities: 'In the UK if 1% more of the working population had A levels rather than no qualifications, the benefit to the UK would be around £665 million per year through reduced crime and increased earning potential' (*ibid.*: 3).

This message was reinforced by one of our European interviewees, who remarked:

> Education systems that do not promote social inclusion are not efficient in economic terms, because the cost of a low popular education system is very, very high.
>
> (Y2)

The European view of exclusion, however, is different from the concept of exclusion in English policy. While the latter views exclusion as a *state* in which individuals find themselves, the former sees it as a dynamic *process* resulting mainly from economic factors. Thus, whereas the English view tends to see exclusion as a problem for excluded individuals, the European perspective sees it as a problem for government and society as a whole. Viewing exclusion as a problem inherent in individuals, for example because of their lack of skills, has led to an emphasis on measures to encourage individuals to gain more skills, rather than measures that deal with structural problems such as poverty or the dearth of decent jobs or barriers within educational institutions.

The second point to note from Blair's Singapore speech is his apparent commitment to equality of opportunity. This also continues to appear in government policy statements. In attempting to achieve equality of opportunity, specific outcome targets have been a key element of policy. For example, the Skills for Life push is towards raising the attainments of the whole population up to a minimal benchmark of literacy and numeracy standards, which, at the time they were set, were accepted as the minimum necessary for active participation in the workforce. Providing opportunities for all those without a Level 2 qualification through schemes such as Train to Gain is an attempt to bring everyone to the level the government sees as necessary to enter the labour market. The concept of inclusion based on outcomes was reflected in the following response of a senior policy interviewee:

> It isn't enough to ensure the participation of all groups in society
> . . . Our focus is very much around outcomes and progression and
> moving on.
>
> (ZA07)

If the policy of the New Labour government has been to improve inclusion through offering better learning and employment opportunities for people who were previously excluded and to do this in an outcomes-focused manner, then it is fair to pose the question: to what extent has this been effective?

Effects of policy on inclusion

A DfES press release dated 20 February 2007 had the following headline: '1.5m learners beat their gremlins and gain qualifications as government hits target'. The press release continues to report that 'since the launch of the strategy in 2001, 4.7 million adults have taken up 10.5 million Skills for Life learning opportunities with 1,619,000 learners achieving their first Skills for Life qualification in literacy, language or numeracy. This figure includes achievements by over 138,000 offenders' (DfES 2007a).

We examined the impact of five government policy levers on inclusion: funding, targets, inspection, planning and initiatives. These levers clearly do not work in isolation (Steer et al. 2007). Skills for Life was an initiative that affected funding for basic skills provision and to which targets were attached. We discuss below our findings on these levers and on other factors that affect inclusion in the LSS.

Funding and initiatives

Funding and initiatives are discussed together because much of the funding for the LSS is channelled through particular initiatives. The discussion draws on both our national policy interviews and findings from sites, so the macro and the micro are linked.

The LSC's annual grant from government more than doubled from £5.5 billion in 2001–2 to £11.4 billion in 2007–8, and between 1997 and 2006 investment in FE colleges in England rose by 48 per cent. This appears to be generous but, over the same period, funding for schools increased by 65 per cent (Coffield 2007). The increased funding for colleges resulted in higher levels of participation and achievements among 16–19-year-olds (DfES 2007a). While those we interviewed in our learning sites reported positively on some aspects of funding, they also raised concerns.

The Childcare sites in FE were very positive about funding. They reported receiving increased money that enabled them to purchase the resources they needed to support the students. This was linked to the demand for trained childcare workers coming from child-care providers. However, one manager would prefer to see 'an end to outcome-driven funding, where you get your funding a year behind even though you've had to increase your numbers of students' (B1M1).

Box 6.3 Pondgate Services

Pondgate Services is a small, owner-managed business in the service sector that opened in 1998 and employs twelve (mainly part-time) staff. The owner-manager approached the LLSC seeking assistance to offer supervisory training to one member of staff and stock-control training to another. The LSC persuaded him to take advantage of the Employer Training Pilot scheme, which offered free training in literacy and numeracy and provided the costs of wage replacement for staff undertaking the training. The owner-manager offered the training to all of his staff and in an interview stated:

> Without [the ETP] I would have put one member of staff on basic English and maths. So what the funding allows you to do is to offer it to every member of staff.

> (PM1)

The Employer Training Pilots played an important role in stimulating, supporting or expanding basic skills provision in five of the eight WBL sites that we studied (see Boxes 6.3 and 6.4). In Moorcroft Depot the manager stated:

> ETP was the catalyst that got training started because management didn't have to pay for it.
>
> (MM3)

National evaluations have indicated that much of the training funded under ETP would have been undertaken without the support offered through the scheme. In the final evaluation of ETP, this 'dead weight' (training that would have taken place without government funding) was estimated as being between 85 and 90 per cent (Hillage *et al.* 2006: 23). While the enterprises that we investigated were organisations committed to training, in each case the scale of training offered

---

Box 6.4 Ewan's story

Ewan had a much-disrupted school education and did not learn to read effectively. However, he managed to hide his problem and gained a craft position in a local authority, using a variety of strategies to cope. His workmate filled out the worksheets and Ewan had a B&Q catalogue from which he copied words when filling in stores' orders. He was a very active trade unionist and when, at a meeting to discuss the introduction of basic skills training in the workplace, he revealed the extent of his problems, colleagues in both the union and management were surprised. He undertook both English and Maths courses and, as a result of the teaching methods used, also gained computing skills. Passing the national test in numeracy gave him a real sense of achievement. Ewan wasn't content just to improve his own skills, but became a tireless champion of the ETP scheme and encouraged many others to take up the opportunities it offered. He was a prime mover in having a book of poems by learners on the ETP programme published. Because he never read much before, he is frustrated by his vocabulary when trying to express himself in poetry. But he does not now have to use his B&Q catalogue. He writes out his stores' order on the counter and is happy to receive advice on spelling.

was claimed to be greater than that which they had previously offered, with those who would previously have been unlikely to be able to access training able to do so under ETP. We recognise that in a sample of eight enterprises it is possible to get results at variance with a much larger, nationally representative study. Our study does, however, indicate benefits in terms of inclusion of ETP. This can be perhaps most powerfully illustrated in the story, in Box 6.4, of one learner whom we interviewed.

The book of poetry referred to in Box 6.4 was mentioned by several of the learners in the ETP at Oakenshaw Works, where Ewan worked. While we had met lots of adult learners who reported that basic skills classes had given them more confidence in helping their children with homework, here we found one who was also encouraging younger members of his family to write poetry. Thus, while the original aim of the ETP was to improve productivity in the workplace, in this instance it had a very important outcome of widening the cultural horizons of participants. Inclusion in this case was more than just economic inclusion; there were also strong elements of social and cultural inclusion, which were equally important to these learners.

While ETP funding was generally viewed positively as an initiative that enabled previously excluded learners to be involved in training, other funding priorities were viewed less favourably. Managers at Queensfield Training saw the LSC's concentration of funding on 16–18-year-old learners as restricting the number of 19–25-year-olds whom they would be able to take on to apprenticeship programmes.

At Roundview Carers, the manager of a training provider saw the lack of funding for Beginner English courses as excluding those learners with the greatest ESOL needs:

> We've found that perhaps 30 per cent of the learners who could come on the course were Pre-Entry [Level]. We were not allowed, not able, to put them on a course because our funding is tied to results. So what we have done is screen the learners out – unfortunately, because those are the very people who need it most – because we know that they are not going to pass the exam and we can't afford to teach them and them not pass the exam.
>
> (RM1/1)

In this case, funding and targets combine to exclude a group of very needy learners. A national policy-maker recognised this problem and in response to an open question on inclusion in our online survey wrote:

> There is a great demand for Pre-Entry ESOL, especially within London. Yet this group is the hardest to teach, slowest to progress yet most in need of help. They get left out because they are so hard to help. Providers will cherry-pick the fastest to progress as this can affect their funding.
>
> (Survey, 15)

ESOL was mentioned in several policy interviews as a means of furthering inclusion. For example, a senior college manager reported:

> I have concerns about ESOL funding. We are doing an increasing amount of ESOL . . . I am extremely proud of our ESOL provision, and the impact that has on the local community . . . I have real concerns, though, about how it is being rolled out and the pressures on it [because of financial cutbacks].
>
> (ZA31)

An LSC official gave an indication of the extent of the issue, saying that in London the scale of the task is huge: 130 languages are spoken in primary schools and 35 ethnic groups have populations of between 25,000 and 35,000. This respondent also highlighted the limited nature of the funding when set against these significant needs. Further funding has since been made available for ESOL provision in London.

Another policy that appears to have had a positive effect on inclusion is the introduction of Education Maintenance Allowances. These are designed to support students from low-income families and enable them to remain in full-time education or training. They comprise elements that encourage both good attendance and sound attainment. Many of the students we interviewed in the North East received EMAs and spoke positively about their impact. One manager in Alder College, however, pointed out the divisive effect that they can have by causing resentment in the students who are not eligible (three out of sixteen in her class). She suggested 'a payment for all to come to college: as long as you are achieving, your behaviour is fine, all of those things, you should get it' (A1M1/3). The administration of EMAs also caused problems. If the administration was done by support staff and attendance records were incomplete, then students could have their EMAs stopped without justification. If the administration was done by teaching staff, then it was one more burden for them. In Central College, EMAs had struggled to make an impact on students for two main reasons: students were poorly informed about them; and the contract set up by the college was, by the manager's admission, weak because it focused only on attendance and not on other aspects of behaviour and achievement (as, for example, at Alder College). In Beechwood College, while the students with EMAs appreciated them, some managers and tutors complained of students playing the system and of the administrative burden.

The national evaluation of the EMA pilots indicated a mixed picture (Maguire and Thompson 2006). While the evaluation estimated that the payment of EMAs led to a 6.5 per cent increase in participation of young people in the target age group, there was no statistically significant impact on post-16 attainment, and the increase in participation in formal education was accompanied by a similar reduction in labour market participation rather than by a fall in young people in the NEET (not in education, employment or training) category.

A further initiative was Entry to Employment (E2E). The manager at Queensfield Training saw E2E as supporting inclusion since it had a strong emphasis on progression into either work or further learning. It was welcomed as a way of engaging young people before they are ready for a work placement or while they are waiting for a placement. It also enables some key skills to be developed before learners start apprenticeships. However, a manager in Alder College thought that it was unrealistic to expect E2E to bridge the wide gap between NEET status and an apprenticeship.

Both Skills for Life and ETP focused on providing free education up to Level 2 for those without a previous qualification at this level. These policies have had a positive effect on inclusion in that they have provided opportunities for many people to achieve qualifications and skills that they did not have. However, can this be considered to be equality? Young people up to twenty-five have free, funded education up to Level 3 (equivalent to A Levels).

Two respondents to our questionnaire highlighted this inequity. A college tutor asked in response to a question on our survey:

> Where do our learners go once they have achieved Level 2? There is nowhere for them. They have finally found they can achieve and then we tell them, 'No further!'
>
> (Survey, 7)

An FE manager commented:

> There seems to be a strong conflict between the rhetoric behind
> lifelong learning and the narrow limits of what is funded. This
> is particularly the case in looking at the prioritisation of full
> Level 2 qualifications.
>
> (Survey, 13)

Also, although the government consider Level 2 to be the minimum
required for labour market involvement, the Leitch Report (2006)
suggested that Level 3 skills should be the minimum necessary in the
future to keep Britain competitive. Thus it appears to be both inequitable and economically inappropriate to continue to have the Level 2
ceiling on funded qualifications for adults who missed out on earlier
education and training opportunities. This issue was partly addressed
in June 2007 when it was announced that 19–25-year-olds will be
funded to do a Level 3 qualification if they do not already have one.
However, this measure still does not address the disadvantages suffered
by adults over 25.

Since funding is limited when compared with needs, there will always
be the necessity to prioritise some groups of learners over others.
Currently economic efficiency seems to trump social inclusion with the
result that sometimes those most in need suffer so that the resources
can be used to get those closest to work accredited with the skills to
help them into jobs.

Targets

Like funding, both positive and negative aspects of targets were reported
by those we interviewed. For example, the manager and a tutor at
Kingsbury Rise reported a positive impact of Skills for Life targets on
social inclusion, with learners with special needs, unemployed learners
and younger people all benefiting. Kingsbury Rise also saw more
learners coming through at the lower levels; although this posed
a problem since 'the targets don't actually start until Entry 3' (KM3/3).
Some FE colleges also reported large increases in the targets allocated
by their LLSC.

However, in five of our sites, concerns were expressed that because
the targets started at Level 1, learners at Entry Level 3 and below were
losing out. It appears that the achievement and inclusion agendas
are in conflict because the achievement targets are set too high for
the learners with the greatest needs. This issue was raised both in

our interviews and in responses to our questionnaire, where some people pointed out the disadvantage faced by those who have the greatest need, given the pressure to have a high throughput of learners and a quick turnaround in terms of gaining qualifications. Some of the learners we met in ACL centres had been attending for long periods of time. A tutor commented:

> Some Entry Level learners need a lot more time to work towards gaining a suitable level qualification. Some may never really be ready to sit a test.
>
> (Survey, 38)

As reported in Chapter 3 and elsewhere in this chapter, the learners we interviewed reported very poor experiences of school education. Sometimes this was reported as the result of poor teaching in the sense that the teachers were not interested in those who were not making progress. Other learners admitted that they had contributed to their negative school experience by 'messing about' or not attending. Learners and their tutors recognise that they cannot compensate for eleven years of poor schooling in courses lasting only a few weeks or months. For some learners, attendance at an ACL centre was as much a social as an educational experience, and attendance was necessary just to maintain skills they already had rather than to make progress up to the outcome benchmarks set by the government.

There is a tension here between economic and social inclusion. If priority is given to economic inclusion, then centres may not have the funds to fulfil long-standing social functions. This tension is recognised by some policy-makers, who argue that those social functions are important but perhaps ought to be funded out of a separate budget. The funds channelled through the LSC are for education and training with economic outcomes.

> Now those students, because they're not going to have an accredited aim within two years, they're actually not going to fit into our classes and so I'm going to have to [approach] my region [to] fund those classes from the personal social development budget, which is going to be very small.
>
> (JM1/3)

Targets appear to have had a mixed impact on inclusion. They have increased accreditation in the group of learners ready to move to Level

1 and Level 2 qualifications, but they have had an adverse effect on the continued participation of Entry and Pre-Entry Level learners.

Planning and inspection

Planning and inspection were the levers least mentioned by our respondents with respect to inclusion, but they did make some relevant points. Alder College staff complained that they could not get into schools to advise potential students on what was available in the college. Moreover, the same staff thought that they had more appropriate facilities than schools for many vocational subjects, a view supported by learners whom we interviewed. The measures taken by schools to retain their own students sometimes acted against the best interests of the learners.

Queensfield Training reported that inspectors' interest in learner progression encouraged the firm to help learners to progress. In Alder College, however, a manager of Construction courses stated that at the next inspection the apprenticeship programme was to be judged by framework success – a disincentive to take on youngsters if they are unlikely to complete the full framework. The latter involves both specific vocational skills and basic skills in literacy and numeracy, and 25 per cent of the funding is dependent on achieving the full framework. In the Alder College Childcare course, the focus on the needs of the learners was already so strong that it was difficult to imagine inspection making any difference to inclusion.

Other factors affecting inclusion

Our research in the learning sites identified two major policy-related factors – qualifications and legislation – and a wide range of more specific, contextual factors, all of which influenced inclusion.

Required qualifications

In some sectors particular qualifications are required before workers can take up posts. In the care sector recent legislation requires both existing care workers and those entering the profession to be qualified to at least NVQ Level 2. This is commonly referred to as a 'licence to practise'. As discussed in Chapter 3, this legislation had an impact in several of our sites. At Top Training learners saw the NVQs as helping them to 'do [the] job properly and it's giving [them] the right way to communicate with clients, to help them and develop [their] career' (TL17). However, some other workers being developed at Top Training said they thought the course was too theoretical and they wanted the opportunity to experience other working environments and a more varied range of clients.

In other settings, although there was no legislative licence to practise, employers expected workers to gain NVQs either to remain in employment or else to progress within the workplace. Thus a group of classroom assistants undertook basic skills qualifications so that they could access the NVQ that would allow them to be considered for promotion to higher-level teaching assistant. As employees at Moorcroft Depot became aware of the need for an NVQ to stay in work, the necessity constantly to update qualifications removed the 'stigma' of coming to the learning centre. (This stigma is an example of a barrier within the workforce that is not the fault of policy or of current educational institutions.)

Anti-discriminatory legislation

The extension of disability legislation to education and training had a positive impact in some FE sites, where we witnessed several students being supported by classroom assistants. In Junior School (an ACL site) the counselling form for entry guidance includes a question on disability and the manager reported on the need to comply with it. However, one of our survey respondents suggested that not enough was being done to implement the legislation:

> Learners with learning difficulties are once again being marginalised regardless of the new legislation and the Duty of Equality. Funding is being reduced before adequate, sustainable, new and achievable qualifications are being introduced.
>
> (Survey, 42)

The impact of institutions and tutors on inclusion

In the FE sites we identified a wide range of strategies undertaken by tutors and managers that were aimed at improving inclusion. These strategies included both formal measures taken by the colleges, such as providing a personal tutor for all students; college mentoring schemes for black students; additional learning support provision; allocation of a base room for students; formal college policies on inclusion and behaviour; formal induction programmes; and student representative committees and informal strategies enacted by tutors, such as giving out their email addresses to students; organising tutoring of weaker students by stronger peers; generating a nurturing, empathetic and inclusive environment; treating learners consistently, fairly and with respect; and providing enrichment activities beyond the basic curriculum.

However, in spite of all these strategies, we discovered that large numbers of students did not complete or progress to the next level (with just 30 per cent progressing in one case). We also found very little involvement of students in the wider life of the college beyond their course. One example of such involvement was that the Construction students in Alder College booked the gym hall to play football at lunchtime. But the Childcare students at the same college appeared to be wary of mixing with other students. Their tutor reported:

> I think they feel vulnerable when they are not together as a group.
>
> (A1T1)

With regard to progression, it is surprising in such a target-driven environment that although there are targets for recruitment, retention and completion, there is none for progression to the next level. Tutors were concerned about progression, yet did not want another target. In some cases, progression is even inhibited by the funding model, which does not provide funds for some students to progress beyond Level 2 courses.

There were some college-related factors that may have been inhibiting inclusion. For example, we had a report of a community college that recruited fifteen students to a Childcare course, yet did not have appropriately qualified staff. All the students failed and the two we interviewed, after they had moved to a well-staffed FE college and were at last making good progress, still spoke bitterly of those two wasted years. This is an example of what can happen in an unregulated, demand-led environment. One can only speculate about the effect of this negative experience on a group of Level 1 students whose school experience had already been one of failure, caused not by their lack of ability or commitment, but by the community college's determination to maximise funding in areas where it had no expertise. In this case, the financial interests of the institution were put before the educational interests of the students.

High staff turnover can also contribute to an inconsistent experience for students. This was an issue in both our London and our North East FE sites. Availability of placements raised interesting issues about equity. In Beechwood College there was no placement for Level 2 Business Studies, and while learners who had part-time jobs were unworried by that, those who did not, including some asylum-seekers who were not allowed to seek paid work, would have appreciated the opportunity. In both colleges with Childcare courses, an optional placement of fifteen half-days in the second half of the course was highly valued. Students complained when they felt their placements were poorly organised, or when they were not allowed to have one because they had not been given the legally required Criminal Records Bureau clearance. Clearly the issue of equal opportunities for all learners is less important than the legal requirement, and less important than the rights of employers and the children they care for to have appropriate placement students.

In the WBL sites, two important factors for inclusion were the availability of a designated learning centre and flexible tutorial staff who were willing to come in, even at 7.30 a.m. or late in the evening, if that was the most suitable time for the learners. A worker at Southern Transport said, 'the college people have been very good. The tutors . . . are very flexible' (SW1/1). A tutor on the same site reported that 'these guys can't go anywhere else' to access training (ST1/3). At Nutmeg Products the tutor commented on the importance of the learning centre, arguing that 'there should be a place where people can just go and learn' (NT1/1). However, both here and in Moorcroft Depot, visiting the learning centre sometimes stigmatised workers in the eyes of their colleagues.

The impact of learning in the workplace varied across our sites. In two of the North East sites the impact tended to be on a minority of heroic individuals who carried on regardless of the views of others. In other sites workplace learning initiatives had had a much wider and more positive impact on workplace culture.

Improving inclusion

This chapter started with a quotation about the tension between social and economic objectives. The current government has both economic efficiency and social inclusion as key objectives, and it considers both of them to be achievable. Our research has shown that multiple and significant steps have been taken to include many more people in the group of those qualified to Level 2. However, it has also been shown that those who are least advantaged in terms of basic skills have not been well served by current policies. The main reason for this is the focus on getting people qualified for jobs that need Level 2 qualifications; yet the most disadvantaged learners are a long way from this level and may never get there. In other words, it may not be possible to address the inequalities in learning achievements with policies that assume the main purpose of education is to prepare people for the workplace.

In a capitalist society workplaces are essentially inequitable. Labour markets reward those who are already most qualified and successful. Consumer markets meet the demands of those who already have the most resources. Increasing the use of markets in the education system is likely to widen current inequities, leading to wasteful competition for public resources with duplication of provision and, as was reported above, biased information, advice and guidance which privileges the programmes offered by the provider of the advice. Planning does not have a good political reputation with New Labour, which has accepted the last Conservative government's education philosophy of using top-down performance management and the market as the main means of systemic improvement. This policy route has the consequence of increasing rather than reducing inequities as, for example, those who get into the local academy have enhanced provision, while their equally or more needy contemporaries in the same area struggle on with poor provision. Yet there is an alternative.

A local authority in one of the regions we studied used the additional funds available for setting up academies to improve provision and facilities in *all* schools in the authority and developed a partnership that involved all the key players in the locality. This example shows how locally devised, planned and implemented policies and practices can use the same overall resources that are available in a manner that maintains local democratic control and accountability, yet which does not disadvantage learners who do not get into the privileged institutions. Permitting local variation is not without dangers in terms of equity. Kooiman (2003: 58) points out the tensions inherent in 'treating citizens as equally as possible . . . while also approaching them in as focused a manner as possible'. Local diversity can result in national inequities. However, it is quite reasonable for national governments to set the parameters within which local diversity can be exercised. The focus of national parameters should be on outcomes, with localities being able to select the appropriate local means to achieve these outcomes subject to equality measures.

An additional consideration in the basic skills/Skills for Life funding is that these learners often need more one-to-one support to aid progress. The distinct lack of funding means that this does not occur to the level it should for the best results. Employable skills should be the main focus but wider learning is important too. Wider learning has health benefits in keeping an ageing population alert and compos mentis for longer.

(Survey, 16)

This observation by an education consultant responding to our survey illustrates another problem with the assumption of employability as the sole reason for post-compulsory education. It is inappropriate to assume that the only route into work or to promotion at work is through education and training programmes that have direct and obvious economic relevance. People do not tend to compartmentalise their learning into boxes labelled 'work' and 'social activities'. Learning changes people who then work and socialise differently through being changed. Many of our interviewees used the learning they received in work-based settings for social and family purposes.

Thus, education that is aimed at improving employment prospects can also have social benefits; and, conversely, learning that primarily has social aims can result in economic benefits. The intentions and outcomes of education cannot necessarily be determined before learning takes place. Alan Tuckett (2007) has argued that adult learning contributes not only to employability, but much more broadly to health, welfare reform, neighbourhood renewal, active citizenship, cross-cultural understanding, cultural enrichment and sustainable communities.

In several of our later interviews the topics of NEETs and the 'workless' were raised. Research into these groups (e.g., Scottish Executive 2006) indicates that long-term membership of these categories is often associated with homelessness, drug addiction, teenage pregnancy and offending behaviour. Education is not the cause of most of these concerns; nor can it provide the solution. Those who are most difficult to reach cannot be reached simply through targets, changes in curricula or qualification systems, but require concerted effort by many agencies at the local level and changes to wider social and economic policies.

Finally, Box 6.5 shows some implications of our findings for policy and practice.

Box 6.5 Implications for policy and practice

- A fairer funding model is required that recognises that getting some learners to Level 2 or Level 3 may require proportionately greater resources. This is in contrast to the proportionately smaller investment in the least advantaged that is currently made. The 'targeted action on persistent inequalities' recommended by the Equalities Review (2007) is relevant here.

- There needs to be recognition that localities can tackle exclusion in ways that are locally appropriate and collaborative, and they should be given the opportunity to do this rather than be forced to respond to top-down policy that may be inappropriate for the area and inherently inequitable.

- Focusing on a narrow conception of the kind of programmes that will result in economic improvement is not necessarily better than allowing people to participate in programmes of their choice and funding those choices. (This is what happens in higher education – another example of the already privileged being given further privileges.)

- Inequities and lack of impact by educational institutions on some potential learners are not the sole fault of education and may only be addressed through a concerted multi-agency approach and broader political, social or economic change. There are limits to what education on its own can achieve.

Chapter 7

The story of the sector in action

This chapter is different from those preceding it, in that it sets out to explain how the learning and skills sector works in practice. In forming and refining our explanation, we have developed a number of concepts, or theoretical building-blocks, which hold together large amounts of our data and which, we think, can make a complex story more manageable and understandable. The story of the sector in action is set in the wider political context of New Labour's strategy of 'modernisation'. Within this we explore the government's use of policy drivers, narratives and levers and how these are mediated and translated at different levels of the LSS. The chapter concludes by exploring the potential of an 'ecological perspective' for understanding complex systems and encouraging collaborative relations between those seeking to build a more effective, equitable and inclusive learning system.

New Labour's hybrid regime and the strategy of modernisation

> New Labour has adapted the fundamental neo-liberal programme to suit its conditions of governance – that of a social democratic party trying to govern in a neo-liberal direction while maintaining its traditional working-class and public-sector middle-class support, and the compromises and confusions that entails.
>
> (Hall 2003: 3)

The LSS was a creation of New Labour and we can, therefore, better understand its behaviour if it is analysed within the wider context of the New Labour political project. Stuart Hall's (2003) seminal work on 'New Labour's double shuffle' describes its approach to policy and policy-making as a 'hybrid regime' of dominant and subordinate strands of discourse. The dominant strand involves the continued use of new public management (NPM); the restructuring of the public sector through privatisation and competition; and drives to improve efficiency by means of performance auditing and measurement. The subordinate strand contains more social democratic aims: promoting increased public expenditure; providing a minimum wage; and a high visibility given to education and training. These two agendas, operating together, have produced an adaptive form of neo-liberalism referred to as New Labour's modernisation of governance and its reform of public services (Newman 2001).

The structures and behaviour of this hybrid regime can be witnessed across all public services, including the LSS. Dominant and subordinate strands interact through a series of trade-offs, in which, for example, increases in public expenditure have to be accompanied by centrally imposed targets and what Hall (2003: 7) refers to as the 'rich panoply of the audit culture'. Trade-offs can be understood as defensive measures to justify progressive measures to a sceptical public and a hostile press. The dominant and subordinate strands also interact through 'counter-actions'. The leading policy assumptions come from the dominant neo-liberal strand, the most notable being that markets are the key to greater efficiency and reducing poverty. The subordinate strand of inclusion (which distinguishes New Labour from Thatcherism) becomes preoccupied with government micro-actions attempting to counter the negative effects of neo-liberal policies or to pursue weak social democratic aims. Trade-offs and counter-actions take place within the hothouse of political triangulation as New Labour and the Conservatives fight for the electoral centre ground. Where there is less visible difference between the dominant political parties, advantage is sought by speeding up the political process, producing what has been termed 'momentum politics' (Hyman 2005) and 'policy busyness' (Hayward *et al.* 2005). The result has been a barrage of policy initiatives as ministers attempt to attract the public's eye, catch their opponent on the hop and make their mark.

The dynamics of the hybrid regime under New Labour and its strategy of modernisation have produced new levels of centralism, bureaucracy and confusion. Policy steering, which involves the relegation of traditional forms of public administration and the promotion of 'arm's-length' regulation, has intensified under New Labour. Its approach to governance is more managerial and interventionist than NPM (Newman 2001) and has also involved a further growth in the role of non-departmental public bodies and public–private partnerships (Ainley 2004; Steinberg and Johnson 2004), together with the use of a wide range of policy levers: performance targets, standards, audit, inspec-tion, quality assurance processes and powers to intervene where public services are deemed to be failing. Policy tensions and confusions have become endemic as the government continues to slide one agenda under the other – the 'double shuffle'.

Modernisation should not be seen, however, as a single and un-changed phase of strategy spanning a decade of New Labour. The hybrid regime is evolving as the balance between the dominant neo-liberal and subordinate social democratic strands moves strongly in a more marketised direction, albeit with a continued appetite for central political control through the use of targets and top-down performance management. This shift has come from the twin hearts of government – the Treasury and the Prime Minister's office – since the second Parliament of 2001. The new policy narrative of 'demand-led' comes from the Treasury-sponsored Leitch Report, while the government's model of public service reform (described in Chapter 1) emanates from the Strategy Unit, as established by Tony Blair.

Right across what can be loosely described as the public sector, we see a complex but unmistakable picture. Government policy is experi-enced primarily as top-down performance management and constant change as it attempts to drive through the reforms of the 'double shuffle'. At the same time, there are constant appeals to various policy actors by the extensive use of rhetoric (e.g., choice, responsiveness and entrepreneurialism). The degree to which the government can produce its intended outcomes depends not only on its power to micro-manage change but on its use of 'more strategic interventions exercised "culturally" and "at a distance"' as it seeks to create a new consensus around 'new values modernising old practices' (Hall 2003: 5).

As much as it would like to think it was in control, the government finds itself dependent on policy actors (including practitioners) who, while excluded from policy formulation, gather a limited degree of power at the point of policy enactment and practice (Bowe et al. 1992). They bring established professional values into play as they 'mediate' policy and engage in 'acts of translation' that produce a variety of outcomes, some intended and some not (see Box 7.1 for definitions of these terms). Moreover, the composition of the hybrid regime varies in different parts of the state. Just as the DfES or Home Office seeks to impose another 'stretching target' on local government and insti-tutions, the Department of Communities and Local Government (DCLG)

Box 7.1 'Mediation' and 'acts of translation'

The concept of 'mediation' is used in two related senses – from the perspectives of policy actors and of the system:

* Seen from the perspective of different policy actors, 'mediation' describes a general and continuing process by which they respond to and act upon policy.
* Seen from the perspective of the system, 'mediation' helps us understand the changes that policy goes through as it moves down the different levels in the system and through stages of the policy process.

'Acts of translation' take place within the general processes of mediation as practitioners, for example, respond to national policy levers by turning them into internal strategies, roles, systems and practices.

---

is trying to promote area-wide agreements and community participation. These are examples of policy tensions producing what Newman (2006) sees as a set of competing logics that open up space for new ideas of the public to emerge. The complex nature of a public sector in action, therefore, is the result of competing approaches to governance, contradictions within policy and the roles played by different policy actors, all interpreting policy in their own way.

Top-down performance management in a changing landscape

It is difficult to discuss life in the LSS without focusing on the changing role of the Learning and Skills Council itself. A brief history, told in Chapter 1, suggests that its evolution parallels the shifting balances of the hybrid regime. The early LSC (2001–3) contained some aspects of a social democratic approach to governance, with its initial emphasis on a more level funding playing field and area-wide planning, exercised through the national LSC and its forty-seven local arms. It was, however, essentially a top-down model, and its planning approach, focused on regular provider performance reviews, was frequently criticised by managers and practitioners for micro-management, bureaucracy and demands for huge amounts of data (Hodgson *et al.* 2005).

Since 2003, the LSC has been reshaped towards a business model with an emphasis on concepts of choice, competition and 'contestability'. It has also been streamlined, with a strengthening of its regional tier. LSC officials interviewed appeared happy with the new model because they thought it could be more locally responsive. This view, however, was not shared on the ground, because what providers see is the reshaped LSC as part of a more centralised system of governance. Government targets are the driving force and the business model is intended to provide a 'clear line of sight' between national PSA targets and government funding priorities (Steer *et al.* 2007). Moreover, as Chapter 4 reports, the LSC has been subjected to control from above in which the DfES devises strategy and the LSC organises delivery. This does not necessarily mean harmony, but it is clear who is in charge. At the same time, and mindful of the criticisms of bureaucracy of its early years, the LSC has sought to focus on institutional improvement through light-touch inspection and the concept of self-regulation. With 'clear line of sight' of national targets and 'self-regulation', the DfES and LSC have their own 'double shuffle' – tight direction from the centre combined with conditional institutional freedoms based on good behaviour.

At the time of writing in summer 2007, the LSS appeared to be entering a third phase. Targets remain in the driving seat but the sector has been slowly splitting into two. Adult and work-based learning are about to be marketised, while 14–19 education and training are becoming increasingly dependent on institutional collaboration and area-based planning, if they are to be successful. This process was, in effect, confirmed by the announcement by Prime Minister Gordon Brown that the DfES would be split into two ministries, one responsible for younger learners and the other for those over the age of nineteen.

Policy drivers, narratives and levers

While exercising control and 'getting results' is the major political objective, New Labour's top-down approach contains inherent contradictions. Tensions within policy are continually present, not only due to political trade-offs but because of mediation of policy by various policy actors at different levels of the LSS. These complex processes can be illustrated by focusing on the key instruments used by government

– policy drivers, narratives and levers – and by analysing the ways in which they are perceived to impact on learning and inclusion.

We see policy drivers as the overarching aims that guide government strategy (Steer *et al.* 2007). For New Labour, as Chapter 4 explains, these are improving competitiveness and social inclusion, which are supposed to cement a consensus behind the hybrid strategy of modernisation. In the LSS, the twin policy drivers have excited little debate but the same cannot be said of the means of pursuing change and maintaining control. Policy narratives and policy levers, more reflective of neo-liberal governance, have proved controversial and are, arguably, defining influences on the structure and behaviour of the LSS.

The government makes extensive use of 'policy narratives' to provide the tone of policy. These are often initiated by trusted public figures leading commissions (e.g., Tomlinson, Foster and Leitch) to broaden the scope of policy text production and to build consensus. Senior policy-makers often attempt to maintain control by carefully selecting the analyses and recommendations of reports to create legislation. Policy narratives can also be organised at the very centre of government to provide a degree of ideological consistency in policy-making across different government departments. Recent examples have been the models of public service reform published by the PMSU (2006, 2007), as discussed in Chapter 1.

As we explained earlier, policy levers are not an inevitable part of governance; rather, they are 'instruments' chosen to meet particular political aims (Kooiman 2003). Within neo-liberal governance, remote policy steering provides a means by which governments transmit national policy into practice while promising a degree of local or institutional flexibility. It is worth noting, though, that the rise of policy steering has been paralleled by a decline in the role of local government. New Labour has chosen to utilise a wide range of policy levers in order to meet the aims of the twin policy drivers of competitiveness and social inclusion in the LSS. The five we decided to examine – targets, funding, inspection, planning and policy initiatives – have to be viewed alongside changes in governance to understand how they function within different phases of policy.

The matrix in Box 7.2 suggests that the five policy levers have changed both in their focus and in their effects as the LSS has moved from a model based on top-down planning to one increasingly based on top-down imposition of markets.

Box 7.2 Different configurations of policy levers during different phases of governance of the learning and skills sector

	FEFC and TEC period	Early LSC	Business model
Planning	Limited planning of TEC-funded provision	Comprehensive area approach (area-wide inspections, strategic area reviews, three-year plans)	Business cycle: national priorities into local targets
Funding	Major driver during period of cutbacks and competition	Promise of stable funding linked to three-year plans	Funding for priority areas; contestability
Targets	Increasing use of performance indicators	Proliferation of Public Service Agreement targets; locally agreed targets	Key national targets linked to funding
Inspection and quality	Divided between agencies	Unification of inspection (Adult Learning Inspectorate, Common Inspection Framework), but quality improvement divided	Rationalisation of quality improvement; 'light touch' for successful providers
Initiatives (e.g., Skills for Life)	Moser Report in 1999 – precursor to Skills for Life strategy	Major impact on adult basic skills: standards, resources, tests, professionalism	Knock-on effects of adult learning cuts; pressure of targets

Five policy levers in action

During our research, we talked to a range of policy actors regarding their views on the role of the five policy levers in relation to learning and inclusion. We present here a balance sheet of perceived effects and indications of how policy, driven from the centre, is mediated and translated at different levels within the LSS.

Planning

Planning, a major aim of the early LSC, has declined as a policy lever as the LSC has moved away from area-based co-ordination and focused more on transmitting government priorities and promoting markets (Steer et al. 2007). The result has been growing instability for the big providers in the LSS, which have to support large infrastructures that cannot be changed easily. One college principal commented:

> We keep being promised the stability of three-year plans, but we never get there because the plans have to be rewritten every year.
>
> (ZA12)

The most serious disruption, however, has not resulted so much from LSC micro-management of college planning but from the shift of government funding priorities from adults to younger learners. At the same time, the reshaped LSC is perceived as 'getting more professional' (ZA28) at enforcing priorities, and several of our senior management interviewees thought that their colleges were increasingly 'straitjacketed' by national policy with decreasing room to manoeuvre locally. Other parts of the LSS, concerned with adult learning, found that the relative absence of planning meant that provision dependent on funding from initiatives could simply come and go (Finlay et al. 2007a).

Targets and funding

These are the dominant policy levers due to the way in which they combine in practice. Funding by itself could be viewed as investment, and this has doubled over the last five years, although serious inequities remain. Targets can be a call to action:

> Targets focus the mind a lot . . . you have an eye on them and the team discusses them and so do I, endlessly.
>
> (B2M3)

In some areas, such as WBL, managers and practitioners set their own targets (Finlay *et al.* 2007a).

It was the combining of targets and funding that produced unpredictable and often perverse outcomes because of the link between fulfilling the targets and the economic viability of the institution. In basic skills learning, accreditation that was linked to targets and funding narrowed approaches to learning (Hodgson *et al.* 2007a); the policy focus on Level 2 was threatening Entry Level learners with course closures; targets produced 'game-playing' as colleges tried to get 16–19-year-olds, 'low-hanging fruit' (i.e., learners who could easily pass target qualifications), counted in the basic skills totals. Targets and funding could also ignore the valuable work of colleges; for example, getting young people into WBL and a career is not counted in institutional retention figures. Targets and funding also threatened the most disadvantaged as basic skills providers working with learners at Entry Level came to realise that these learners would not contribute towards the government's Level 2 target.

Inspection

Inspection was viewed more positively because of its ability to galvanise staff to focus on teaching and learning and to provide a framework for improvement:

> The inspectorate has forced the drive in colleges because it is heavily biased on good teaching and learning.
>
> (A2M1)

However, the 'light-touch' approach promised in policy texts has not always been recognised on the ground. Comments such as 'inspection, inspection, inspection' (C1M2) and having to cope with 'the horrendous bits of admin' and 'massive, massive workload' (D1T1) were made as colleges implemented systems and practices to meet OFSTED criteria. Self-regulation may come to mean embedding bureaucracy and external standards at the heart of institutions. Across the LSS as a whole, inspection appeared to have a variable impact. For FE, as the comments above reflect, its effects could be powerful. In ACL inspection was a weaker but relatively benign policy lever and, despite the early record of the Adult Learning Inspectorate in weeding out weak WBL providers (Hodgson *et al.* 2005), in our work-based sites the impact of inspection was patchy and in some cases hardly 'on the radar' of some independent training providers.

Policy initiatives

These were broadly welcomed because they brought much-needed funding and attention to neglected areas of the LSS. We found that Education Maintenance Allowances (EMAs) helped financially needy young people to participate in post-16 education and training; the Skills for Life strategy has raised the profile of adult learning; and the Union Learning Fund (ULF) and ULRs have encouraged their colleagues to take advantage of basic skills provision which became available in workplaces (Edward et al. 2007). Policy initiatives should, therefore, be regarded as a different type of policy lever from those associated with accountability and performance management because they represent additional interventions and resources aimed at particular groups of learners. But even here, the positive was compromised by accountability and politically inspired changes. As we have seen, with policy initiatives came endless form-filling and bureaucracy, targets threatened to narrow professional practice (Hodgson et al. 2007a) and funding taps were turned on and then off, leaving basic skills provision in workplaces like 'flowers in the desert' – there one minute and gone the next (Finlay et al. 2007a).

Practitioner perceptions of policy levers were, therefore, mixed. Those designed closest to the needs of learners and learning (e.g., inspection and policy initiatives) were better received than those associated with accountability or central control. However, practitioners were not simply passive transmitters of each of the policy levers. We found that these instruments, which have been so important to New Labour's concept of governance, functioned in complex and unpredictable ways as they were acted upon at different levels within the LSS.

How policy levers function in the LSS

From the perspective of a policy-maker, a policy lever could be likened to a physical lever attached to a 'delivering' institution. The lever (e.g., targets or funding) is activated in order to produce the desired institutional response. If institutions were not responsive to these forms of policy steering, they could be pressurised by the LSC through its provider review process, using a range of centrally designed performance measures, and by OFSTED inspection. On the surface, the system of policy levers looked logical and failsafe – the government would set national steers reinforced by financial incentives and quality checks. At the same time, however, it also accepted that policy and policy levers will be translated in different ways by different actors. In response to our survey statement, 'Policy levers are "translated" by different actors at multiple levels in the system and this at times produces perverse outcomes', a total of 91 per cent agreed with little additional comment. One policy-maker retorted:

> This is almost stating the obvious, it is a consistently observed fact in all complex human activity systems!
>
> (Survey, 15)

Policy-makers have responded to the paradox of wanting to control change closely, while acknowledging that the sector is complex, by attempting to tighten control over the 'delivery chain' of policy that moves down the different levels of the LSS. This has been done by rebalancing LSC reorganisation at the regional level rather than the local level; by focusing on funding priorities and a reduced number of targets; and by introducing common performance measures across the sector. However, as we will see in a more detailed examination of issues of mediation and translation, the more tightly the system is drawn the more likely is the production of perverse outcomes, including the marginalisation of disadvantaged learners and the accumulation of transactions costs.

Mediation and translation of policy

Our research, which corroborates the findings of others researching the effects of policy on education (e.g., James and Biesta 2007; Wallace and Hoyle 2005), has found that policy levers interact with other factors at all levels of the system, as well as within institutions. In doing so, they are also mediated and translated within the LSS as different actors achieve a degree of agency or freedom at the practice stage of a policy process (Bowe et al. 1992). We should not, however, overestimate the power or the ethics of professionals in these situations, because they are working within systems of top-down power. Nevertheless, policy levers, as remote forms of steering, present policy actors with spaces to interpret them as they apply their own values and intentions in a system, which the government also attempts to influence ideologically. In doing so, policy actors at different levels of the LSS do not reverse policy, as such, but make its outcomes far less predictable. These actions can lead to varying degrees of compliance and subversion, including: various forms of 'gaming behaviour' to maximise funding; policy-makers in national agencies trying to make policy workable; FE college managers attempting to shield teaching staff from the effects of funding or targets; or adult learning providers putting their learners in for tests in order to generate funding to subsidise learners at lower levels. The picture is further complicated by the way in which policy levers such as funding, targets and inspection interacted with other national factors (e.g., competence-based qualifications), as well as institutional factors, such as the style of management and different professional cultures within various departments (Spours et al. 2007). These interactions explain, in part, why outcomes can vary significantly from one institution to another.

Policy levers, therefore, go through a complicated life cycle as they interact with changes and tensions in policy; are interpreted at each layer of the sector; combine with one another; and interact with other important factors (e.g., qualifications). In this complex process of mediation, each participating actor has his or her effect and each 'act of translation' can turn a policy lever into something else. It is unsurprising, then, that remotely operated policy levers can produce both intended and unforeseen outcomes, some of which are positive, while others are costly in financial, educational and/or human terms.

Translating policy levers into institutional systems

Policy levers are created with the assumption that institutions will apply them to reflect both the policy intention and local circumstances. Policy levers, therefore, invite what we have termed acts of translation. At the institutional level, LSC local plans, the Skills for Life initiative, funding regimes and targets were translated into institutional plans and strategies. This process produced a variety of outcomes. On the one hand, there was the 'reproduction' (see Box 7.3 for a definition of this term) of policy levers into the heart of the institution. On the other, policy actors responded by applying their professional values, producing what Wallace and Hoyle (2005) refer to as 'principled infidelity', in order to make sense of the situation in which they found themselves and to pursue what they understood to be their professional mission.

Box 7.3 Reproduction of policy levers

By 'reproduction' we mean the ways in which institutions translate policy levers so that the dysfunctions of the LSS are recreated within the institution itself (e.g., the policy levers start to become the aims of the institution, leading to continual reorganisation; multiple data-gathering and bureaucracy; interference in professional practice; and a remote management style).

Below we describe from our research evidence a range of different reactions to policy levers across different parts of the LSS from 2004 to 2007. These examples elaborate on Shain and Gleeson's (1999) concepts of 'compliance' and 'strategic compliance', used to understand professional responses in the new managerialism in the FE sector in the late 1990s.

Compliance and ideological agreement

Shain and Gleeson (1999) used the term 'compliance' to refer to the acceptance, often by new members of staff, of the new enterprise and marketised culture in FE that followed the incorporation of colleges in the early 1990s. We found compliance alive and well in the LSS. There were instances of educational and ideological agreement, particularly in sections of FE management – a belief in an FE market and using policy levers to improve attainment and completion rates. Some senior and middle managers, echoing the managerialism of incorporation, revelled in performance management and in pressurising those they perceived to be under-performing. Others reproduced the logic of policy levers within their departments by creating mechanical and paper-heavy learner tracking and accountability systems that served to maximise funding. How far an institution went in reproducing bureaucracy was, to a degree, an issue of preference, with some making heavier weather of it than others. One newly appointed manager reflecting on his wider experience of institutions said that he'd 'never seen a college like it for the amount of data I get to evaluate' (D2M2).

In many cases, compliance was enacted with a heavier heart when acknowledging the power of the combination of targets and funding. Commenting on the power of funding, associated targets and bureaucratic burdens, one Skills for Life manager lamented:

You can't chance it, you can't fight it. We lose a few thousand pounds if we don't have whatever form, so you have to do it.

(LM2)

These responses also echo the findings of previous research on FE incorporation (e.g., Randle and Brady 1997; Shain and Gleeson 1999) of college staff working within prescribed limits and having to get on with the job. Compliance was more likely to be found in middle and senior management. It was certainly not the case that all managers were serial compliers, but they were most immediately responsible for the viability of the institution and were subjected to the greatest direct pressure from policy levers. However, they were certainly seen by some as compliers, as these scathing comments from questionnaire respondents working in the higher education sector reveal:

Management is commonly weak and self-serving, little vision for the sector or the institution – just target followers and OFSTED pleasers.

(Survey, 37)

Sadly, most managers do what they are told by their Philistine bosses, ministers and the LSC.

(Survey, 59)

The changing nature of strategic compliance under modernisation

The broadest spectrum of responses to policy and policy levers appeared to fall under what Shain and Gleeson (1999) termed 'strategic compliance'. They used this term to describe the evolving responses of college lecturers in the late 1990s, as they applied their professional values to offset the effects of the NPM in colleges in a period marked by deterioration in conditions of service for lecturers. Strategic compliance undoubtedly continues, but its dynamic within the LSS in a period of modernisation appears more complex. Policy levers operate through top-down managerialism, markets and elements of social democratic discourse. These can focus on student retention and achievement as means of inclusion, and are intended to appeal to policy-makers, managers and tutors to justify or make sense of prevailing policy.

As with previous research (e.g., Lumby and Tomlinson 2000), we found areas of agreement within colleges and other sites of learning about what should be done to improve learning and achievement but dissent resulting from the effects of top-down performance management: constant reorganisation, meeting targets and accountability-related paperwork. Within this context it could be argued that strategic compliance has moved, to a degree, from a struggle between tutors and managers to a struggle between institutions and the system, in which all parties within institutions and within the wider LSS find themselves under pressure from accountability and politically driven changes in priorities.

How these pressures were dealt with differed significantly according to the wider economic and social situation of the institution, the personal values that managers and tutors applied to any situation and their professional traditions. The four college principals in our study faced different local contexts and adopted different management styles. Within colleges, a strong influence affecting responses to top-down performance management was vocational ethos in course teams, and 'licence to practise' and 'professional standards' demands in certain courses, such as Care and Construction. Tutors here balanced their responsibilities to their college performance managers for retention and progression with their responsibilities to the standards of the professions that their learners were preparing to enter. Within adult basic skills, adult learning traditions played an important role in the way that policy was mediated, as both managers and tutors in ACL sites attempted to get the best they could from Skills for Life; and union learning representatives in workplaces worked creatively to persuade their colleagues into learning.

Ethical gaming, shielding and damage limitation

Strategic compliance under top-down performance management often involved trying to ameliorate the negative effects of policy levers. We found examples of what can be termed 'shielding', where senior (and sometimes middle) management would take the brunt of the effects of funding rather than passing them on to tutors, or would reduce paperwork in response to tutor feedback, or shield learners from the effects of funding turbulence (e.g., by creating long induction periods at the beginning of the academic year, while staff recruitment and accommodation difficulties were still being addressed). Tutors, concerned about how targets might negatively affect learning and inclusion, saw part of their professional role as limiting the damage of particular policy levers (Edward et al. 2007). There were also instances of 'ethical gaming' (Dixit 2002), in which managers and tutors in some of the learning sites played the system or bent rules to ensure the courses could continue to function in the interests of learners.

In policy circles we also found examples of 'damage limitation', in which senior national officials were caught between ministerial imperatives and trying to make policy workable in practice. The most politically combustible area resulted from the effects of economic migration and the increased demand for ESOL provision. One LSC official commented on the dilemma:

> The growth in ESOL is unsustainable. The change to the populations, with migrant workers actively recruited on a promise of free English by employers, is not a sustainable situation. Furthermore it was compromising the strategy, and so there would be changes.
>
> (UA14)

At the same time, officials felt a particular responsibility to create defensible policy:

> We can't just target migrant workers and that's why we had a fee introduction policy. You have to take a whole-policy approach if you want to achieve that end, so it's about changing the policy to respond to ministerial edicts.
>
> (UA14)

These types of policy mediation were intended to take the raw edges off politically motivated policy-making.

Resistance and exit

We did not find compelling evidence of outright resistance to policy and policy levers. This was the result not of any lack of conviction on behalf of professionals, but of the fact that they found themselves largely agreeing with the policy drivers (the broad aims of policy, particularly around achievement and inclusion), but disagreeing about how the sector was working in practice. Resistance was thus dissipated. For some people, however, endless policy changes and the effects of funding levers pushed them to breaking point. Following the edicts from the DfES and LSC on removing entitlements for free ESOL tuition for certain groups of learners, for example, one FE senior manager played a 'game of chicken' with an LSC official:

> So I said to him, 'Are you interested in what we are going to cut?' And he said, 'Yeah, tell me.' So I said, 'We're going to cut a million pounds' worth of ESOL,' and you could see the panic across his face. He said, 'You can't do that.' And I said, 'Well, what the hell do you think I was going to cut? We don't do yoga and pilates, and we haven't done that for twenty bloody years, so what do you think we are going to cut?'
>
> (ZA28)

Resistance, in this particular case, was not futile. Eventually the college and the LSC arrived at an agreement, with the latter having to acknowledge that it was not going to deliver its targets without the co-operation of the former. But this college manager later admitted that this form of resistance was a desperate measure and that the LSC came to his college 'with zero flexibility in their pocket' (ZA28). It transpired, however, that colleges across the capital had lobbied the Mayor, Ken Livingstone, for additional funds for ESOL, resulting in an extra £15 million being granted by ministers for this provision in London (Ford 2007). Many others in the LSS, however, did not have this kind of countervailing power, and for them the ultimate form of resistance was to get out. Hodkinson et al. (2005b) found high levels of staff turnover that was not just the result of normal job mobility, but because many decided that enough was enough (see also Arrowsmith 2006).

'Lost in translation' and the 'misinterpretation' of national policy

Policy itself fell victim to the exercise of top-down performance management in a rapidly changing climate. We found instances in which policy was 'mistranslated' or 'over-interpreted' (Coffield et al. 2007), the clearest examples of which took place in relation to adult learning and ESOL. As the government placed more emphasis on Level 2 achievements in basic skills and declared that fees would be payable for certain groups of learners in ESOL provision, so providers reacted in anticipation. Not only were ESOL courses closed, exemplified by the LSC/college exchanges above, but basic skills provision for the most disadvantaged learners at Entry Level has gone into decline. Reports of these closures appeared to puzzle senior LSC officials:

And we know, for example, that there is an issue around really understanding what's happening in relation to LLDD [learners with learning difficulties and/or disabilities] provision. Colleges are required to maintain their LLDD provision, yet ministers are getting complaints about the closure of courses. So there's something happening out there that we haven't got to the bottom of yet. We're probing that.

(UA15)

At a project seminar held in November 2006 on problems of policy translation at different levels of the LSS, LSC national officials went to great lengths to explain the policy position and how provision of learning for disadvantaged communities would have a degree of protection. But this was late in the day and some managers on the ground, feeling they had little control over funding, had made up their minds and were closing courses.

Unintended outcomes and transactions costs

Significant gains by the LSS in terms of participation, retention and achievement rates have come at a price. In addition to the unintended outcomes which threaten more marginal groups of learners, there have been high 'transaction costs'. We use the term to refer to the time, energy and resources devoted to contracting in markets and responding to the demands of accountability. Within a sector that combines both features of markets and political bureaucracies, these costs have become considerable, although they are difficult to calculate precisely. We can, however, outline their scale.

Within institutions, they include the constant redrafting of plans by senior management in response to changing national priorities; responding to multiple versions of data demanded by the LSC, the inspectorate and awarding bodies; the time spent by middle managers translating these demands into institutional systems of accountability and the time of tutors as they react to the demands of these systems; and the work of restructuring the LSC and other agencies, including redundancy pay to thousands of dismissed staff. Moreover, there is the loss of social capital when networks, partnerships and goodwill are broken, when the forty-seven LLSCs were disbanded and all the council members, including many leading employers, were told their services were no longer needed. Constant restructuring spreads general feelings of uncertainty, lowers the commitment of many of those working in the sector who feel threatened by repeated streamlining, and makes it less likely that able people will join such a volatile sector. These institutional costs have been compounded by micro-management and 'policy busyness', such as the expense of what appears to be an army of DfES officials shadowing LSC officials (Hodgson *et al.* 2005) and the costs of the many private consultants employed to speed up policy implementation.

The politically driven, bureaucratic and marketised arrangements that currently dominate the LSS thus stand accused of being wasteful. This is not just financial waste but the displacement of professional energy and expertise that could be better spent focusing on the needs of learners, particularly the most disadvantaged.

Improving learning and inclusion in complex systems

Policy, policy levers and manufactured complexity

The story of the sector in action is one of achievements and all-too-evident limitations. The achievements, as we make clear at the beginning of the book, include improved levels of investment, quality, retention and achievement. It is also possible to argue that the LSC itself has been an achievement of sorts as it adapts to a changing political and policy landscape. Achievements have resulted from government policy, the effects of policy levers and the professional responses of those who work at different levels within the sector. However, our research suggests that these gains are being compromised by the way in which the sector is governed – 'policy busyness', constant change and instability; top-down performance management and the dissipation of professional resources; and the production of unintended outcomes, particularly for more marginal groups of learners. It is likely that the early gains of the LSS could be jeopardised because of the limitations of governance. Moreover, the next phase of the LSS, which could see a policy of imposed demand-led strategies, could produce greater instability still. In keeping with New Labour's hybrid strategy, however, it is more than likely that such moves will be followed by more top-down intervention to counter its negative effects. Top-down performance management and managed markets constitute a cycle that actively manufactures complexity and unpredictability. But this approach to governance does not take into account the complex interaction of factors (such as qualifications, labour markets and the needs of learners and communities) that impact on learning and inclusion at the local and institutional levels.

Improving learning and inclusion beyond current levels, particularly at a time of resource constraint, will require a breakout from this logic. Our research points to the possibilities of a different course of action, able to harness the innovative power of professionalism and to resonate with wider political debates about the organisation of public services more generally. As Shah and Goss (2007: 79) suggest:

> The top-down centralised behemoth could be replaced with a looser, more organic network of services that fit the needs of the people who use them. Instead of crude assumptions about central control ensuring 'delivery', we need to pay more attention to how complex systems work.

An ecological perspective – working with complexity

Ecological concepts, originating in biology, are being used to think holistically about complex and interdependent human relations in different 'spaces' or levels of systems or societies. Bronfenbrenner (1979) developed the idea of different scales of human ecologies – macro, meso and micro. Finegold (1999) applied ecological thinking on a macro scale when examining the interaction of factors that constituted a regional eco-system – economic, technological and organisational – to support high skill and innovation in Silicon Valley, California. Stronach et al. (2002) used the concept at a more micro level when studying nursing practice, making a distinction between performative practices and 'ecologies of practice' based on extended forms of professionalism. In the context of the LSS, we have applied ecological concepts at a meso level to think about interdependent relationships of different providers in a locality 'in which the behaviour of one provider can affect the success or failure of others' (Stanton and Fletcher 2006: 15). Stanton and Fletcher's concept, used to examine 14–19 institutional arrangements, has been expanded to embrace a wide range of local factors that education and training providers must consider when attempting to function effectively within their locality. These include different local competitive or planning environments; configurations of institutional provision; local labour markets, patterns of skill levels and employer demand; local demography and geography; social conditions; the needs of learners and their patterns of travel to college (Spours et al. 2007). An expanded concept of local ecologies helps with thinking about the interrelationship of multiple factors that play out at local and institutional levels. The metaphor is used, therefore, in a more descriptive than normative sense, in that a locality does not have to develop a particular quality of relationships to be classified as one. The condition of local ecologies will vary. Relations can be more competitive or collaborative, rich or impoverished, strained or harmonious. However, the term 'local ecologies' encourages thinking about interdependent relationships and thus may encourage an implicitly collaborative approach to policy and practice to assist the direction of future reform.

In the first instance, the metaphor can be used to critique the effects of policy and policy levers on the development of durable local relationships. At different points throughout our research, and echoing wider findings on 14–19 education (e.g., Hodgson and Spours 2006), policy actors commented on the tensions within policy between the promotion of competition and collaboration and how these can inhibit collaborative relationships. Several senior managers in our sites suggested that national policy levers, targets and funding, in particular, were impairing the ability of their institutions to work effectively with local ecologies, particularly in relation to adults. More recently, the policy of contestability and creating a demand-led system has led to complaints that the brokering role of the LSC in Train to Gain is disrupting established college–employer relationships. Top-down performance management and top-down markets, as Figure 7.1 illustrates, weaken the 'local'.

Moving beyond critique, an ecological perspective points to ways in which national policy and governance arrangements in the LSS could be changed to help providers improve the quality and inclusiveness of the local educational landscape. In the final chapter we argue for the development of explicitly collaborative ecologies as part of effective and inclusive learning systems. In the wider political context, there is the added advantage that ecological perspectives echo debates taking place about the role of local government and governance more generally (see Chapter 8 for a discussion of these wider governance debates).

It will be important, however, to avoid creating a naïve concept of the local, seen as autonomous from other levels of governance. Strong local systems, capable of responding to the needs of learners will have to be component parts of strong national and regional systems capable of strategic planning, achieving minimum standards and promoting equity. In the final chapter, we will argue for a new and more devolved

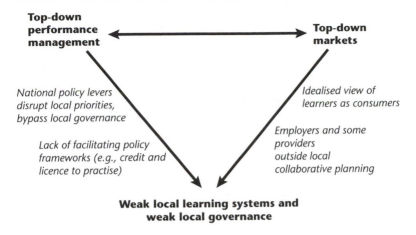

Figure 7.1 The weakening of the 'local'

balance between national, regional and local levels of governance so that different policy actors in the LSS can exercise greater local control to support learners, and, at the same time, be more actively supported themselves by national policy.

An ecological concept of the sector with its suggestion of holistic thinking and interdependent relations offers an alternative to the images of mechanical control that are part of top-down performance management. Its collaborative ethos also steers thinking away from markets and more towards the realm of the public and human agreement. In this sense, it may be a concept for our time, capable of providing a language and imagery of different parties working together in the interests of learners and of the common good, while at the same time harnessing the commitment of professionals who are so often frustrated by policy.

Before moving on to discuss how an increasingly fragmented sector might be transformed into an inclusive, equitable and effective learning system, we return to the relationship between learners and their tutors that constitutes the real fulcrum of the sector (Finlay *et al.* 2007c). The centrality of this partnership is something that the learners in our study have attested to on several occasions (Hodgson *et al.* 2007c). Viewed through an ecological lens, these could be seen as the most micro of interdependent relationships. The learners relied on their tutors to motivate and guide them. Tutors were dependent on their relationship with learners, even the more challenging ones, to reinforce their sense

Box 7.4 Implications for policy and practice

The new 'demand-led' model of the LSS that combines two forms of centralism – centrally constructed policy levers to drive through government priorities and a centrally imposed 'quasi-market' – will produce new levels of instability. There is a need to provide sufficient stability to encourage professional innovation and empowerment based on commitment rather than fear.

Policy actors devote significant amounts of energy to offsetting the negative effects of imposed policy and policy levers, reducing the energy going into the organisation of learning. New forms of governance need to be developed that allow far more energy to be devoted to supporting learning.

The most powerful policy levers – targets and funding – combine, and these, in turn, are mediated and translated by different layers of the LSS. Policy-makers know little about their behaviour, effects and costs. Policy actors, particularly at the local level, have to be able to exercise much greater control over levers to make them more responsive to local needs and conditions.

Current policy levers appear to encourage some practitioners to create accessible but mechanical and narrow forms of learning experience. These can deliver some initial gains for learners but not necessarily the skills for sustained participation, progression and critical thinking. Attention should be focused on encouraging professional communities of practice that can deliver more 'expansive' forms of learning.

We found an appetite for professional and institutional collaboration and the exercise of local discretion that resonates with wider debates taking place in local, regional and national government. Debates within the LSS need to be linked to wider discussions and changes, focused on the democratic development of the political system as a whole.

of professional identity and to provide them with the strength to confront the difficulties they faced working with instability and uncertainty.

Recognition of this micro scale of interdependence will be a vital step to improving learning. It is not only learners who need to be supported but those supporting the learners. This takes us right back to the wider ecological landscape. New local learning relationships cannot be fully forged without the reciprocal role of the other levels of policy and governance, and this is why we now turn our attention to gradual reform of the whole system.

Part III

Overall implications

Chapter 8

An alternative future for learning and skills

Introduction

The stories we have told in earlier chapters have been multi-layered, intricate and conflictual. Within the welter of detail we can now discern two main narratives about the sector. The first is the picture painted by politicians of rising investment, increasing participation and substantial achievements. The second comes from a growing number of the managers, practitioners and policy-makers we interviewed, who spoke of deepening feelings of frustration, of constant struggles to keep services going and of increasing concerns for the future of the sector. The gap between these two sets of perceptions has steadily widened over the last three years and has recently been intensified by the latest structural reform of departmental responsibilities and by government plans for a radical move to a demand-led system. The first story uses statistical data to support its argument that outcomes are improving significantly; the second claims that the processes, mechanisms and 'levers' that are being used to achieve these goals are exacting too heavy a price for success. At stake between these two competing views lie the future prospects of no fewer than six million learners.

At the end of Chapter 2, we promised to return to six crucial questions which we have wrestled with over the years; here, we offer our responses. First, are government reforms creating the radical and enduring change which David Blunkett hoped to see? We think not. The word 'radical' suggests getting to the root of the problems; instead, we have witnessed recurrent structural change. In the three-and-a-half-year lifetime of this project two departments of state, the Department for Education and Skills (DfES) and the Department of Trade and Industry (DTI) have disappeared, and several national and local government agencies have also vanished or are scheduled to do so: the Adult Learning Inspectorate (ALI), the National Employment Panel

(NEP), the local Learning and Skills Councils (LLSCs), the Learning and Skills Development Agency (LSDA) and the Sector Skills Development Agency (SSDA). The atmosphere and culture created by these constant upheavals speak of short-termism, uncertainty and impermanence rather than of enduring stability.

Second, are the reforms creating a healthy, innovative and self-confident sector? Again, our answer is unfortunately 'no'. Top-down performance management, driven too fast from the centre on short timescales and without reference to varying local conditions, stifles innovation and renders all but the most self-confident risk-averse.

Third, learners are only rhetorically at the heart of the sector. The heavy emphasis on skills, the restructuring of the organisational landscape and the formation of policy continue to occupy centre stage.

Fourth, are we moving towards a system of lifelong learning that provides clear progression routes for all types of learner? The noble idea of David Blunkett, as spelled out in New Labour's first Green Paper on Education in 1998, is being quietly forgotten:

> Our vision of the Learning Age is about more than employment. The development of a culture of learning will help to build a united society, assist in the creation of personal independence, and encourage our creativity and innovation.
>
> (DfEE 1998: 6)

This broad vision has narrowed to the 'economically valuable skills' of the Leitch Report. Moreover, lifelong progression routes will be arguably harder to discern, following the division of the DfES into the Department for Children, Schools and Families (DCSF), which will be responsible for 14–19 skills, and the Department for Innovation, Universities and Skills (DIUS), in charge of apprenticeships and post-19 adult skills.

Fifth, we asked how much radical change the sector can tolerate. We refer readers back to Box 1.1 (p. 11 above), which lists forty main tasks currently proposed for the sector between now and 2020. The annex to the DIUS's plan to implement the Leitch Report contains seventy-six actions that have to be carried out before 2015 (DIUS 2007: 68–73). It is as though burden after burden is being heaped on the sector, making it probable that it will fall down on some of the tasks it has been set. In this way, further political intervention is legitimated.

Our final question is concerned with the changes needed to create a more equitable, effective and democratic system. The latter half of this chapter is devoted to addressing what we consider to be the most important topic of all.

A further reflection drawn from the stories in previous chapters is that this sprawling, over-centralised and over-regulated sector has still some way to go before becoming an integrated and cohesive learning system. At present, the whole is less than the sum of the parts; and the parts continue to be changed and supplemented. In other words, the turbulence that has bedevilled the sector since 2001 shows no signs of abating. For example, as we were completing this chapter in summer 2007, news came of the latest round of structural changes, when, as discussed in Chapter 1, the new Prime Minister, Gordon Brown, dissolved the DfES and set up three new departments: the DCSF, the DIUS and the Department for Business, Enterprise and Regulatory Reform (DBERR), promising further upheaval for the LSC. This move shows that the political culture of top-down management without prior consultation and agreement is, despite rhetorical claims to the contrary, still alive and well; and that the English disease of resorting to periodic structural change without addressing fundamental problems is still virulent. The sudden, unexpected and non-consultative nature of the changes makes the case for a new approach to policy-making and to the governance of the LSS all the stronger.

Before outlining the main principles and features of our alternative approach, we want first to draw together the various strands of our argument from the previous chapters by presenting a brief summary of each of the stories we have sought to tell. We have therefore structured this chapter around three questions:

- What have we found?
- What do we propose?
- How do we get there?

What have we found?

From the preceding chapters on our findings, we can identify three overarching themes:

- the centrality of the learner–tutor relationship;
- the impact of a top-down, frequently changing national system;
- inclusion (or lack of it) for learners and for staff.

We shall now consider these in turn, drawing together threads from the previous chapters.

The centrality of the learner–tutor relationship

The learners' stories in Chapter 3 showed how many struggled with various combinations of personal, social, health and economic disadvantages and had fragile or even damaged learning identities, following disruptions or difficulties in their schooling. Yet, despite their generally negative prior learning experiences, the learners we met were extremely positive about their current learning. Across all three groups of learners, the relationship with tutors emerged as being centrally important. Learners valued an experience of learning that was different from that which they had had at school. In college, adult and community learning (ACL) and work-based learning (WBL) they found a relaxed and safe atmosphere, a culture of mutual respect, more one-to-one attention and (for the younger learners in particular) a relationship in which the students were treated as adults. Similarly, the practitioners' accounts in Chapter 5 suggest that the learner–tutor relationship is the cornerstone of success for many learners who have previously failed at school. Tutors confirmed that these learners were challenging to teach, often needing support with confidence and self-respect, as well as with personal, health or social problems. This learner–tutor relationship and the ability to make a difference to learners' lives appeared to sustain staff who complained about other aspects of their work, such as bureaucracy and coping with changes arising chiefly from government policy or local interpretations of it. In vocational areas, tutors' knowledge of practice and of local employers' needs helped to motivate learners and to prepare them for their future careers.

Qualifications and the ways in which learners were assessed were also major factors shaping their learning experiences. While they were in the main very positive about the ways in which they were assessed, there were some tensions for learners, which became challenges for tutors. In ACL, for example, we found some tensions between the Skills for Life core curricula and meeting the learners' individual needs; while in FE staff faced the challenge of breaking down assessment for students, just enough to help them succeed, while taking care to avoid excessive 'spoon-feeding', which could stunt their development as independent learners.

The implication of this important theme is that policy needs to recognise, support and build upon this learner–tutor relationship.

Policy-makers need to find better ways of listening to tutors, and of involving them in the policy process, so that their knowledge and experience of working closely with demanding learners at Entry Level, Level 1 and Level 2 can be used to improve policy.

The impact of a top-down, frequently changing national system

The policy-makers' stories in Chapter 4 showed how, although the twin drivers of policy – promoting a competitive economy and social inclusion – remained constant throughout our period of study, policy language, structures and initiatives all changed considerably. Governance of the LSS moved from an area-planning approach to a 'top-down market' model, reliant on 'contestability' to drive up standards of provision and meet employer and learner 'demand'. In an attempt at 'simplification' of structures and processes, some agencies were merged (e.g., OFSTED and ALI); others, including the Quality Improvement Agency for Lifelong Learning (QIA), were created; and the LSC underwent significant organisational change with the addition of a regional tier and a replacement of the LLSCs by partnership teams, normally in each local authority area. And, as this book goes to press, there is yet further major upheaval, as the DfES splits into its new departments. From 2010–11, funding for 14–19 education and training will be channelled through local authorities, so the role of the LSC in funding and commissioning post-16 provision will be correspondingly reduced. The LSS will no longer be the unified sector for lifelong learning envisaged by David Blunkett when he sponsored the Learning and Skills Act in 2000.

Policy actors raised questions about many aspects of the system, including who was to pay for learning and whether current funding was being equitably distributed within the LSS and between it and other phases of education, such as higher education and schools. They queried whether the 'voluntarist' measures that have historically been used in England in relation to employers would be strong enough to ensure that these social partners play a more active role in the LSS. The current qualifications system was seen as inflexible, anxieties were expressed about the new diplomas and several policy actors remarked on the slow progress of the new Qualifications and Credit Framework (QCF). Finally, many questioned the future capacity of the workforce to deliver the transformation required within the LSS, both in terms of 'the crisis of succession' in governance and leadership of the sector and in relation to the number of part-time, agency and temporary staff.

Both policy actors and practitioners expressed considerable frustration with the pace of change – too much policy, too fast, with no time for reflection or evaluation, so that valuable lessons were not being learned and energy was being squandered in trying to understand and respond to change. In Chapter 5 we described how tutors and middle managers struggled to maintain stability and continuity for their learners through frequent policy changes. It was on these practitioners that the policy levers we were researching – funding, targets, planning, inspection and initiatives – ultimately had impact, but in their interviews tutors also identified many other local factors, including student need, which influenced their teaching. Staff with a wide range of roles and different levels of experience had in common the fact that their funding, and the continuing existence of their courses or institutions, depended on meeting targets and the heavy accountability requirements of national and local institutions. Most welcomed the additional funding for the sector, helping them improve learner participation, retention and achievement. Yet our research found them struggling to keep pace with policy change and to protect their learners from its impact. Practitioners felt remote from policy-makers, and often did not know why policy decisions had been taken, or even by whom. Targets loomed large in their accounts: they had to be met but were not widely accepted as useful indicators of the quality of provision. Concerns about levels of paperwork and bureaucracy were widespread, and many staff became anxious about the impact of the move to a demand-led system on disadvantaged learners, on rural learners and on courses which are expensive to mount.

The achievements and limitations of the LSS were explained in Chapter 7 by reference to its system of governance. The sector has, over the last six years, experienced a top-down planning phase and, more recently, a more overt top-down market phase. The marketised phase – symbolised by the move to a demand-led system – combines two forms of centralism: centrally constructed policy levers to drive through government priorities and now a centrally imposed 'quasi-market'. The LSC, presiding over significant new levels of investment and major national initiatives, has produced early gains for learners in the LSS, including the removal of the weakest provision and increases in participation, retention and achievement rates. However, it is doubtful whether top-down strategies of either kind (planning or market) can deliver further improvements for certain groups of learners or for the sector as a whole. Our research suggests that policy levers generate heavy 'transactions costs', as significant amounts of energy are diverted away from the organisation of learning, to be devoted instead to offsetting the negative effects of imposed policy and policy levers. Moreover, policy actors at all levels of the system 'translate' policy in ways that produce unpredictable and unintended outcomes.

Overall, this theme in our research points to a need for more openness, better communication between policy actors and practitioners and more trust in professional judgement; rebalancing national, regional and local relations; slowing down the policy-making process; and reconfiguring policy instruments to encourage teamwork and social partnership.

Inclusion (or lack of it) for learners and for staff

In Chapter 6 we discussed the impact of policy levers, highlighting both the positive and negative aspects. Initiative-based funding, such as that channelled through the Employer Training Pilots, the Union Learning Fund, Skills for Life and Education Maintenance Allowances, resulted in positive effects on participation and achievement by many individuals who had previously been excluded from opportunities to learn. However, some government decisions were having adverse effects on inclusion. For example, the focus on Level 1 and Level 2 achievements had led to an over-emphasis of provision for individuals who were close to achieving these levels, with neglect of people at Entry and Pre-Entry levels. Recent policy decisions on ESOL and adult education provision were also seen as excluding very needy groups.

The accounts from learners themselves in Chapter 3 contain many success stories, of how they were enjoying learning more, progressing in their courses and achieving qualifications. Spurred on by these successes, many learners wanted to take their learning further and move on to higher levels. However, we found that there was a significant degree of uncertainty about whether many of these learners would be able to progress as they hoped. In ACL wider funding cutbacks were narrowing provision for basic skills learners; in WBL there was the dual problem of uncertain funding (because of the reliance on short-term initiatives) and limited learning opportunities within the workplace; while in FE there were clearer progression pathways, but low rates of progression on some courses. Across all types of site, learner progression was not as strong a focus as meeting retention and achievement targets.

Institutions and staff involved in education and training also had both positive and negative impacts on inclusion. Colleges and tutors engaged in a wide range of pastoral and tutorial activities aimed at helping students to persevere and succeed. We also identified, however, examples where institutions contributed to exclusion by failing to allow full and open information, advice and guidance that included the provision offered by competitors, or by laying on courses which they could not adequately support and which led to student failure. In Chapter 7 we noted too how over-zealous pursuit of achievement targets can create accessible but mechanical and narrow forms of learning experience. Learners might gain qualifications, but not the skills for sustained participation, progression and critical thinking.

In Chapter 5 we also considered learning and inclusion for practitioners in the sector. We raised questions about the efficacy of the use of staff development as a policy lever, both in the past, in the Success for All agenda, and in the future as a result of Qualified Teacher Learning and Skills (QTLS) status and annual Continuing Professional Development (CPD) requirements for licence to practise, both introduced in September 2007. The gap between the pay and conditions for LSS staff and those in schools has not yet been eliminated, although it has narrowed; the position of part-time and agency staff remains particularly precarious; and anxieties about the impact on staffing of a demand-led system are widespread. Our research suggests that licence to practise in the LSS will need careful handling to ensure that CPD does not become a bureaucratic exercise rather than a useful learning experience for tutors and their learners. We need a really effective feedback system from practitioners to policy-makers to monitor this.

We concluded that an inclusive, equitable and effective learning system would be one in which wider social, economic and cultural inequalities beyond the education system are recognised and addressed. This would require the establishment of a fairer model of funding with provision for those who are disadvantaged being funded at levels either equal to, or greater than, higher-level provision. Furthermore, wider social and cultural outcomes of learning should be recognised as being equally important as economic benefits.

The features of the current top-down market model and our proposal for a devolved social partnership approach are summarised in Box 8.1, which is used to guide the rest of this chapter.

Box 8.1   Features of the top-down market model and of a devolved social partnership approach

Top-down market model	Devolved social partnership
Learners	
• Some priority groups benefit from Level 2 entitlement; other disadvantaged adults excluded by focus on 'economically valuable skills'.	• More flexible and inclusive approach; priority groups of learners identified at regional and local levels, according to area needs.
• Focus on articulation of learner choices (Skills Accounts, Train to Gain).	• Stronger emphasis on learner voice and participation in decision-making.
Teaching and learning	
• Policy levers often 'translated' in ways which create accessible but narrow forms of learning, delivering initial gains for learners but not necessarily skills for sustained participation, progression and critical thinking.	• Success at lower levels depends upon flexible, patient and informal approach tailored to their needs, which builds their confidence through small-group learning, one-to-one support and time to build skill levels.
• Retention and achievement targets lead to weak focus on learner progression.	• Focus on learner progression (e.g., by providing credit framework with smaller steps between qualification levels).
• Qualifications system currently not fit for purpose.	• Development of QCF, to support inclusive approach to lifelong learning.
Tutors and trainers	
• 'Self-regulation' and 'light-touch' inspection mean that monitoring and auditing are internalised by institutions. This creates heavy paperwork demands, diverting	• New forms of governance allowing more energy to support learning; professional communities of practice encouraged to deliver more 'expansive' forms of learning.

continued

Top-down market model (cont.)	Devolved social partnership (cont.)
energy and attention from core activity of teaching/learning. • Terms and conditions and career structures not as good as in other sectors of education; other inequities within the LSS.	• Professional practice supported by stable funding; more local decision-making and CPD. • Greater equity in pay, conditions and career structures.

Institutional arrangements at the local level

• 'Demand-led' combines two forms of centralism: policy levers to drive through government priorities; and centrally imposed 'quasi-market', producing new levels of instability. • Funding and planning horizons shortened; policy tension between competition and collaboration. • Providers increasingly 'strait-jacketed' by top-down policy and initiatives, limiting ability to respond effectively to local needs.	• Strong emphasis on professional–institutional collaboration and exercise of local discretion, linked to wider debates on democratisation of services. • Sufficient stability to encourage professional innovation and empowerment, based on commitment rather than fear. • Localities given powers and resources to tackle exclusion in ways that are locally appropriate and collaborative.

Employers and other social partners

• Rhetorically, employers have a central role, but approach remains voluntarist (e.g. Skills Pledge). Voluntarism given final chance until 2010.	• Training stimulated by wider use of 'licences to practise' (following model in the social care sector).

Top-down market model (cont.)	Devolved social partnership (cont.)
• Intermediaries such as Skills Brokers and SSCs may not adequately represent employer views.	• Employers fully represented, but not privileged over other social partners (e.g., trade unions and voluntary sector).
LSC and other agencies • LSC in role as 'market-maker' withdraws from planning; increasingly intervenes to correct 'market failure'. • Agencies such as the QIA and SSCs strongly directed from the centre, acting as conduits for national policy. • Accountability is primarily to government, not to wider range of stakeholders.	• Continuing need for body to oversee planning at local levels and to arbitrate among social partners – needs to be more democratic and accountable than current LSC. • Agencies perform a more independent advisory function, offering professional expertise and advice to create appropriate checks and balances in the system.
Regional level • Manages implementation of national priorities, ensuring a 'clear line of sight' between local plans and national targets. Focus on economic planning and bringing partners together around skills.	• Broader role for strong city/regions, focused on wider benefits of learning, and not just skill needs of regional economy.
National policy • Top-down, centralised policy the hallmark of governance.	• Need for rebalancing of national, regional and local relations.

continued

Top-down market model (cont.)	Devolved social partnership (cont.)
• Up-skilling seen as panacea to nation's economic and social problems. • Constant policy change and turbulence, accelerating with move to 'demand-led'. • Most powerful policy levers (targets and funding) combine; translated by different layers of the LSS; policy-makers know little about their behaviour, effects and costs. • Low trust relationships between national policy and professionals; few opportunities for feedback. • Idea of a 16-plus LSS abandoned by government in favour of separate school-based system up to 19 and skills-based system for adults.	• LSS cannot remediate wider socio-economic problems, which need concerted multi-agency approach and broader political, social and economic change. • Slower pace of reform to allow for consolidation and reflection, based on energy, knowledge and commitment of sector. • Policy actors to exercise greater control over policy levers, to monitor and influence their effects via feedback loops and fora of staff from different levels of the LSS. • Teaching/learning to become central aim of policy. • Reclaiming idea of lifelong learning system balancing education and skills at different ages.

What do we propose?

Broad principles of a new learning and skills system

Our research findings indicate the need for nothing less than a new settlement, underpinned by some explicit principles and new forms of governance. Reflection on our data suggests the need for a set of principles that would form the moral and procedural basis of the alternative system we will outline in the next section. We propose – for public discussion and improvement – three fundamental principles. The first, which would put teaching and learning at the heart of the system, seeks to reclaim the broad concept of education, which has disappeared from the titles of the three new ministries (DCSF, DIUS and DBERR) and from the most recent policy texts, which prefer to talk of adult skills (e.g., DfES 2006c). The second argues that for far too long the claims for equity have been subordinated to the demands for economic efficiency and that this imbalance needs to be corrected. The third principle calls for a new policy process to accompany the new system and for a more moderate pace of change; in other words, for a new model of reform. We go on to suggest that these principles can be best enacted within a system of governance based on 'devolved social partnership' that brings partners together at national, regional and local levels to serve the needs of learners.

Principle 1: teaching and learning at the heart of the system

We return to our central finding: namely, that students in three different settings (FE, ACL and WBL) reported that it was the relationship with tutors that was the key to their learning, progress and success. For learners of any age who had been poorly served by their schooling, a tutor who gave them respect, confidence and self-belief could help them achieve where in the past they had failed. This is a considerable achievement for tutors working with students whom no-one else wants to teach.

For some years in educational and policy circles the fashion has been to talk of moving the focus of attention away from teaching and on to learning. We are very much in favour of the principles enunciated by the team, in the Teaching and Learning Research Programme (TLRP) project Transforming Learning Cultures in FE (TLC), to maximise student agency: that is, 'to maximise their opportunities to contribute to their own learning' (James and Biesta 2007: 151). Similarly, we agree with the conclusion from Thompson and Wiliam's review of the literature that 'teacher professional development [is] the fundamental lever for improving student learning . . . teacher quality trumps virtually all other influences on student achievement' (Thompson and Wiliam 2007: 2). Our data suggest, however, something more: that teaching and learning should not be seen as two separate activities, but as interdependent elements of a single, reciprocal process – two sides of a single coin.

Policy and practice need to consider how to establish, maintain and enrich learner–teacher relationships. We described earlier how tutors were adept at building a culture of mutual respect. How could such effective relationships be improved? Our data suggest that policy needs to focus on supporting professional communities of practice and CPD, which are tailored to personal and team needs and emphasise capacity-building for the sector as a whole. In order to support these professional communities, policy has to offer greater trust, more local determination, more secure career structures and the time to innovate and take pedagogical risks. Tutors and managers need to be given the space to develop a shared concept of quality in terms of teaching and learning, which is subject to more local, as well as national, accountability. We have four further suggestions to make. First, tutors need a language with which to discuss learning with their students, and Noel Entwistle's (1998) research on deep, surface and strategic approaches to learning provides an appropriate lexicon. Second, to counteract one-sided and cognitively undemanding interaction in classrooms, Robin Alexander (2006) has proposed five criteria to guide and inform dialogue. His research suggests that it should be collective (tutor and students working together), reciprocal (learning from each other), supportive (helping each other), cumulative (building on each other's ideas) and purposeful (with specific educational goals in mind). Third, Jerome Bruner (1996) has argued that teaching is a direct reflection of the assumptions teachers hold about how students learn and how their minds work. Students can be seen as imitative learners; or as novices who can (with help) become experts; or as passive receptacles to be filled with knowledge; or as collaborative thinkers, able to construct their own models of the world; or as knowledgeable about the provisional nature of knowledge and how new knowledge is generated. For Bruner, the point is that these 'folk pedagogical theories of teachers . . . need to be made explicit and to be re-examined' (Bruner 1996: 46 and 50). Fourth, the TLRP has established a new series of publications, called *Improving Practice*, which explores new ways of enhancing learning experiences and improving educational outcomes of all sorts. One particular study that is of relevance here is a practical guide for schools and colleges – *Learning How to Learn* (James 2006).

If improving teaching and learning were to be acknowledged as the core business of the sector, then FE and ACL institutions would be seen first and foremost as centres of teaching and learning and only secondarily as businesses competing for learners and funding. Furthermore, in order to demonstrate the overriding importance of teaching and learning, senior management should themselves teach; they are, after all, educational leaders first and business leaders second. Moreover, improving teaching and learning is more than an individual task for all tutors: it is also a collective responsibility, which requires an institutional strategy to create a learning culture within the institution (see Grubb 1999). The job of the senior management team is to provide 'the necessary structures, resources, spaces and opportunities for all members of the community to collaborate in a focus on learning' (Reed and Lodge 2006: 8). Written policies on teaching and learning also need to go beyond administrative matters and explain in some detail how not just students but tutors, senior managers and the institution itself can become better at learning. Seymour Sarason, an American psychologist, seeking to explain what he called the predictable failure of educational reform in the United States, argued that teachers cannot create and sustain the conditions for students to become creative lifelong learners if those conditions do not exist for teachers themselves (Sarason 1990).

We have argued throughout for teachers, as accountable professionals, to be treated as full, equal and trusted partners in the policy process. We do not, however, take a romantic notion of the profession which sees all tutors as heroic, overworked and underpaid reformers. Poor provision should not be tolerated and working for the best interests of students is the cardinal principle which unites politicians, policymakers and practitioners.

Nor do we wish to be misunderstood as suggesting that the long-established patterns of disadvantage which we have outlined in this book can be reversed through education alone. As Lave and Wenger (1991: 100) have argued, the problems of education 'are not, at the most fundamental level, pedagogical'. Rather, educational reform needs to be part of a co-ordinated strategy of socio-economic policies to tackle persistent inequalities. As Mortimore and Whitty (1997: 29) argued at the beginning of the first Blair administration, 'policies which tackle poverty and related aspects of disadvantage at their roots are likely to be more successful than purely educational interventions in influencing overall patterns of educational inequality'. That conclusion remains every bit as valid now that Gordon Brown is Prime Minister. Perhaps this time it will be acted upon.

Principle 2: equity and efficiency

In 2006 the European Commission, while outlining the twin challenges of competitiveness and social cohesion facing Europe's education and training systems, argued that, rather than being mutually exclusive, 'equity and efficiency are, in fact, mutually reinforcing' (CEC 2006a: 2). To support this claim, the Commission produced a working paper, which sets out the underlying evidence in considerable detail. This work contains two conclusions that are important for our purposes.

First, returns to investment at different levels of lifelong learning show that 'pre-primary education has the highest rates of return of the whole lifelong learning continuum, especially for the most disadvantaged, and the results of this investment build up over time' (CEC 2006a: 3). It follows that the most efficient policy is to invest at an early stage in the most disadvantaged children. Hence, the heavy government investment in Sure Start, which hopefully, over the years, will help to reduce the large numbers of young people arriving at FE colleges, workplaces or ACL without basic skills in literacy and numeracy.

Second, the review of international research conducted by the European Commission concluded that 'there is an urgent need for *a better balance between the economic and socio-cultural objectives of learning*' (CEC 2006b: 8; original emphasis). The review argued that education and training policies should '*reduce inequality* by improving the life opportunities of those most in need and narrowing the gap between the best and worst qualified individuals' (*ibid.*: 5; original emphasis). The English system contains two glaring inequalities: the estimated 220,000 young people aged 16–18 not in any form of education, employment or training – the so-called NEET group (LSC 2006a: 5); and the 30,000-plus students who leave school every year without any qualifications (Barber 2007: 278). For the European Commission, equity now deserves to be considered alongside efficiency when member states take decisions about the resourcing and reform of their education and training systems. For us, funding decisions are a direct expression of the values and priorities of governments; and, as we shall see, equity and efficiency are not miraculously reconciled by being placed side by side in the same sentence.

New Labour rightly boasts that investment in FE colleges has increased by 48 per cent in real terms since 1997 (DfES 2006c: 18); but we need to remember that investment in schools increased by 65 per cent during the same period (HMT 2006: 131). Mick Fletcher (2007: 8) has intensified this argument by pointing out the two-tier approach to funding, whereby government provides stability in funding for schools and universities, but deliberately creates instability for colleges and independent providers because 'it sharpens the spur of competition'.

Again, New Labour has promised to implement a new set of principles for 14–19 funding, one of which is that 'comparable funding must be allocated for comparable activity, irrespective of the type of institution' (DfES 2006b: 66). The White Paper on FE goes on to explain that the 13 per cent funding gap between school sixth forms and colleges has been reduced to 8 per cent, and it promises a further reduction of 3 per cent from 2008: 'when resources allow, further steps will be taken' (*ibid.*: 68). Fletcher and Owen (2005) estimate that it would cost some £200 million to eliminate this funding gap. If the government wants the sector to reach 'its full potential as the powerhouse of a high skills economy' (DfES 2006b: 1), then it should act more speedily to bridge this gap. Not to do so allows critics to point to the reduced sum spent per student and lower salaries in FE as hard evidence of the lower esteem in which it is held by the government, despite the fulsome rhetoric. And rewards, career prospects, conditions of service are all poorer in ACL and WBL than they are in FE. Transferring the funding for the 14–19 phase in FE colleges, school sixth forms and sixth-form colleges to local authorities will, we trust, increase the pressure on government for parity of funding across these different types of institution.

We would also like to suggest another funding principle: that those young people and adults who have little to show for years of formal schooling should be entitled to greater resources and opportunities to repair the damage; so all courses at or below Level 2 should be funded as favourably as Level 3 courses in order to cope with the concentration of educational, financial, social and physical disadvantages suffered by such students. The target is to reduce the NEET group to 8 per cent by 2010, but the latest figures show that their numbers *grew* in 2005 from 10 to 11 per cent. Substantial additional resources are needed to make serious inroads into the often chaotic lives of those in the NEET group. The continued existence of such a large group suggests strongly that in the UK the twin goals of equity and efficiency are very far from being aligned.

There remain many thousands of young people and adults, apart from the NEET group, who do not have a Level 2 qualification, which is considered the minimum for entry into employment. For them, the QCA and the LSC are jointly developing the Foundation Learning Tier (FLT) for any learner at Entry or Level 1, aged fourteen and older, as part of the new QCF. While we welcome this development, we also have two concerns. First, the FLT needs to be well resourced and staffed, at the same standard as Level 3 provision, to prevent it becoming stigmatised as a disadvantaged service for disadvantaged people. Second, it needs to become an integral part of an inclusive set of learning opportunities open to all learners and not a separate, compensatory programme.

The inequalities which suffuse the sector also need to be seen in an international comparative perspective, which raises such questions as: are such persistent inequalities an inevitable consequence of globalisation, increased international competitiveness, rapid change in labour markets and repeated waves of technological innovation? Research on the Nordic countries (see Box 8.2) suggests that there are alternative strategies for responding to these challenges.

Box 8.2 Evidence from the Nordic countries

Andy Green's important research shows that, faced with the same conditions, other countries in Europe have developed distinctive models of lifelong learning and of the knowledge economy, which have been far more successful in combining economic competitiveness and social cohesion. In sharp contrast to the Anglo-Saxon market model with relatively high employment and high income inequality, 'characterised by polarised high skills/low skills labour markets that trade off economic competitiveness against social cohesion' (Green 2006: 250), the Nordic states have succeeded in combining 'high levels of economic competitiveness with relative equality and high levels of social cohesion' (ibid.: 252). Green also shows how their education and training systems play an important part in their success.

Milana and Desjardins (2007: 2) amplify his argument by defining the characteristics of the Nordic model and point to 'a strong political commitment to lessen inequality', which has attenuated the differences between disadvantaged groups and the rest of the population. A raft of policies support this objective, three of which are relevant to our argument:

- intervention targeted at particular disadvantaged groups;
- the central role in planning adult education and labour market policies is given to the state and the social partners, but funding is decentralised;

> • in Sweden, since the 1970s, employed adults have had the right
> to paid educational leave which has created high demands for
> adult education and training.

The alternative settlement for which we argue in this book is not,
therefore, some unimaginable fantasy or impossible dream, but a lived
reality in other societies that have made different political, economic
and educational choices.

Principle 3: a more moderate pace of change

Our research has exposed yet again the different normative worlds
of politicians and practitioners, in particular their different cultures and
timescales (see Bell and Raffe 1991). Someone who has recently
experienced both worlds, Peter Hyman, who was Tony Blair's chief
speech-writer before becoming a teacher in an inner-city comprehensive, wrote of a 'yawning gulf' between the two. In the political world
he experienced:

> the tyranny of momentum politics . . . constant reforming activity
> to show a department was serious about change . . . momentum
> is essential or politicians are accused of drifting. This meant
> constantly coming out with initiatives, talking points, speeches,
> nuggets of policy.
>
> (Hyman 2005: 272 and 384)

He had not been teaching long before he realised that schools need,
not a string of new initiatives, but 'empowerment, partnership and
consistency' (*ibid.*: 384).

Michael Barber, the head of Blair's Delivery Unit from 2001 to 2005
and the architect of self-styled 'deliverology', presents the options in
such a restricted and simplistic way that only the conclusion that he
favours can be drawn: 'Advance or fail. Momentum or drift. Here
there is no middle way . . . the only alternative to successful transformation was the running down of our service so that it became a safety
net for the poor' (Barber 2007: 211 and 242). We refuse to accept this
crude form of argumentation which attempts to dismiss the many
intermediate options available to all governments.

A similar clash of perspectives can be discerned over the timescales thought appropriate by the two groups for creating successful change. Politicians are driven by different forms of accountability; they are judged by manifesto commitments, the need for quick results before the next General Election, and the demands of a twenty-four-hour media, hungry for news. Hence the macho talk of 'transformational change', 'quantum leaps' and 'step changes'; and the need for 'hard' evidence to demonstrate that change has taken place within the four-year period of an administration.

In contrast to the short-termism endemic in the political world, education practitioners realise that effective reform takes time and that radical and enduring change cannot be rushed. In the epigrammatic words of Michael Fullan (1993: 24), 'change is a journey, not a blueprint'. The political language of reform seriously underestimates the complex processes and multidimensional nature of change in education, which involves not just adopting new materials and teaching approaches, but changing the assumptions, beliefs and practices of teachers (see Fullan 1991).

Moreover, educational institutions must keep the twin pressures of change and maintenance in a healthy balance. As Hargreaves and Hopkins (1991: 17) argued:

> schools need to maintain some continuity with their present and past practices, partly to provide the stability which is the foundation of new developments and partly because the reforms do not by any means change everything that schools do now.

These two worlds need a better understanding of the different types of pressure that each has to bear. There is, however, still no sign of a rapprochement. On the one side, Tony Blair, Gordon Brown and Ruth Kelly (then Prime Minister, Chancellor of the Exchequer and Secretary of State for Education and Skills, respectively), in their foreword in the White Paper on FE, claimed that 'Evolutionary and incremental change will not be enough. We need fundamental reform' (DfES 2006b: 2). On the other side, practitioners in our project complained that it is not possible to plan adequately with short-term funding. Witness the criticism from a middle manager at our final seminar in Newcastle in 2007:

> We now just react to problems. The ability to be proactive has long since gone. The system is getting worse: I used to write a three-

year plan but everything changes every six months so I don't bother any more.

We are arguing for a more sustainable, middle position between the political rhetoric of rapid and radical transformation and a painstakingly slow pace of change that would not serve the interests of learners. The issue is not one of accepting or rejecting change, but of introducing it at a rate that allows it to be absorbed successfully. We agree with Wallace and Hoyle (2005: 14 and 7), who argue for 'more temperate policy-making . . . an incremental strategy for continual and evolutionary improvement', to avoid the current position where 'today's policy change gets added to yesterday's improvement strategy'.

In discussing these key principles, we have already begun to highlight some of the features of an inclusive, equitable and effective learning system: a focus on how policy can support the learner–tutor relationship through developing and sustaining professional communities of practice; a more equitable approach to the distribution of funding; and a more moderate pace of change. The other major features of such a system, as outlined in Box 8.1, will be discussed through our proposals for a new devolved social partnership approach to governance.

Features of an inclusive, equitable and effective learning system – towards devolved social partnership

We see devolved social partnership resulting from the fusion of two approaches to governance. The first is social partnership at the national level, based on the principle of power sharing between government and a range of national representatives, including employers, trade unions, professional associations and community organisations, as practised in the Nordic countries and the Republic of Ireland, where a wider range of partners, including the community, not only implement policies but contribute to their formation (Boyd 2002).

Social partnership, defined in this way, can be linked to a second principle: the civic republican ideal of positive freedom and democratic self-government (Devine *et al.* 2007), with its emphasis on citizen involvement, the promotion of social trust, civil society and local identity. Taken together, they suggest a more democratic set of relationships between national, regional and local governance with the accent on devolution and subsidiarity: 'that unless there is a strong counter reason (usually with regard to equity) democratic institutions should be located as closely as possible to the people they represent' (Lawson 2005: 28). The concepts of devolution and subsidiarity recognise that those at the centre cannot, by themselves, adequately address complex or 'wicked' issues (Newman 2001): these require local and regional determination.

We see devolved social partnership as a way of overcoming the major problems summarised earlier in this chapter: top-down performance management and markets that produce unintended outcomes and heavy costs; the marginalisation of the most disadvantaged groups of learners; a lack of democratic accountability in public bodies like the LLSCs and the RDAs; and a general sense of powerlessness which corrodes commitment. Janet Newman (2001) conceptualised these shifts in another way as movement away from 'hierarchy' and 'rational goal' models towards a combined 'open system' and 'self-governance' approach, although elements of all four approaches have been used by Blair governments.

We should also, however, be aware of the dangers of the social partnership approach. Agreements forged at a local level may be prone to 'club partnership' (Lowndes and Sullivan 2004) and the agenda may be taken over by producers and activists (Newman 2001), thus sidelining less powerful voices in the local community. Deciding on representation presents a further problem to the social partnership approach: who, for example, speaks for part-time or agency staff or for the unemployed? Moreover, strong vested interests may be determined to block any change. We think that these dangers can be addressed by a better balance of national, regional and local governance.

A new set of national, regional and local relationships

Devolved social partnership is not a remote and idealistic goal: it is already present in debates about how local government can be reinvigorated. Over the past ten years the concept of 'New Localism' has emerged as a response to the complexities of modern governance and as a way of promoting democratic and civic renewal:

> New Localism can be characterised as a strategy aimed at devolving power and resources away from central control and towards front-line managers, local democratic structures and local consumers

and communities, within an agreed framework of national minimum standards and policy priorities.

(Stoker 2004: 2)

New Localism can also be seen as a response to a prolonged period of centralisation and a growing realisation that the government's national performance framework for public service delivery is fast decaying, due to high transaction costs and an inability to secure better outputs (Sorajbi 2006). This has resulted in a number of New Labour ministers coming out in favour of a shift of power to local government and localities (e.g., Miliband 2006; Blears 2005; Rainsford 2006).

An integral part of this rebalancing is the growing importance of city/regions, increasingly seen as a way of responding to the 'no' vote in the North East referendum in 2004 (Leese 2006). City/regions are seen as both effective economic drivers and sources of identity, a point not lost on Mayor Ken Livingstone, who has taken control of a London-wide Employment and Skills Board and will actively seek to expand decision-making over skills in order to meet global challenges (LDA 2007). Janet Newman (2001: 73) speculated that this 'might develop as a strong power base from which alternative policy agendas might be pursued'. It appears that the new Brown administration also takes the regional agenda seriously, with the appointment of ministerial portfolios for each of the regions (Leslie 2007). In addition, there has been progress in terms of legislation, although it is too early to assess its impact. The local government White Paper, *Strong and Prosperous Communities* (DCLG 2006), has been welcomed by supporters of New Localism as a step forward (NLGN 2006). Within local government, there is also some evidence of devolution taking root in the development of 'democratic services' by some local and city councils (e.g., City of Birmingham 2007), although the Local Government Association's most recent report, *Prosperous Communities* (LGA 2007), argues that there is much further to go in devolving powers to regional and local government.

We have a practical suggestion to make to bring these ideas to life. A more participative model of change would build into the system feedback loops whereby local policy actors (including employer, union and community representatives), professionals and researchers could report back to regional and national policy-makers on the strengths and weaknesses of particular reforms. They need to be involved at all stages in the development, enactment, evaluation and redesign of policy, because they know most about how to make national policy work in different localities. Our research suggested that fora of this kind, where participants from all the many levels in the sector (national, regional, sub-regional and local) come together on a regular basis to iron out policy tensions, misunderstandings or over-interpretations, could reduce the distance between policy and practice.

A new culture of national politics

A learning system based on more power to regions and localities will require support from a new national political culture. Changes lower down require reform at the top. For example, we need a decisive break with the culture of constant interference and endless national initiatives, tied to ministerial careers. Within the slower policy process that we have argued for earlier, we see the need for ministers to offer leadership rather than engaging in micro-management. In the area of learning and skills, political leadership would involve communicating and explaining policy priorities, promoting equity and securing national standards. Confident leadership is not about drawing power more closely but actively giving it away. This means being serious about devolving powers to regions and localities, but also about distributing power within the centre of national politics, including a greater role for Parliament in policy-making, accompanied by a focus on parliamentary deliberation and the select committee system (Lawson 2005; Heald 2006). Gordon Brown has made a start on this process by publishing for the first time a paper on the government's draft legislative programme (Office of the Leader of the House of Commons 2007)

Policy frameworks rather than policy levers

Part of the process of devolution should be a radical reduction in the use of remote policy levers, currently employed to enforce professional compliance and competition between institutions. Top-down policy levers, which our research suggests have provided some initial gains in performance but at significant cost, could be replaced by 'policy frameworks', which provide the 'rules' and 'freedoms' that stimulate collective practice between social partners and encourage local innovation. Our research suggests four areas where policy levers might be replaced by policy frameworks:

*   **Targets** We need to get rid of the micro-managed, target-driven and quantitative culture of accountability. An alternative approach

is to see targets as broad aspirations and as areas of improvement rather than as numerical entities tightly measured from above. Regions and localities could be asked to provide overall responses to the national 'direction of travel' by producing area-wide targets, generated bottom-up and based on collaboration between social partners, rather than delivering specific 'numbers'. Such a development would signal a significant degree of 'translation' of national policy to fit local circumstances and priorities and would bring a very different feel to the LSS.

- **Funding** Time and again, our interviewees called for greater stability and flexibility in national funding to meet local needs. Funding could be linked to more broadly based targets over a period of three years with more discretion as to how resources might be used to meet local need. An independent Committee of Enquiry recommended that 'at least 20 per cent of colleges' budgets should be at college discretion, with accountability for use after the event' (NIACE 2005: 4).

- **A qualifications and credit framework** Similar calls were made for a more flexible qualifications and credit framework to promote lifelong learning. A framework could contain not only nationally recognised full awards but units to be accumulated in a more incremental manner, some of which could be designed specifically to respond to local need. This may go some way to addressing the problems of learner progression discussed in Chapters 3 and 6.

- **Labour market regulation and licences to practise** Like qualifications and credit, licences to practise offer a regulatory framework that brings employers, providers and learners into a common pact to increase the demand for learning. Taking the Care Standards Act 2000 as a model, such an arrangement communicates: clear signals to all the key partners; the qualifications and skills employers should demand; the level of qualification and skills learners have to achieve; and the courses providers have to offer. This regulatory arrangement produces improved predictability in terms of planning provision locally and regionally. The problem remains of who should pay for the considerable cost of such licences, with the government concerned that employers and learners should share the financial burden.

The role of employers

Part of this new settlement has to be a different relationship between government, employers, employees and their representatives. This requires fundamental change on the part of many employers, for, despite repeated attempts by governments of different political complexions to increase the investment of employers in the skills of their workforce, 'some 35 per cent of employers offer no training to employees, covering more than one quarter of the workforce; a further 6 per cent only offer induction or health and safety training' (DIUS 2007: 37). However, there is also a need for a different type of engagement between government and employers within the type of social partnership arrangements we have described above. Employers are being asked by government to play an ever-increasing role in learning and skills (as well as in many other policy areas), but the complexity of the LSS, with its many competing priorities, makes this an unrealistic task (Brown et al. 2004). Moreover, although employers have rhetorically been placed centre stage, and apparently have been given unprecedented influence through the Sector Skills Councils and their involvement in the development of specialised diplomas, there are difficulties with the mechanisms for representing the views of such a heterogeneous group as employers.

A criticism of some of our interviewees was that the SSCs are not, in fact, employer bodies and cannot, therefore, represent them adequately. This view was borne out by the evidence cited in a Sector Skills Development Agency-sponsored survey of employers (SSDA 2006), which found that only 13 per cent of business establishments are aware of SSCs generally, with 27 per cent having heard about their own SSC under its current brand name. Of these latter employers, only 14 per cent had had any dealings with their SSC, and just 9 per cent in the past twelve months. There is a particular problem with small and medium-sized enterprises because they do not have the resources to meet all the varied demands government places on them.

The latest in a long line of initiatives which have so far proved unsuccessful is the Skills Pledge, launched in June 2007, whereby employers voluntarily commit their firm to invest in the skills of their employees. More than 150 employers had signed up to the Pledge within the first month, including large employers from the public sector (e.g., the police and armed services) and the private sector (e.g., Ford, McDonald's and Sainsbury's), covering 1.7 million employees (DIUS 2007: 55), out of a total of 29.08 million (National Statistics 2007):

that is, 5.8 per cent. Employers have been given until 2010 to sign this Pledge, at which point the government will review whether it is necessary to introduce statutory entitlement to workplace training for employees.

To go back no further than the 1990s, the Training and Enterprise Councils were set up as the last throw of voluntarism, but after ten years that experiment failed to change the culture of employers (see Coffield 1992). By 2010, the LSC will have been given another ten years and the Skills Pledge a further three years to make moral persuasion and financial incentives work. If by then the voluntary approach has failed yet again, the time will have come for the government to act on behalf of the whole community and introduce a statutory entitlement to training.

The role of non-departmental public bodies (NDPBs)

A new political culture will also have to consider the role of NDPBs, such as the LSC, which have become integral parts of neo-liberal governance. The future of NDPBs is an emotive political topic, with different approaches coming from left and right. The right basically invented them in their current form; New Labour expanded their role; and the left, as witnessed by debates in Wales (Hayward et al. 2006), would broadly like to see a 'bonfire' of them.

The LSC, despite its achievements, has been a regular focus of debate since its creation in 2001. It has drawn particular fire because of its large budget, with one of our policy interviewees intimating that there was no shortage of players seeking to control this scale of funding. All the major political parties have voiced views on its future. The Conservatives have proposed the removal of the regional tier and the creation of a single national funding body more responsive to business needs (Heald 2006). The Liberal Democrats, on the other hand, suggest a merger between the LSC and the Higher Education Funding Council for England (HEFCE) into a funding and planning body that brings together learning and skills and higher education (Liberal Democrats 2006). With the publication of the Leitch Report, New Labour has embarked on a demand-led strategy and has yet to decide on the fate of the LSC. As we have seen, however, the Brown administration's division of the DfES means that the outlook for the LSC looks uncertain, to say the least. One possibility, and we stress it is only one of several, is that the national LSC could eventually be merged with the HEFCE; the regional LSC could be integrated with other regional bodies; and the LLSC partnership teams might join local authorities, now responsible for 14–19 provision. This alignment would move some way towards a more democratic role for this particular NDPB. We suggest that other quangos (e.g., QCA, QIA) are empowered to take a stronger two-way advisory role in relation to policy and practice, rather than being simply the transmitters of top-down policy.

Democratic accountability

The short life of the LSC has been dominated by accountability, and any new system would have to be accountable in some way. But in what way? Stuart Ranson (2006: 213) suggests that the culture of accountability will have to be replaced by 'the obligation to communicate with and explain to the public [which] is the foundation of a democratic polity because the authority and consent for public service derives from the public, and without that the legitimacy of the public sphere withers'.

This should not be seen as a dilution of accountability. On the contrary, the concept of democratic accountability is very demanding because of the need to answer for greater freedom of action locally, not only laterally to fellow social partners, but directly to the public at large. Social partnerships, at local and regional levels, would have to demonstrate that collective target-setting could produce better outcomes for learners and that inclusion could be accompanied by efficiency.

There would still be a need for accountability to national government, but we envisage it free from micro-management. If local partnerships had, for example, agreed three-year plans and these had been purchased by local and regional government, then those partnerships would have to account for themselves through explanation, dialogue and openness, rather than relying on authoritarian mechanisms of inspection and audit. In the final analysis, however, poor or unsatisfactory performance, if identified by peer review and rigorous inspection, should not be tolerated because the interests of learners are the overriding concern.

Collaborative local and regional ecologies

It is tempting to think of the 'local' through the lens of local government, particularly given that powers over education up to nineteen years are to be passed from the LSC to local authorities. In Chapter 7 we argued for the need to think in different ways about the local, not just as important administrative and democratically representative entities, but also as ecological systems. An ecological perspective attempts to think about the multidimensional nature of learning beyond schooling (e.g., decisions about where to learn and how to get there; interdependent relations between providers; and the influence of wider community, social and labour market factors). An ecological perspective thus recognises the complexity of educational decisions and relationships that have become more complicated as a result of neo-liberal market reforms (Spours et al. 2007). It provides the framework for professional and institutional collaboration, which could create the spaces for local deliberation of equity, innovation and capacity-building. Such structures also offer the possibility of more efficient use of scarce resources.

Educational relations do not always conform to local administrative boundaries. Learners, for example, may live in one area but choose to study in another, particularly if they wish to pursue a specialism. Large providers, such as general FE colleges, are not just local institutions but have sub-regional and, sometimes, regional roles. On the other hand, effective provision of adult and community education may be on a very local scale, near to or within particular communities.

Thinking about different scalings of activities also helps to conceptualise partnership at different levels of the system and the optimum levels of decision-making needed to serve the interests of learners. A learning partnership, viewing itself as a 'collaborative local ecology', would be part of systems above and below. In defining their parameters, some local ecologies would correspond to the boundaries of local authorities, while others might exist on either a larger or smaller scale depending on their function. Examples of these different scalings can be found in 14–19 education. For instance, 14–19 consortia, comprising several schools and a college, will normally be responsible for the day-to-day learning opportunities and are usually smaller entities than local authorities. On the other hand, 14–19 strategic partnerships can be the same size as some smaller local authorities and will involve the wider range of partners (e.g., health, housing and social services) who will provide the whole 14–19 entitlement. Learning partnerships may operate on a sub-regional scale and will draw in FE colleges, HE institutions and voluntary and community organisations who work on a broader canvas and represent the ecology of wider journey-to-learn patterns.

Fostering collaboration and dealing with complexity, however, requires a strong shared sense of purpose. The principle should be a commitment to raising the educational level of *all*, not just of a minority; and providers should be held jointly responsible for local levels of participation and achievement (Stanton and Fletcher 2006). Fulfilling such a commitment means collaboration between various providers both large and small, support services, employers and community groups. Local ecologies thrive on collective agreement. This does not preclude responding to national targets or using markets, but the extent of the market could be decided collectively through, for example, the process of commissioning by local authorities. Working by agreement can be a long and arduous process but the prizes are high levels of awareness and consensus about what and why decisions are being taken and a sense of commitment to bringing about sustainable change and future capacity-building. There is, nevertheless, the question of leadership within local ecologies. There are roles for local and regional authorities to provide strategic planning; to arbitrate between the partners; to move decision-making forward; to commission provision by agreement; to work for local consistency and equity; and to provide accountability to democratically elected representatives. Ecologies at whatever scale have to be entrusted with what Pratchett (2004) calls 'freedom to' bring about effective and equitable change and not just 'freedom from' central government.

There is, however, nothing sacred about local ecologies which can be as subject to bitter political in-fighting as any national political arrangement, not to mention narrow parochialism and local inertia; but within them they contain the potential to develop a vision of the educational needs not just of particular students or of one institution, but, more importantly, of a local community as a whole.

How do we get there?

We do not want to suggest a set of principles and features of an alternative learning system without exploring the costs and benefits of yet another structural reform; and without explaining how parts of our proposed system are already in place or slowly coming into being.

Further rationalisation or consolidation?

During this project we have witnessed a series of structural and organisational changes and we will use our data to draw up a brief balance sheet of the costs and benefits of this political manoeuvre, which has become a standard feature of the governance of the English education and training system, just as it has been of the National Health Service.

Let us begin by listing the benefits which are routinely claimed. The changes will address structural weaknesses and 'sharpen the focus of Government' (Cabinet Office 2007: 2), which will allegedly be better equipped to face new challenges. Reforms are also introduced to bring together key aspects of policy to make 'efficiency' savings by eradicating duplication and overlap, sharing central services, and 'streamlining' staff; to improve communication by establishing clearer roles and responsibilities; and overall the aim is to improve standards and performance in the interests of users. Another positive effect claimed for 'permanent revolution' is that staff have to change their roles so frequently that they are less likely to stagnate.

The benefits are stressed to such an extent by politicians that one might almost assume there are no costs. In fact, as we outlined in Chapter 7, the economic and human costs are considerable. First, there are the economic costs of paying staff who are made redundant, relocated or transferred. Then come the human costs in terms of careers disrupted, families left to cope with sudden unemployment and individuals who have had their confidence and security shaken. Institutions also have to bear costs in terms of increased bureaucracy and loss of loyalty and collective memory. Moreover, as Richard Sennett (1998: 4) argued, 'social bonds take time to develop, slowly rooting in the cracks and crevices of institutions', but they can be broken at the first restructuring.

Major change also creates widespread uncertainty and insecurity which become part of professional life; and recurrent change lowers morale and long-term commitment. Up to two years can be lost while changes bed down, and during that time staff are diverted from their main tasks to the job of making the new arrangements work. In addition, organisations are usually busily engaged in rectifying weaknesses at the very time the next round of change arrives.

The costs mentioned above appeared repeatedly in our data and yet they seem not to be considered by the advocates of constant change. The dangers of such disruption and short-termism have been eloquently criticised by Richard Sennett (1998: 25), who has questioned how the long-term purposes of government can be pursued by short-lived strategies and agencies: 'Detachment and superficial cooperativeness are better armour for dealing with current realities than behaviour based on values of loyalty and service.' Most of our interviewees craved a period of consolidation but were convinced that they would have to work through further rounds of change. Administrations come and go, agencies come and go, staff come and go, but the political language of 'relentless focus', 'unprecedented rate of change' and 'transformational change' gathers apace. A democratic, equitable and effective system cannot be forced into being; it needs to grow organically out of existing practices. What is needed is a longer-term strategy for gradual reform that provides the time and space for reflection, evaluation and consolidation and in which all social partners feel they are collectively shaping a more democratic future for lifelong learning.

A new settlement is slowly taking shape

Our principles and proposals for a new system are neither unattainable nor unrealistic; in fact, with every day that passes of the new Brown administration aspects of them are being promised, as the retreat from command and control quickens. Shortly after becoming Prime Minister, Brown announced, in a publication called *The Governance of Britain*, 'a new settlement', which proposes to limit the powers of the executive, to make it more accountable, and to reinvigorate our democracy by, for example, placing 'a duty on public bodies to involve local people in major decisions' (Office of the Leader of the House of Commons 2007: 8). The Prime Minister also proposed a new concordat between local and central government and new committees to review the economies and public services of each region.

Another example of a culture change in the new administration is the reduction in the number of targets. At their height in 1999 there were no fewer than 600 public sector agreements, which were reduced to 110 in 2004; the proposal now is to restrict them to only 30. As Andy Burnham, the Chief Secretary to the Treasury, explained:

> The direction of travel is for public services to look and feel differently in different parts of the country. At local level, people will be far more ambitious than perhaps the centre would have dared to be. If not, they will be open to challenge locally.
>
> (Burnham quoted in Carvel 2007: 13)

Fewer targets, on their own, do not necessarily mean less command and control. However, the wider movement towards greater devolution of power has been gathering momentum for some time and suggests that the reduction of targets is part of a significant culture change. For example, arguments for a stronger role in the provision of public services were well made by the Lyons Review of Local Government, which accepted that, if real space is to be made available for local choices and priorities, then 'variability between areas is not only inevitable, but also desirable if pressures are to be managed' (Lyons 2007a: 8). Six months earlier, the White Paper on local government, *Strong and Prosperous Communities*, had called for 'a new settlement between central government, local government, and citizens [by reducing] the amount of top-down control from central government' (DCLG 2006: 5–7). The White Paper also argued for Local Area Agreements with 'a duty for local authorities and other local parties to work together to agree their priorities' (*ibid.*: 11). London's regional Skills and Employment Board is yet another example, which may well be copied by other large city/regions.

These ideas resonate closely with our proposals for devolved social partnership and collaborative local and regional ecologies. In other words, many of the features of our proposed system are coming into being or are already in place, as we finish this book, but most lie outside the LSS.

When we started this project in 2004, one of our major tasks was to suggest how this new *sector* could be developed into a more inclusive and effective learning *system*. In common with the policy-makers and practitioners we interviewed in 2004–5, we welcomed the creation of a unified sector which embraced all aspects of post-16 education and training outside higher education, particularly because it was allied to David Blunkett's radical vision of lifelong learning. But the rejection of Tomlinson's proposals, which would have started the unified sector at the age of fourteen, and the splitting of the DfES along age lines, have seriously damaged this vision of an integrated lifelong learning system.

The LSS, which we have studied for over three years, is entering a new phase and it is no longer clear that it can still even be called the LSS. John Denham refers in his first open letter as Secretary of State at the DIUS to 'the Further Education system'; and his new department, in its plan to implement the Leitch Report, talks of the 'employment and skills system'. Whatever it is to be called, the sector has lost its single identity, has to absorb yet another round of structural change, must develop a successful demand-led strategy for skills and needs to carry out all the myriad tasks which government has set before it. We are concerned that in the midst of such permanent turbulence, the central and gradual reforms for which we have called will be lost from sight in a confusing mass of activities; that central government will remain firmly in charge and the social partners will not be involved as trusted equals; that there will be much official noise about the devolution of power, but only minimal discretion will be given to localities over funding; that no new obligations will be placed on those employers who do not train, but the full force of the market will be brought to bear on colleges, adult and community learning centres and independent providers; that the pursuit of economically valuable skills will displace a broader approach to the curriculum; all of which will distract attention from the centrality of the learner–tutor relationship which places teaching and learning at the heart of the system. If, on the other hand, the fears for the sector that so many of our interviewees have shared with us prove to be unfounded, the prospects of six million learners and the thousands of tutors on whom they rely will be greatly enhanced.

How we did the research

Introduction

Chapter 2 contains a short introduction to our research methodology. This appendix seeks to amplify that brief account, and to discuss some of the choices we had to make and problems we tried to overcome.

The overarching aim of our project, which ran from January 2004 until July 2007, was to explore the impact of national policy on teaching, learning and inclusion in the learning and skills sector (LSS), with a particular focus on three groups of learners who have been poorly served by their previous education: unemployed people in adult and community learning (ACL) centres, low-skilled adult employees in work-based learning (WBL) and younger learners on Level 1 and Level 2 vocational courses in further education (FE) colleges.

The six main objectives of the project, set out in our research proposal, were:

- To produce models of the roles and relationships between the main partners within the new LSS, by studying the impact of key national Learning and Skills Council (LSC) steering mechanisms on teaching, learning and assessment (TLA).
- To test how inclusive the new LSS is by studying its impact on the learning outcomes, motivation and experiences of three types of disadvantaged learner.
- To develop a theoretical model of an effective and inclusive local learning system to be tested more widely.
- To involve participants in the new LSS in developing ways of improving outcomes for learners, by joint, critical reflection on six levels of policy and practice in TLA (European, national, regional, local, organisational and classroom/workplace).

- To interrogate the meaning, use and influence of policy terms related to TLA (e.g., 'best practice', 'learners at the heart of the system') as a means of reflecting on professional practice.
- To build research capacity within the post-16 sector which will extend beyond the life of the project, by means of an iterative and collaborative research methodology.

We shall consider how far we have been able to achieve these objectives after introducing the participants and describing the structure of our data collection, analysis and dissemination of findings.

The range of participants

We wanted to understand the perspectives of learners in our three target groups and tutors who work with them, but also of officials responsible for making and enacting policy at all levels in the sector – local, regional, national and including the international perspective of European partners. Although perspectives of policy-makers were also accessed through analysis of over 300 policy documents, interviews were our main tool for gathering these multiple perspectives on the impact that policies have had on learners, on those who teach and support them and on the institutions which employ those staff.

Box 2.1 (p. 30 above) shows the range of participants at different levels in the sector who contributed to our research over the forty-three months. We deliberately included so many different levels – from government ministers and those who make and influence policy, to learners and their tutors, with as many intermediate levels as possible – to trace the ways in which policy percolates down to practice.

Our extensive data collection spanned three years. Data fell into two broad categories:

- that collected from policy-makers and officials forming and enacting policy, about the aims and objectives of policy, and the mechanisms by which these are to be achieved; and
- that collected in learning sites, from managers, teachers and learners, about what happens in practice and the perceptions of impact both of policy and of other factors on learning and inclusion for learners in 2004–6.

An important third type of data emerged, however, through our project events which brought together the policy and practice perspectives.

We held a series of annual seminars, one in Newcastle and one in London each year, bringing practitioners, managers and tutors from the learning sites together with officials and other players in the policy scene, to hear about our findings to date and to have an opportunity to discuss, confirm or challenge them in a forum of those who work in different areas of the LSS but who have no official opportunity to meet.

The format proved very useful. In 2005, for example, three practitioners in each seminar agreed to supplement our reports by giving short personal presentations, putting their own views directly to participants and stimulating further debate; and in 2006, in London, DfES and LSC officials, surprised by the gap between their own understandings of policy and the impacts which practitioners were describing, encouraged us to organise an additional one-day seminar, in November 2006, on the Skills for Life target, to allow a more systematic exploration of 'the practitioners' story' and the 'policy-makers' story' in relation to that target. The many interviews described below are therefore not the only data we were able to draw on for analysis. We have also circulated project research reports in draft form as 'consultation papers' for comment from participants, and drew on their responses to refine our publications.

A final example of data collection drawing together the perspectives of practitioners and policy-makers was our online survey, which will be described further after an outline of the policy interviews and data collection from the learning sites.

The policy interviews, 2004–7

The project began in 2004 with analysis of key policy documents and an intensive series of confidential interviews with officials, identifying the policies which they believed were having impact and exploring how they believed policy 'levers' were working. This first round of policy interviews was analysed and reported (Coffield *et al.* 2005; Hodgson *et al.* 2005).

Some further policy interviews were conducted in 2005 and early 2006 with officials and representatives of Sector Skills Councils, employers' and union organisations, provider organisations, awarding bodies and other players in the sector, but the second intensive period of policy interviews then began late in 2006, when we returned to many of the organisations visited in 2004, to update their perspectives and discuss our emerging findings. These interviews were completed several months later than originally planned, to include perspectives on the much-anticipated Leitch Review of Skills (Leitch 2006). In spring 2007 we also extended data collection to Brussels, talking to five officials working in and around the European Commission.

Box A.1 shows the range of the 131 policy interviews. For discussion of the range of officials interviewed, see also Chapter 4. At regional and local level (corresponding to levels 5 and 6 in Box 2.1), we sought to include officials who worked with our learning sites in London and the North East, although other regions were included in the online survey in 2007.

Box A.1 Policy interviews, 2004–7

Type of organisation	Number of interviewees
LSC (national, regional and local)	44 (in 52 interviews)
National departments and NDPBs	27 (in 26 interviews)
Other national, regional or local bodies, including employers' and union organisations	47 (in 48 interviews)
European officials	5 (in 5 interviews)
Total	**123 (in 131 interviews)**

The codes used throughout this report to attribute quotations from interviews while protecting the identity of individuals begin with letters U–Z (letters A–T having been used for the learning site interviewees): U indicates LSC staff, at national, regional or local level; V is used for staff in the Inspectorate and other arm's-length agencies; W for national government officials, mostly those employed in the DfES at time of interview; X for staff in learning partnerships and Regional Development Agencies; Y for European officials; and Z for officials of other national, regional and local organisations.

The learning sites, 2004–6

While the policy interviews provided essential background to the intentions and processes of policy-making, the evidence of impact (or lack of impact) could only be found in the sites where learning takes place. Data were collected from learners, tutors and course managers in twenty-four learning sites, twelve each in London and the North East of England. In each of these two regions we visited four FE (two Level 1 courses and two Level 2 courses), four ACL and four WBL sites.

The reasons for the choice of learning sites merit further discussion. First, the two regions in which we collected data are very different, in their local economy, their labour markets, their skill profiles and their demographies. Second, the sites we chose were recommended, either by LSC officials or by college senior managers, as places where we might find 'good practice'. We were often impressed by the quality of teaching and learning in the sites, but are aware that we cannot generalise from this to all similar provision. Third, we opted for depth, rather than breadth, making repeated visits to twenty-four sites to monitor change and learn how policy was received over time, rather than investigating a larger sample of tutors, managers and learners. Our schedule planned 104 visits, four to each ACL and WBL site, and five to each FE site. This strategy gave us a far better understanding of challenges facing tutors, managers and learners than making single visits to 104 different sites could have done. Nevertheless, twenty-four learning sites represent only a drop in the ocean in the vast learning and skills sector.

In all, we made 102 visits; two planned visits, one to each of two WBL sites, were replaced by a telephone call at the request of their staff. On each visit, typically we interviewed up to six learners, their tutor and the manager of their course, including, in the WBL sites, union learning representatives (ULRs) and line managers involved in the initiative. Box A.2 shows the numbers of interviews, which have been transcribed and used in the analysis.

The learners on FE sites were studying for Level 1 qualifications in Health and Social Care or Childcare, or for Level 2 qualifications in Business Studies or Painting and Decorating. Although our choice of sites was influenced by recommendations of senior managers and LSC staff, this sample provided a good mix of courses with a very clear vocational destination (e.g., Childcare) and others, such as Business Studies, which have been described as 'weakly vocational' (Stanton 2004), attracting learners with more diffuse career goals, and taught by staff with a broader range of work experience.

Box A.2 Interviews in learning sites, spring 2004–summer 2006

Site type	Learners*	Tutors and managers	Workplace managers and ULRs	Total
FE Levels				
1 and 2	168	81	–	**249**
ACL	92	59	–	**151**
WBL	89	44	26	**159**
Total	**349**	**184**	**26**	**559**

Note: *Figures in this column indicate number of learner participants, in 333 group and individual interviews.

As discussed in Chapter 3, we met three cohorts of FE learners on our visits. On the first visit in spring 2004 we held group interviews with classes of learners nearing the end of their course; on subsequent visits in 2004–5 (visits 2 and 3) and 2005–6 (visits 4 and 5) we aimed to talk individually to the same six learners in the first few weeks of their one-year course, and then again the following summer when they could report on their personal experiences of the course. This pattern revealed tremendous growth in confidence in some students, and also allowed us to ask the tutor to review expectations of achievement and progression for the whole group. Our interviews with learners centred on their personal experience of learning there, and clearly we did not ask them to discuss government policy and its impact on their learning; but we did, for example, ask directly about the Education Maintenance Allowance (EMA) and gleaned data about its usefulness to those who received it and the resentment of some of those who did not.

We used observation, as well as interviewing. On our fourth visit, we observed a classroom session for most of the groups, seeing at first hand, for example, the challenges of teaching a class with several support staff in attendance, because a majority of learners required learning support or physical assistance. We saw the patient efforts required to encourage everyone to participate fully, and the mutual support among learners. Seeing tutors and learners working together also confirmed for us the importance of this relationship, which both parties had talked about in interviews. On our final visit, we also asked learners to show us their portfolios of work completed over the year, as a visual aid to demonstrate their progress, and also to let us to see the feedback on assignments which had helped them to this point.

In interviews with FE staff (see also Chapter 5), we explored their perceptions of the impact of policy, both on their own work and on learning and inclusion for their learners. Areas of questioning in the semi-structured interviews included:

- key challenges of working with Levels 1 and 2 learners;
- factors which impact on teaching, learning, retention and progression, both helping and hindering (including the national policy levers, such as funding and targets, and also other factors that tutors considered significant);
- changes affecting their teaching and changes they would have liked to see;
- whether they were able to make changes to their teaching of their own choosing, and what those changes were; and
- college policies for supporting learning and inclusion for Levels 1 and 2 learners, and learning for the staff who taught them.

We also used the interviews to feed back our analysis of data previously collected on that site, and of themes emerging from the project as a whole.

On our four visits to the ACL and WBL sites, we aimed to speak to a tutor, a manager and up to six learners, although we often found fewer learners available on the day, especially in centres where drop-in provision was the norm. In WBL sites, we also spoke to ULRs and to line managers or training managers based in the workplace, who could give us insights into how supportive that workplace culture was for employees' learning. Patterns of basic skills courses, sometimes in weekly twilight classes, sometimes drop-in sessions, sometimes intensive weeks of preparation for taking a national test, also made it impossible for us to interview learners at the beginning and end of their courses in the way we had done in FE colleges, although we did follow up learners in these sites where it was possible. Data from adult learners here were rich in reasons for deciding to improve their basic skills and in their appreciation of tutor support. Staff interview schedules used in colleges were adapted to suit the other settings.

Although the challenges of working with adult basic skills learners were different from those presented by the younger FE learners, there was much common ground to explore, about the impact of policy levers and other factors on teaching, learning, retention and progression. Predictably, much of the discussion of change in ACL and WBL settings centred on Skills for Life, its funding mechanisms and associated staff qualification requirements.

Finally, since we have used pseudonyms for the sites and alphabetic codes to distinguish individual interviewees, we list in Box A.3 the pseudonyms and codes for the three categories of sites. Codes used when citing individual interviewees also indicate the role of the speaker: thus, A2M1 indicates the first manager we interviewed for the Level 2 course at Alder College; HT2, the second tutor we interviewed at Hammerend; OU1, the first ULR interviewed at Oakenshaw; and SL6, the sixth learner at Southern Transport.

Box A.3 Pseudonyms of learning sites

Site type	Pseudonym (Code)
FE Level 1	Alder College (A1); Beechtree College (B1); Central College (C1); District College (D1)
FE Level 2	Alder College (A2); Beechtree College (B2); Central College (C2); District College (D2)
ACL	Eastway Learners (E); Forest Community Centre (F); Greensward Adult and Community Learning (G); Hammerend Adult Basic Education (H); Island Estate (I); Junior School Centre (J); Kingsbury Rise Centre (K); Lawnview Centre (L)
WBL	Moorcroft Depot (M); Nutmeg Products (N); Oakenshaw Works (O); Pondgate Services (P); Queensfield Training (Q); Roundview Carers (R); Southern Transport (S); Top Training (T)

The online survey, 2007

The final stage of data collection was an online survey in spring 2007. In this we aimed to test our findings by canvassing the views of a broader range of policy-makers, officials and practitioners. The questionnaire was constructed around twenty-one of our provisional key findings, agreed within the team when our analysis was almost complete; and a further eight more tentative statements about what local learning systems might look like in the future. The findings related to the impact of policy on teaching, learning and assessment; on inclusion; on staff and institutional behaviour; and on governance in the LSS. Respondents indicated their level of agreement with each statement and commented on their reasons for agreement or disagreement. We received 102 responses, analysed in a research report (Steer and Lakey 2007).

The survey fulfilled multiple functions within our methodology, stimulating analysis and debate within the team in the long process of agreeing its contents; feeding back to respondents, both policy-makers and practitioners, some of our most important emergent findings; confirming those findings for the respondents and testing them, on a small scale, with a wider sample of their colleagues in regions other than London and the North East; and allowing us to collect further data from their comments on our statements. Of the 21 findings, 17 were agreed with by 70 per cent or more of the respondents, with 90 per cent or more agreeing with 3 of the statements. The explanatory comments have enriched our qualitative data, with the responses to the questions about possibilities for future learning systems proving particularly useful in constructing a model of an effective and inclusive learning system.

Features of our methodology

We tried to learn from the experience of other TLRP projects, and, in particular, Transforming Learning Cultures in FE (TLC), which started three years before us and had a similar focus on learning sites, although it covered 19 FE sites with a team of 14, while we had 24 sites in colleges, the community and workplaces, and a team of 6. We read their methodological papers (Hodkinson and James 2003; Hodkinson *et al.* 2005a) and discussed shared problems of analysis with Phil Hodkinson. Our projects had one major issue in common: our aspiration to increase the capability of FE and LSC staff to undertake research was thwarted by recurrent funding crises in those organisations. While we have not published case studies of individual practitioners or sites, as they have (e.g., Wahlberg and Gleeson 2003), we consciously built on some aspects of their work, particularly in relation to the synthesis of data 'through a series of stages' (Hodkinson *et al.* 2005a: 5). In our project, this meant analysing the data systematically, by site, by sector and by role. In these systematic comparisons, we were working within the traditions and procedures of grounded theory (Strauss and Corbin 1998; Silverman 2001). Although our project was primarily about looking at the whole system, and the interactions between policy and practice, we noted the differing learning cultures in our learning sites, and the differing professional responses of staff. In the TLC project, the emphasis was reversed, with the impact of policy on practice being in the background and cultural approaches to learning in the foreground.

We turn now to describe in more detail those four important features of our approach which we highlighted in Chapter 2, because they strengthen our confidence in our findings:

* repeated visits by the same small team of researchers;
* analysis of learning site data by site, by sector and by role;
* feeding back interim findings to participants, for corroboration or challenge;
* bringing together participants from different levels or parts of the sector who would not normally have a chance to meet.

Repeated visits

Both in the North East and in London, the research officer and at least one of the directors took responsibility for conducting all visits to any one site. We therefore became familiar to – and, we hope, trusted by – staff in those sites with low turnover, and we were able to keep track of the changes in those where staff left and were replaced. Staff turnover varied widely: in several ACL and WBL sites and one of our eight FE sites we found the same manager and tutor in place throughout the five visits, but in another college we interviewed four different managers for one course, all of whom occupied that post within the space of two years. In other settings we sometimes found the same people, but learned that the management structures above them had changed, because of local authority restructuring.

We also found changes in their concerns. In ACL sites, for example, the dominant concerns in the early visits were the introduction and availability of Skills for Life materials and the requirement for staff to acquire Level 4 qualifications in literacy or numeracy. On later visits, these concerns had receded, to be replaced, for example, by anxiety about changes in the way funding was allocated, about cuts to adult budgets and about staffing problems. In WBL sites the repeated visits highlighted the huge problem of sustainability of funding for workplace provision. While some sites moved forward, as workplace management took over responsibility for funding what had previously been made possible by the Union Learning Fund or Employer Training Pilot/Train to Gain funding, in others we saw a loss of momentum after the first wave of employees had gained their national tests and employers were unwilling to continue to support courses financially.

Iterative data analysis

Data analysis could not have been left until the end of the project. The first batch of policy interviews in 2004 was analysed using NVivo and led to a consultation paper which, after comments from the interviewees and other colleagues to whom it was sent, became our first research report (Hodgson *et al.* 2005) and the basis of a journal article (Coffield *et al.* 2005). By summer 2005, we had completed two visits to ACL and WBL sites and three to the FE sites, and a keynote symposium at the British Educational Research Association (BERA) conference in September 2005 provided the spur to analyse data up to that point. Three papers from that symposium, after being sent out to research participants for consultation, were made available as research reports, and have since become the basis, after substantial updating, of published papers on policy (Finlay *et al.* 2007b), staff views (Edward *et al.* 2007) and learners (Hodgson *et al.* 2007c).

The most intensive period of analysis of learning site data was in spring 2006. Between the penultimate site visit in autumn 2005 and the final visit in summer 2006, the whole research team was immersed in data analysis, site by site, and each of the six of us, four part-time directors and two full-time research officers, produced between two and seven reports, giving us a full set of twenty-four. The next stage was collaboration between the North East and London 'sub-teams': for example, the lead researchers on London ACL sites and North East ACL sites worked together to produce a summary of emerging themes, similarities and differences in the learning site data, and subsequently went on to produce a paper for BERA in 2006, later revised for publication (Hodgson *et al.* 2007a). The corresponding papers on FE (Spours *et al.* 2007) and WBL (Finlay *et al.* 2007a) had a similar genesis, and the paper by Steer *et al.* (2007) on policy levers also arose from this analysis.

Feedback on interim findings

In addition to the formal consultation process for our research reports, we valued informal feedback on emergent findings. The continuity in the researchers visiting the sites ensured that we could discuss our previous visits with participants. The most extensive use of formal feedback was on our final visit to each site. Summaries of the reports prepared in spring 2006 were sent to managers and tutors in advance of our final site visit, and were well received by staff, who brought them up to date, rather than contradicted or challenged them. That overwhelmingly positive response increases the 'warrant' of our findings.

A striking feature of the data in all three strands was the number, diversity and importance of factors interviewees identified as having impact on their practice and on learning. Unsurprisingly, the main policy levers – funding, targets, inspection, planning and initiatives such as Skills for Life – were frequently mentioned; these were not, however, always seen as the most important factors affecting day-to-day practice. Among tutors, and some managers, meeting learners' needs was seen as a far more influential factor. To check this finding, at a team meeting where we discussed the findings of the three 'sub-teams' working on FE, ACL and WBL, we produced three diagrams as a stimulus for further discussion with interviewees on our final visit. An example, the ACL diagram, is shown as Figure A.1.

Large arrows indicate strong impact, and the powerful link between Skills for Life, targets and funding; the smaller arrows indicate that inspection and planning were seen as less important. Consequently, we had two feedback documents to show on our final fieldwork visits – a summary report relating solely to that site, and a diagram which represented findings from all eight similar sites – so that interviewees could comment further on the impact of these levers. This proved productive: some details and qualifications were added, and the diagrams stimulated debate, both in our learning site visits and subsequently in our summer seminars in 2006. Some tutors suggested that the 'Learners' needs' arrow should be significantly larger than all the others.

Finally, in this context, the online survey also met our goal of maximising feedback, providing a final opportunity to check our understandings, both with participants and with a wider audience.

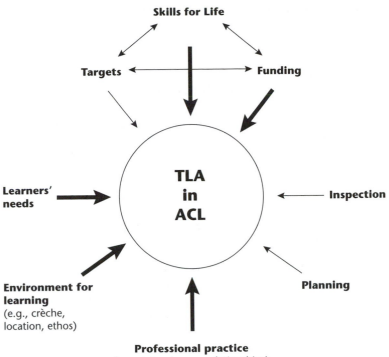

Figure A.1 Impact of factors on teaching, learning and assessment in eight ACL sites

Bringing participants together

The value of bringing practitioners and policy staff together at our seminars has already been mentioned as an example of data that goes beyond what could be obtained by interviews. Seminars were useful in many ways. They allowed practitioners doing similar work in different settings to meet and talk; and gave them access to officials whom they would never meet in the normal course of their work. One unintended consequence was that one of our participants heard for the first time at one of our seminars about the opportunity to become a Standards Unit subject coach – and subsequently went on to train for that role. For policy officials, the seminars provided opportunities to listen directly to the concerns of practitioners, and to explain their own intentions. For the research team, they provided opportunities to bring alive data which had been collected at the other end of the country by meeting participants whom we should otherwise have known only through their transcripts. And, above all, they allowed us to present emergent findings for discussion, challenge or confirmation. Diagrams (such as Figure A.1) which we had discussed with interviewees on learning sites were also aired and further debated at our 2006 seminars. The real value of these events, however, lies not in the fact that participants talked to, or listened to, *us*, but in the fact that they talked to, and listened to, *one another*. The 2005 seminars, which included ten-minute personal statements by three practitioners, speaking directly to their colleagues and any officials who were present, were particularly successful.

Do we have confidence in our findings and conclusions?

Returning to the aim and objectives set out at the beginning of this Appendix, we are confident that we have covered the ground. With a total of nearly 700 interviews with over 500 individual participants, documentary analysis, an online survey, observations, project seminars and a policy of airing our developing ideas in conferences and consultation papers, we have considerable confidence in the picture we have painted of the roles and relationships in the sector and the impact of policy on the three groups of learners and those who teach them. This has been achieved despite the fact that many features of 'the new LSS' envisaged when the project was planned back in 2003 have changed almost beyond recognition. We have involved participants as much as possible, in face-to-face discussions and seminars, and have given them further opportunities to comment, in the survey, on elements of our model of an effective and inclusive learning system. Our tentative conclusions were aired at our two final project conferences, in June 2007 in Newcastle and in London that July, and participants' comments there have helped us to refine those findings.

Within our multi-disciplinary team, we have subjected all our published outputs to rigorous internal scrutiny and debate. This process has continued in the writing of this book, for although each of the six of us has taken responsibility for the initial drafting of one or more of the chapters, all of us have commented on and contributed to drafts at every stage. We have also engaged throughout the project with the policy-making community – for example, by holding a meeting with the Prime Minister's Strategy Unit about public service reform, and by submitting evidence to the Foster Review, and Frank Coffield was invited to give evidence to the House of Commons Select Committee on Education and Skills in 2007. The objective that we might help build research capacity in the sector by including FE staff in the research team proved impossible, because of financial constraints on the organisations that had hoped to collaborate with us. We have, however, been able to interrogate the meaning, use and influence of a number of policy terms in published papers, including 'learners at the heart of the system' (Finlay *et al.* 2007b) and 'best practice' (Coffield and Edward forthcoming).

Bibliography

Adult Learning Inspectorate (ALI) (2006a) *Annual Report of Chief Inspector*, Coventry: ALI.

—— (2006b) Inspection statistics. Available online at: <http://www.ali.gov.uk/Inspection/Inspection+statistics> (accessed 7 November 2006).

Ainley, P. (2000) 'Missing the point about the Learning and Skills Council, a comment on Coffield', *Journal of Education Policy*, 15 (5): 585–8.

—— (2004) 'The new "market-state" and education', *Journal of Education Policy*, 19 (4): 497–514.

Aldridge, F. and Tuckett, A. (2006) *Green Shoots? The NIACE Survey on Adult Participation in Learning 2006*, Leicester: NIACE.

Alexander, R. (2006) *Education as Dialogue: moral and pedagogical choices for a runaway world*, London: Dialogos/Hong Kong: Institute of Education.

Arrowsmith, R. (2006) 'Look back in anger', *Education Guardian*, 8 August.

Avis, J. (2003) 'Rethinking trust in a performative culture: the case of post compulsory education', *Journal of Educational Policy*, 18 (3): 315–32.

Barber, M. (2007) *Instruction to Deliver: Tony Blair, public services and the challenge of achieving targets*, London: Methuen.

Bathmaker, A. (2001) 'Neither dupes nor devils: teachers' constructions of their changing role in further education', paper presented at the fifth Annual Conference of the Learning and Skills Research Network, Cambridge, 5–7 December.

Bell, C. and Raffe, D. (1991) 'Working together? Research, policy and practice: the experience of the Scottish evaluation of TVEI', in G. Walford (ed.) *Doing Educational Research*, London: Routledge.

Bernstein, B. (1996) *Pedagogy, Symbolic Control and Identity: theory, research, critique*, London: Taylor & Francis.

Blair, T. (1996) *The Singapore Speech*. Available online at: <http://www.psa.org.nz/library/psa/02%20partnership%20for%20quality%20materials/tony%20blair%20-%20the%20singapore%20speech%201996.doc> (accessed 12 July 2007).

Blears, H. (2005) 'Foreword', in *New Localism in Action: An NLGN Collection*,

London: NLGN. Available online at: <http://www.nlgn.org.uk/mod_ media_releases.php?article=168> (accessed 2 January 2007).

Bloomer, M. and Hodkinson, P. (1997) *Moving into FE: the voice of the learner*, London: Further Education Development Agency.

Blunkett, D. (2000) *Remit Letter to Learning and Skills Council*, London: DfES.

Bowe, R., Ball, S.J. and Gold, A. (1992) *Reforming Education and Changing Schools: case studies in policy sociology*, London: Routledge.

Boyd, S. (2002) *Partnership Working: European social partnership models*, Glasgow: Scottish TUC.

Bronfenbrenner, U. (1979) *The Ecology of Human Development: experiments by nature and design*, Cambridge, MA: Harvard University Press.

Brooks G., Davies R., Ducke L., Hutchinson. D., Kendall, S. and Wilkin, A. (2001) *Progress in Adult Literacy: do learners learn?*, London: Basic Skills Agency.

Brown N., Coney, M. and Stanton, G. (2004) *Breaking out of the Silos: 14–30 education and skills policies*, London: Nigel Brown Associates.

Bruner, J. (1996) *The Culture of Education*, Cambridge, MA: Harvard University Press.

Cabinet Office (2006) *Reaching Out: an action plan on social exclusion*. Available online at: <http://www.cabinetoffice.gov.uk/social_exclusion_task_force/ documents/reaching_out/intro_forewords.pdf> (accessed 22 May 2007).

—— (2007) *Machinery of Government: departmental organisation*, London: Cabinet Office.

Carvel, J. (2007) 'Thinking out of the tickbox', *Society Guardian*, 18 July.

Castells, M. (1998) *End of Millennium*, Vol. III, Oxford: Blackwell.

Caulkin, S. (2007) 'Labour's decade, the best and worst of times', *Observer*, 29 April.

Centre for Research in Social Policy and Institute for Fiscal Studies (2005) *Evaluation of Education Maintenance Allowance Pilots: young people aged 16 to 19 years – final report of the quantitative evaluation*, DfES Research Report No. 678, Annesley: DfES.

City of Birmingham (2007) *Democratic Services*. Available online at: <http:// www.birmingham.gov.uk/text/GenerateContent?CONTENT_ITEM_ID=155 39&CONTENT_ITEM_TYPE=0&MENU_ID=311> (accessed 12 January 2007).

Clarke, J. and Newman, J. (1997) *The Managerial State*, London: Sage.

Clarke, K. (2007) *An End to Sofa Government: better working of Prime Minister and Cabinet*, Conservative Party Democracy Taskforce. Available online at: <http://www.conservatives.com/tile.do?def=democracy.taskforce.page> (accessed 12 January 2007).

Coffield, F. (1992) 'Training and Enterprise Councils: the last throw of voluntarism?', *Policy Studies*, 13 (4): 11–32.

—— (2007) 'Running ever faster down the wrong road: an alternative future for education and skills', inaugural lecture, 5 December 2006, published London: Institute of Education, University of London.

Coffield, F. and Edward S. (forthcoming) 'Rolling out "good", "best" and "excellent" practice. What next? Perfect practice?', *British Educational Research Journal.*

Coffield, F., Steer, R., Hodgson, A., Spours, K., Edward, S. and Finlay, I. (2005) 'A new learning and skills landscape? The central role of the Learning and Skills Council', *Journal of Education Policy*, 20 (5): 631–56.

Coffield, F., Edward, S., Finlay, I., Hodgson, A., Spours, K., Steer, R. and Gregson, M. (2007) 'How policy impacts on practice and how practice does not impact on policy', *British Educational Research Journal*, 33 (5): 723–41.

Colley, H., Hodkinson, P. and Malcolm, J. (2003) *Informality and Formality in Learning: a report for the Learning and Skills Research Centre*, London: LSDA.

Commission of the European Communities (CEC) (2006a) *Efficiency and Equity in European Education and Training Systems*, COM (2006) 481 final, Brussels: Office for Official Publications of the European Communities.

—— (2006b) *Efficiency and Equity in European Education and Training Systems*, COM (2006) 481 final, accompanying Commission Staff Working Document, Brussels: Office for Official Publications of the European Communities.

—— (2006c) *The History of European Co-operation in Education and Training: Europe in the making – an example*, Brussels: Office for Official Publications of the European Communities.

Crowther, J. and Tett, L. (1997) 'Literacies not literacy learning', *Adults Learning*, 8 (8): 207–9.

Davis, J. (2007) 'Doctors don't want golf – they want empowerment', *Guardian*, 24 April.

Department for Communities and Local Government (DCLG) (2006) *Strong and Prosperous Communities: the local government White Paper*, Cm 6939, London: DCLG.

Department for Education and Employment (DfEE) (1998) *The Learning Age*, London: The Stationery Office.

—— (1999) *Learning to Succeed: a new framework for post-16 learning*, Cm 4392, London: The Stationery Office.

—— (2001) *Skills for Life: the national strategy for improving adult literacy and numeracy skills*, Annesley: DfEE.

Department for Education and Skills (DfES) (2002) *Success for All: reforming further education and training*, London: DfES.

—— (2004) *Five Year Strategy for Children and Learners: putting people at the heart of public services*, Cm 6272, London: The Stationery Office.

—— (2005a) *14–19 Education and Skills*, London: DfES.

—— (2005b) *Evaluation of the Employer Training Pilot Skills for Life Interventions Programme*, DfES Research Report RW26, London: Carol Goldstone Associates.

—— (2006a) *Delivering the Further Education (FE) Book for Facts*, London: DfES.

—— (2006b) *Further Education: raising skills, improving life chances*, Cm 6768, London: The Stationery Office.

—— (2006c) *The Five Year Strategy for Children and Learners: maintaining the excellent progress*, Annesley: DfES.

—— (2007a) *1.5M Learners Beat Their Skills Gremlins and Gain Qualifications as Government Hits Target*, press release. Available online at: <http://www.dfes.gov.uk/pns/DisplayPN/.cgi?pn_id=2007_0027> (accessed 23 March 2007).

—— (2007b) *New Centres for Excellence in Teacher Training*, press notice, 4 May, London: DfES.

—— (2007c) *Raising Expectations: staying on in education and training post-16*, London: DfES.

Department for Innovation, Universities and Skills (DIUS) (2007) *Increased Support for Students in Higher Education*, press release, 5 July. Available online at: <http://www.dius.gov.uk/pressreleases/press-release-20070705.htm> (accessed 16 July 2007).

Devine, P., Permain, A., Prior, M. and Purdy, D. (2007) 'Feel-bad Britain: a view from the democratic left', *Hegemonics*. Available online at: <http://hegemonics.co.uk> (accessed 17 July 2007).

Dixit, A. (2002) 'Incentives and organizations in the public sector: an interpretative review', *Journal of Human Resources*, 37: 696–727.

Dworkin, R. (2000) *Sovereign Virtue: the theory and practice of equality*, Cambridge, MA: Harvard University Press.

Ecclestone, K. (2005) *Understanding Assessment and Qualifications in Post-Compulsory Education and Training: principles, politics and practice*, 2nd edn, Leicester: NIACE.

Edward, S., Coffield, F., Steer, R. and Gregson, M. (2007) 'Endless change in the learning and skills sector: the impact on teaching staff', *Journal of Vocational Education and Training*, 59 (2): 155–73.

Eldred, J. (2002) *Moving on with Confidence: perceptions of success in teaching and learning adult literacy*, Leicester: NIACE.

Engineering Employers Federation (EEF) (2006) *Learning to Change: why the UK skills system must do better*, London: EEF.

Entwistle, N.J. (1998) 'Improving teaching through research on student learning', in J.J.F. Forrest (ed.) *University Teaching: international perspectives*, New York: Garland.

Equalities Review (2007) *Fairness and Freedom: the final report of the Equalities Review*, Wetherby: Communities and Local Government Publications.

Eraut, M. (1994) *Developing Professional Knowledge and Competence*, London: Falmer.

Etzioni, A. (ed.) (1969) *The Semi-Professions and Their Organization*, New York: Free Press.

Evans, K., Hodkinson, P., Rainbird, H. and Unwin, L. (2006) *Improving Workplace Learning*, London: Routledge.

Finegold, D. (1999) 'Creating self-sustaining, high-skill ecosystems', *Oxford Review of Economic Policy*, 15 (1): 60–81.

Finlay, I., Hodgson, A. and Steer, R. (2007a) 'Flowers in the desert: the impact of policy on basic skills provision in the workplace', *Journal of Vocational Education and Training*, 59 (2): 231–48.

Finlay, I., Spours, K., Steer, R., Coffield, F., Gregson, A. and Hodgson, A. (2007b) '"The heart of what we do": policies in teaching, learning and assessment in the new learning and skills sector', *Journal of Vocational Education and Training*, 59 (2): 137–53.

Fletcher, M. (2007) 'On funding, it's sticks for the poor and carrots for the rich', *Education Guardian*, 10 July.

Fletcher, M. and Owen, G. (2005) *The Funding Gap: funding in schools and colleges for full-time students aged 16–18*, London: LSDA.

Ford, L. (2007) 'London to get £15m extra for English teaching', *Guardian Unlimited*, 4 May.

Foster, A. (2005) *Realising the Potential: a review of the future role of further education colleges*, London: DfES.

Fullan, M. (1991) *The New Meaning of Educational Change*, London: Cassell.

—— (1993) *Change Forces: probing the depths of educational reform*, London: Falmer.

Fullick, L. (2004) *Adult Learners in a Brave New World: lifelong learning policy and structural changes since 1997*, Leicester: NIACE.

Fullick, L., Grainger, P., Hodgson, A., Spours, K., Truelove, J. and Waring, M. (2007) *14–19 Partnership Working in London: towards inclusive and effective local and regional collaborative learning systems*, London: Institute of Education, University of London.

Gleeson, D., Davies, J. and Wheeler, E. (2005) 'On the making and taking of professionalism in the further education workplace', *British Journal of Sociology of Education*, 26 (4): 445–60.

Grace, G. (1995) *School Leadership: beyond educational management, an essay in policy scholarship*, London: Falmer.

Grainger, P., Hodgson, A. and Spours, K. (2007) 'A pan-London approach to 14–19 learning: a figment of the imagination or potential reality?', in T. Brighouse and L. Fullick (eds) *Education in a Global City – essays from London*, Bedford Way Papers, London: Institute of Education, University of London.

Gravatt, J. (2007) 'Leitch is proposing nothing less than a revolution in the way adult learning is funded', *Adults Learning*, 18 (5): 20.

Green, A. (2006) 'Models of lifelong learning and the knowledge economy/society in Europe: what regional patterns are emerging?', in M. Kuhn and R.G. Sultana (eds) *Homo Sapiens Europaeus: creating the European learning citizen*, New York: Peter Lang.

Green, A., Hodgson, A. and Williams, G. (2000) *Where Are the Resources for Lifelong Learning?*, Paris: OECD.

Grubb, W.N. (1999) *Honored but Invisible: an inside look at teaching in community colleges*, New York: Routledge.

Hall, S. (2003) 'New Labour's double shuffle', *Soundings*. Available online at: <http://www.lwbooks.co.uk/journals/articles/nov03.html> (accessed 9 July 2007).

Hamilton, M. (2007) 'Reflections on agency and change in the policy process', *Journal of Vocational Education and Training*, 59 (2): 249–60.

Hamilton, M. and Hillier, Y. (2006) *Changing Faces of Adult Literacy, Language and Numeracy: a critical history*, Stoke-on-Trent: Trentham.

Hanberger, A. (2006) 'Democratic accountability in decentralised government', paper presented to the Conference on the Interpretative Practitioner: From Critique to Practice in Public Policy Analysis, Birmingham University, 8–10 June. Available online at: <http://www.inlogov.bham.ac.uk/june%2006%20conference/conference%20papers.htm> (accessed 2 January 2007).

Hargreaves, D.H. and Hopkins, D. (1991) *The Empowered School: the management and practice of development planning*, London: Cassell.

Hayward, G., Hodgson, A., Johnson, J., Oancea, A., Pring, R., Spours, K., Wright, S. and Wilde, S. (2005) *Annual Report of the Nuffield 14–19 Review 2004–5*, Oxford: OUDES.

Hayward, G., Hodgson, A., Johnson, J., Keep, E., Oancea, A., Pring, R., Spours, K., Wright, S. and Wilde, S. (2006) *Annual Report of the Nuffield 14–19 Review 2005–6*, Oxford: OUDES.

Heald, O. (2006) 'Giving responsibility to local people and local communities', speech to the Conservative Party Conference, 12 October. Available online at: <http://www.conservatives.com/tile.do?def=news.story.page&obj_id=132927&speeches=1> (accessed 8 November 2007).

Her Majesty's Government (HMG) (2005) *Skills: getting on in business, getting on in work*, London: The Stationery Office.

—— (2006) *Further Education and Training Bill*, London: The Stationery Office.

Her Majesty's Treasury (HMT) (2006) *Budget 2006: a strong and strengthening economy: investing in Britain's future*, HC968, London: The Stationery Office.

Higham, J. and Yeomans, D. (2007) 'Policy memory and policy amnesia in 14–19 education: learning from the past?', in D. Raffe and K. Spours (eds) *Policy-Making and Policy Learning in 14–19 Education*, Bedford Way Papers, London: Institute of Education, University of London.

Hill, D. (1999) *New Labour and Education: policy, ideology and the third way*, London: Tufnell Press.

Hillage, J. and Mitchell, H. (2003) *Evaluation of Employer Training Pilots*, London: DfES/HMT/LSC.

Hillage, J., Loukas, G., Newton, B. and Tamkin, P. (2006) *Employer Training Pilots*, final evaluation report, London: DfES.

Hodgson, A. and Spours, K. (1999) *New Labour's Education Agenda: issues and policies for education and training from 14+*, London: Kogan Page.

—— (2003) *Beyond A Levels: Curriculum 2000 and the reform of 14–19 qualifications*, London: Kogan Page.

—— (2006) 'The organization of 14–19 education and training in England: beyond weakly collaborative arrangements', *Journal of Education and Work*, 19 (4): 325–42.

—— (2007) 'Specialised diplomas: transforming the 14–19 landscape in England?', *Journal of Education Policy*, 22 (6): 657–74.

Hodgson, A., Edward, S. and Gregson, M. (2007a) 'Riding the waves of policy? The case of basic skills in adult and community learning in England', *Journal of Vocational Education and Training*, 59 (2): 213–29.

Hodgson, A., Spours, K. and Wilson, P. (2006) *Tomlinson and the Framework for Achievement: a unified answer to a divided system*, Leicester: NIACE.

Hodgson, A., Spours, K., Coffield, F., Steer, R., Finlay, I., Edward, S. and Gregson, M. (2005) *A New Learning and Skills Landscape? The LSC within the learning and skills sector*, ESRC TLRP Project Research Report 1, London: Institute of Education, University of London.

Hodgson, A., Spours, K., Steer, R., Coffield, F., Edward, S., Finlay, I. and Gregson, M. (2007b) *A Seismic Shift: policy actor perspectives on the changing learning and skills landscape*, ESRC TLRP Project Research Report 5, London: Institute of Education, University of London.

Hodgson, A., Steer, R., Spours, K., Edward, S., Coffield, F., Finlay, I. and Gregson, M. (2007c) 'Learners in the learning and skills sector: the implications of half-right policy assumptions', *Oxford Review of Education*, 33 (3): 315–30.

Hodkinson, P. (2005) 'Making improvement through research possible: the need for radical changes in the FE system', paper presented at West Yorkshire Learning and Skills Research Network Conference, Leeds, 8 July.

Hodkinson, P. and Bloomer, M. (2002) 'Learning careers: conceptualizing lifelong work-based learning', in K. Evans, P. Hodkinson and L. Unwin (eds) *Working to Learn: transforming learning in the workplace*, London: Kogan Page.

Hodkinson, P. and James, D. (2003) 'Transforming learning cultures in further education', *Journal of Vocational Education and Training*, 55 (4): 389–406.

Hodkinson, P., Biesta, G., Gleeson, D., James, D. and Postlethwaite, K. (2005a) 'The heuristic and holistic synthesis of large volumes of qualitative data: the TLC experience', paper presented at RCBN 2005 Annual Conference, Cardiff, 22 February.

Hodkinson, P., Biesta, G., James, D., Gleeson, D. and Postlethwaite, K. (2005b) *Improving Learning in Further Education: a new cultural approach*, TLRP Research Briefing 12, London: TLRP.

Hooker, B. (2005) 'Fairness', in T. Honderich (ed.) *Oxford Companion to Philosophy*, Oxford: Oxford University Press.

House of Commons Education and Skills Committee (HoC) (2007) *14–19 Diplomas*, Fifth Report of Session 2006–07, HC 249, London: The Stationery Office.

House of Commons Select Committee on Education and Skills (HoC) (2006) *Examination of Witnesses (Questions 540–559)*, Minutes of Evidence, 15 March. Available online at: <http://www.publications.parliament.uk/pa/cm200506/cmselect/cmeduski/649/6031505.htm> (accessed 5 July 2007).

Hoyle, E. and John, P. (1995) *Professional Knowledge and Professional Practice*, London: Cassell.

Hyman, P. (2005) *1 out of 10: from Downing Street vision to classroom reality*, London: Vintage.

James, D. and Biesta, G. (2007) (eds) *Improving Learning Cultures in Further Education*, London: Routledge.

James, D. and Diment, K. (2003) 'Going underground? Learning and assessment in an ambiguous space', *Journal of Vocational Education and Training*, 55 (40): 407–22.

James, M. (ed.) (2006) *Learning How to Learn: tools for schools*, London: Routledge.

Johnson, T. (1972) *Professions and Power*, London: Macmillan.

Keep, E. (2006) 'State control of the English education and training system: playing with the biggest train set in the world', *Journal of Vocational Education and Training*, 58 (1): 47–64.

Kooiman, J. (2003) *Governing as Governance*, London: Sage.

Lave, J. and Wenger, E. (1991) *Situated Learning: legitimate peripheral participation*, Cambridge: Cambridge University Press.

Lawson, N. (2005) 'Dare more democracy: from steam-age politics to democratic self-government', *Compass*. Available online at: <http://www.compasson line.org.uk/publications.asp> (accessed 2 January 2007).

Learning and Skills Council (LSC) (2004a) *Concordat on Future Working between the Regional Development Agencies and the Learning and Skills Council*, Coventry: LSC.

—— (2004b) *Extending Trust: bureaucracy task force final report*, May, Coventry: LSC.

—— (2004c) *Quality Improvement Strategy to 2006*, Coventry: LSC.

—— (2004d) *Shaping a Better Future: the new Learning and Skills Council business cycle*, Coventry: LSC.

—— (2004e) *The Learning and Skills Council Announces a New Regional Management Structure*, press release, 7 January, Coventry: LSC.

—— (2005a) *Further Education, Work Based Learning for Young People and Adult and Community Learning: learner numbers in England 2004/2005*, National Statistics first release, Coventry: LSC.

—— (2005b) *Learning and Skills: the agenda for change*, Coventry: LSC.

—— (2006a) *Delivering Learning and Skills: progress report 2006*, Coventry: LSC.

—— (2006b) *Framework for Excellence: a comprehensive performance assessment framework for the further education system*, Coventry: LSC.

—— (2006c) *National Learner Satisfaction Survey: adult and community learning 2004/05*, Coventry: LSC.

—— (2006d) *National Learner Satisfaction Survey: further education 2004/05*, Coventry: LSC.

—— (2006e) *National Learner Satisfaction Survey: work-based learning 2004/05*, Coventry: LSC.

—— (2006f) *Record Numbers of 16–18 Year Olds in Training: Education Maintenance Allowance helps to boost participation in learning*, press release, 8 June, Coventry: LSC. Available online at: <http://readingroom.lsc.gov.uk/ LSC/2006/externalrelations/press/nat-recordnumbersof1618yearolds intraining-pr-june2006.pdf> (accessed 5 July 2007).

—— (2007a) *Apprenticeship Completions 2002/03 to 2005/06*, Coventry: LSC. Available online at: <http://www.lsc.gov.uk/providers/Data/statistics/ learner/Apprenticeship_completions.htm> (accessed 19 July 2007).

—— (2007b) *EMA Learner Numbers to June 2007*, Coventry: LSC. Available online at: <http://www.lsc.gov.uk/providers/Data/statistics/learner/ EMA_take_up.htm> (accessed 16 July 2007).

—— (2007c) *Record Success Rates in Further Education*, press release, 17 April, Coventry: LSC. Available online at: <http://readingroom.lsc.gov.uk/ lsc/National/nat-recordsuccessratesinfe-pr-17apr2007.pdf> (accessed 24 June 2007).

Learning and Skills Council (LSC) and Department for Education and Skills (DfES) (2007) *Delivering World-Class Skills in a Demand-Led System*, Coventry: LSC.

Leese, R. (2006) 'City regions: the English answer?', *Renewal: A Journal of Labour Politics*, 14 (2): 33–6.

Leitch, S. (2006) *Prosperity for All in the Global Economy: world class skills*, Final Report, London: The Stationery Office.

Leslie, C. (2007) *Local Freedom Is Key to Delivering Community Cohesion Says NLGN*, press release, 14 June, London: NLGN.

Liberal Democrats (2006) *Your Community, Your Choice: policies for local government in England*, Policy Paper 73, London: Liberal Democrat Policy Unit.

Local Government Association (LGA) (2007) *Prosperous Communities II: vive la dévolution!* Available online at: <http://www.lga.gov.uk/Documents/ Publication/prosperouscommunitiesII.pdf> (accessed 15 July 2007).

London Development Agency (LDA) (2007) *London Skills and Employment Board*, London: LDA. Available online at: <http://www.lda.gov.uk/server/ show/nav.001002002002002> (accessed 28 January 2007).

Lowndes, V. and Sullivan, H. (2004) 'Like a horse and carriage or a fish on a bicycle: how well do local partnerships and public participation go together?', *Local Government Studies*, 30 (1): 51–73.

Lumby, J. and Tomlinson, H. (2000) 'Principles speaking: managerialism and leadership in further education', *Research in Post-Compulsory Education*, 5 (2): 139–52.

Lyons, Sir M. (2007a) *Place-Shaping: a shared ambition for the future of local government*, Final Report of the Lyons Review of Local Government, London: The Stationery Office.

—— (2007b) Press release on the Lyons Enquiry on Local Government, 27 March.

McGivney, V. (2003) *Adult Learning Pathways: through-routes or cul-de-sacs?*, Leicester: NIACE.

—— (2005) *Keeping the Options Open: the importance of maintaining a broad and flexible curriculum offer for adults*, Leicester: NIACE.

McIntyre, D., Pedder, D. and Ruddock J. (2005) 'Pupil voice: comfortable and uncomfortable learnings for teachers', *Research Papers in Education*, 20 (2): 149–68.

Maguire, S. and Thompson, J. (2006) *Paying Young People to Stay on at School – Does It Work? Evidence from the evaluation of the piloting of the Education Maintenance Allowance*, Oxford: SKOPE.

Marquand, D. (2004) *Decline of the Public: hollowing out of citizenship*, Cambridge: Polity Press.

Milana, M. and Desjardins, R. (2007) 'Enablers and constrainers to participation: has policy in Nordic countries reached its limit for raising participation in adult learning among certain groups?', paper presented at the Second Nordic Conference on Adult Learning, Linköping University, 17–19 April.

Miliband, D. (2006) 'My new year's resolution for local government' *Localist*, January/February: 1.

Mortimore, P. and Whitty, G. (1997) *Can School Improvement Overcome the Effects of Disadvantage?*, London: Institute of Education, University of London.

Mulgan, G. and Bury, F. (2006) *Double Devolution: the renewal of local government*, London: The Young Foundation.

National Institute of Adult Continuing Education (NIACE) (2005) *Eight in Ten: adult learners in further education*, Report of the Independent Committee of Enquiry invited by the National Institute of Adult Continuing Education to Review the State of Adult Learning in Colleges of Further Education in England, Leicester: NIACE.

National Statistics (2005) *Population Trends*, No. 121, Autumn, London: Office of National Statistics.

—— (2007) *Employment to May*. Available online at: <http://www.statistics.gov.uk> (accessed 24 July 2007).

New Local Government Network (NLGN) (2006) *Does the White Paper Pass the Litmus Test?*, press release, 30 October.

Newman, J. (2000) 'Beyond the new public management? Modernising public services', in J. Clarke, S. Gewirtz and E. McLaughlin (eds) *New Managerialism, New Welfare?*, London: Sage/Open University.

—— (2001) *Modernising Governance: New Labour, policy and society*, London: Sage.

—— (2005) (ed.) *Remaking Governance: peoples, politics and the public sphere*, Bristol: Policy Press.

—— (2006) 'Restating the politics of "the public"', *Soundings*, 32: 162–76.

Office of the Leader of the House of Commons (2007) *The Governance of Britain – the government's draft legislative programme*, Cm 7175, London: The Stationery Office.

Percy, K. (1997) *On Formal, Non-formal and Informal Lifelong Learning: reconceptualising the boundaries for research, theory and practice*, 27 Annual SCUTREA Conference Proceedings, London, July.

Piatt, W. and Robinson, P. (2001) *Opportunity for Whom? Options for funding and structure of post-16 education*, London: IPPR.

Pierre, J. and Peters, B.G. (2000) *Governance, Politics and the State*, Basingstoke: Macmillan.

Power, M. (1994) *The Audit Explosion*, London: Demos.

Pratchett, L. (2004) 'Local autonomy, local democracy and the "New Localism"', *Political Studies*, 52: 358–75.

Prideaux, S. (2005) *Not So New Labour: a sociological critique of New Labour's policy and practice*, Bristol: Policy Press.

Prime Minister's Strategy Unit (PMSU) (2006) *The UK Government's Approach to Public Service Reform – a discussion paper*, London: Cabinet Office.

—— (2007) *Building on Progress: public services*, London: Cabinet Office.

Qualifications and Curriculum Authority (QCA) (2004) *A Framework for Achievement: recognising qualifications and skills in the 21st century*, stakeholder consultation document, London: QCA.

Quality Improvement Agency for Lifelong Learning (QIA) (2007) *Pursuing Excellence: the national improvement strategy for the further education system*, Coventry: QIA.

Raffe, D. and Spours, K. (eds) (2007) *Policy-making and Policy Learning in 14–19 Education*, Bedford Way Papers, London: Institute of Education, University of London.

Rainsford, N. (2006) 'Foreword', in D. Sorajbi, *Pacing Lyons, a Route-Map to Localism: forecasting the future shape of local governance*, London: NLGN.

Rammell, B. (2007) 'Leitch offers an unprecedented opportunity to change the nation's attitude to skills', *Adults Learning*, 18 (5): 9.

Randle, K. and Brady, N. (1997) 'Managerialism and professionalism in the "Cinderella Service"', *Journal of Vocational Education and Training*, 49 (1): 121–39.

Ranson, S. (2006) 'Public accountability in the age of neo-liberal governance', in B. Lingard and J. Ozga (eds) *Education Policy and Politics*, London: RoutledgeFalmer.

Rawls, J. (2001) *Justice as Fairness: a restatement*, 2nd edn, Cambridge, MA: Harvard University Press.

—— (2005) *Political Liberalism*, 2nd edn, New York: Columbia University Press.

Reed, J. and Lodge, C. (2006) *Towards Learning-Focused School Improvement*, INSE Bulletin, No. 28, London: Institute of Education, University of London.

Rees, G., Gorard, S., Fevre, R. and Furlong, J. (2000) 'Participating in the learning society: history, place and biography', in F. Coffield (ed.) *Differing Visions of a Learning Society – research findings*, Vol. II, Bristol: Policy Press.

Rescher, N. (2002) *Fairness*, Edison, NJ: Transaction Publishers.

Robson, J. and Bailey, B. (2007) 'Personalised learning and social justice: a critical discussion of recent policy', paper presented at the seventh International Conference of the *Journal of Vocational Education and Training*, University of Oxford, 6–8 July.

Sarason, S.B. (1990) *The Predictable Failure of Educational Reform: can we change course before it's too late?*, San Francisco: Jossey-Bass.

Scottish Executive (2006) *More Choices, More Chances: a strategy to reduce the proportion of young people not in education, employment or training*, Edinburgh: Scottish Executive.

Sector Skills Development Agency (SSDA) (2006) *Skills for Business Network 2005: survey of employers*, Research Report 18, Wath-upon-Dearne: SSDA.

Sennett, R. (1998) *The Corrosion of Character: the personal consequences of work in the new capitalism*, New York: W.W. Norton.

Shah, H. and Goss, S. (2007) *Democracy and the Public Realm*, London: Lawrence and Wishart.

Shain, F. and Gleeson, G. (1999) 'Under new management: changing perceptions of teacher professionalism and policy in the further education sector', *Journal of Education Policy*, 14 (4): 445–62.

Sherlock, D. (2007) 'Does Leitch show the way to upskilling the nation?', *Talisman*, 58: 1.

Silverman, D. (2001) *Interpreting Qualitative Data: Methods for Analysing Talk, Text and Interaction*, London: Sage.

Skelcher, C., Mathur, N. and Smith, M. (2004) 'Negotiating the institutional void: discursive alignments, collaborative institutions and democratic governance', paper presented to the Political Association National Conference, University of Lincoln, April. Available online at: <http://www.inlogov.bham.ac.uk/research/esrc%20pubs/instvoidpaper.pdf> (accessed 17 January 2007).

Sorajbi, D. (2006) *Pacing Lyons, a Route-Map to Localism: forecasting the future shape of local governance*, London: NLGN.

Spours, K., Coffield, F. and Gregson, M. (2007) 'Mediation, translation and local ecologies: understanding the impact of policy levers on FE colleges', *Journal of Vocational Education and Training*, 59 (2): 193–211.

Stanton, G. (2004) *The Organisation of Full-Time 14–19 Provision in the State Sector*, Nuffield Review of 14–19 Education and Training Working Paper 13. Available online at: <http://www.nuffield14-19review.org.uk/files/documents30-1.pdf> (accessed 22 June 2007).

Stanton, G. and Fletcher, M. (2006) *14–19 Institutional Arrangements in England: a research perspective on collaboration, competition and patterns of post-16 provision*. Nuffield Review of 14–19 Education and Training Working Paper 38. Available online at: <www.nuffield14-19review.org.uk> (accessed August 2006).

Steer, R. and Lakey, J. (2007) *Voices from the Sector: findings from a survey on the learning and skills sector*, ESRC TLRP Project Research Report 6, London: Institute of Education, University of London.

Steer, R., Spours, K., Hodgson, A., Finlay, I., Coffield, F., Edward, S. and Gregson, M. (2007) '"Modernisation" and the role of policy levers in the learning and skills sector', *Journal of Vocational Education and Training*, 59 (2): 175–92.

Steinberg, D. and Johnson, R. (2004) 'Introduction', in R. Johnson and D. Steinberg (eds) *Blairism and the War of Persuasion*, London: Lawrence and Wishart.

Stevens, B. (2007) *Qualifications and Assessment Reform: implications for an inclusive and coherent 14–19 phase – a business perspective*, paper presented to a Nuffield 14–19 Review seminar, Nuffield Foundation, 14 March.

Stoker, G. (2004) *New Localism, Participation and Networked Community Governance*, paper published by the Institute for Political and Economic Governance, University of Manchester. Available online at: <http://www. ipeg.org.uk/papers/ngcnewloc.pdf?PHPSESSID=61dcf6465a5695d16a9d9 5b367497f38> (accessed 7 November 2007).

Strauss, A. and Corbin, J. (1998) *Basics of Qualitative Research: techniques and procedures for developing grounded theory*, London: Sage.

Stronach, I., Corbin, B., McNamara, O., Stark, S. and Warne, T. (2002) 'Towards an uncertain politics of professionalism: teacher and nurse identities in flux', *Journal of Education Policy*, 17 (1): 109–38.

Styles, B. and Fletcher, M. (2006) *Provision for Learners Aged 14–16 in the FE Sector: an initial analysis*, London: LSDA.

Swain, J. (2007) 'Telling it like it really is', *Reflect*, 7: 10–13.

Taubman, D. (2007) '1984 and all that', *Adults Learning*, 18 (9): 12–13.

Tawney, R. (1938) *Equality*, reprinted in D. Riesman (ed.) (1994) *Theories of the Mixed Economy*, London: William Pickering.

Thompson, M. and Wiliam, D. (2007) 'Tight but loose: a conceptual framework for scaling up school reforms', paper presented to the American Educational Research Association, Chicago, 9–15 April.

Torrance, H., Colley, H., Garratt, D., Jarvis, J., Piper, H., Ecclestone, K. and James, D. (2005) *The Impact of Different Modes of Assessment on Achievement and Progress in the Learning and Skills Sector*, LSRC Research Report, London: LSDA.

Tuckett, A. (2007) 'Adult learning, skills and inclusion', paper presented at the Final Project Conference, Institute of Education, University of London, 3 July.

University and College Union (UCU) (2007) *Response to the DfES Consultation on 'World Class Skills in a Demand-Led System'*, London: UCU.

Wahlberg, M. and Gleeson, D. (2003) '"Doing the business": paradox and irony in vocational education – GNVQ Business Studies as a case in point', *Journal of Vocational Education and Training*, 55 (4): 423–45.

Wallace, M. and Hoyle, E. (2005) 'Towards effective management of a reformed teaching profession', paper presented at a seminar of the Teaching and Learning Research Programme, King's College, London, 5 July.

Williams, G. (1999) 'Paying for lifelong learning: problems and possibilities', in A. Hodgson (ed.) *Policies, Politics and the Future of Lifelong Learning*, London: Kogan Page.

Wolf, A. (2002) *Does Education Matter? Myths about education and economic growth*, London: Penguin.

Working Group on 14–19 Reform (2004) *14–19 Curriculum and Qualifications Reform*, The Tomlinson Report, Annesley: DfES.

Index